MW01227200

Culturequake

Chuck Burr, Ashland, OR
www.culturequake.com

First edition edit, Peggy Sue Richards.
Interior design, Ben Smyth, Grand Opening Public Projects, NYC.
Index and bibliography, Noalani Terry.
Third edition edit and Forward, Larry Korn.
Thank you to my friends, family and mentors.
Front cover clockwise from top: children at Tamera Community Portugal; Zach
Rosen sheet mulching at Restoration Farm, Ashland Oregon; connecting deeply
at ZEGG Community, Belzig Germany; garden at Aprovecho Research Center,
Cottage Grove Oregon; bounty at Central Rocky Mountain Permaculture Insti-
tute, Basalt Colorado; Aprovecho chicken coup; yurt at ZEGG Community; cen-
ter Daniel Kra weeding organic blueberries at Restoration Farm, Mail Tribune.

Printed by Amazon kindle. Rev 2020/07/01

ISBN: 9798-6574-5027-9 (soft)

Printed digitally on-demand on recycled, 100% chlorine-free, paper

CULTUREQUAKE

The Restoration Revolution

CHUCK BURR

DEDICATION

To my children, Charlie, Bridget, and Erin.
To Mother Earth and the 30 million other species
with whom we share this beautiful home.
And especially to the species
that will be forced into extinction
this century by our modern culture.

CONTENTS

FORWARD

Few books have caused me to rethink my entire view of human history and human culture as *Culturequake* has. It provides a fascinating review of the approximately three million years humanity has been living on the planet and shows how the fateful decision to proceed headlong with agriculture about 10,000 years ago created a nightmare for human society and other forms of life. The author, Chuck Burr, charts a hopeful and practical course for how society could reorganize itself to create a brighter future than we could have ever imagined.

People had lived successfully and intimately bound with the natural world for more than 150,000 generations. Society was largely tribal and intuitively followed the basic rules of ecology taking only what was needed and not depriving livelihood from other forms of life. All that changed with the shift to agriculture. It led to the disastrous consequences we see today...degraded natural systems, mass extinction of species, human population explosion, widespread famine and cultural fragmentation. Besides taking over vast areas strictly for growing food for human beings a shift in consciousness also occurred. People somehow began to believe that they were the masters of creation, that the natural world was here solely for human benefit and that we had the right to exploit nature in any way we chose. In short, for the first time, people separated themselves from nature, considering themselves superior.

There were other options, but somehow the ancestors of our current world culture gained ascendancy. With plowed-field and irrigated agriculture surpluses developed. These needed to be defended. A hierarchic social structure was formed which quickly led to "haves" and "have nots," slavery and war. Since plowed-field agriculture despoiled the landscape the new culture constantly needed new lands to conquer. The horticulture/forager/gatherer cultures viewed the natural world as sacred and preserved wilderness as a practical necessity. The "Taker" agricultural society considered wilderness and the humans and other forms of life who lived there as a nuisance.

That "Taker" culture of 10,000 years ago is the dominant worldwide culture today. It is not, however, the real story of human history. For 99.7 percent of human history people lived intimately bound to the natural world and to each other in social families, or tribes, that provided "cradle to grave" security for its members. We can live that way again and regain our true human history. It will involve walking away from the cultural teachings we have grown up with that only serve to maintain the dominant destructive status quo. Above all we need to reject the common notion that humanity has "divine permission" to use nature in any way he sees fit.

The second part of *Culturequake* gives a concise summary of the social and ecological problems we face today such as accelerated population growth, environmental degradation, social fragmentation and injustice. The point of this chapter is not to belabor these familiar issues but to show how they came about so we do not make the same mistakes again while trying to solve them. We already know how to live sustainably on the earth; after all we did it successfully for almost three million years. But it is not simply going back. The vision of *Culturequake* is a synthesis of ancient wisdom and practical experience from living in the modern world.

The final chapter gives a practical and inspiring strategy for changing course. The way a culture grows its food defines that culture so it not surprising that Burr proposes a no-tillage, perennial agriculture that will both heal the land and create a more egalitarian society. Foraging and gathering yields more calories of food produced per calorie invested than any other form of agriculture. The most effective way to do that is by planting millions of trees on worn out farmland and by creating edible forest gardens and farms. These systems are highly productive, require almost no effort once established, improve the soil and use less water than any other.

Socially, ecovillages are a modern way of living as a community which is informed by our tribal heritage. Intentional communities are springing up all over the world. Access to land, conservancies, trusts, community gardens and guerilla gardening are also part of the new vision which are discussed at length in this book.

Ecologically and socially the best model for this new vision is nature. By observing nature closely and patterning our society after its interconnected webs and relationships we can create a highly productive and resilient society which is based on regeneration and mutual respect. Yes, we can do this. And we need to get started right away.   —Larry Korn

PREFACE

Starting with 9/11, I began to realize that something in the world was changing. I had a feeling that things were not as they appeared and that I did not have the whole story. I started doing some research and the story turned out to be much larger and more interconnected than I imagined. *Culturequake: The Restoration Revolution* is the summary and conclusions of my research.

After a certain point I became overwhelmed with information. So, I created a knowledge-base I called Earth Literacy to synthesize it. This book reflects about ten percent of the data I recorded which is about one percent of what I reviewed. I did not choose what to research; connecting the dots showed me where to look next. Growing like a tree grows, *Culturequake* wrote itself.

When you are done, pass the book along to friends or family and consider asking your library to order it. More *Culturequake* readings can be found at www.culturequake.org.

Restoration Farm and permaculture education center in Ashland, Oregon is our attempt to create a positive model for the future. We offer permaculture and related courses, internships and food to our local community. Visit us at www.restorationfarm.org.

INTRODUCTION

The purpose of *Culturequake* is to start a new vision that will restore humanity and the earth. I believe that modern culture does not offer the ordinary person the most fulfilling and secure way to live.

A culturequake is a major shift in humanity's story and its place in the community of life. The last shift happened during the agricultural revolution 10,000 years ago. Revolutions such as the Renaissance, American revolution, industrial revolution, green revolution and now technology revolution are not culturequakes because they left our cultural story intact, that the world belongs to people for our use alone.

To develop real long-term solutions, we need to find the connections between and the root causes of the problems caused by the last culturequake.

Culturequake has three essential parts to find the shifts that we need to make: understanding where in our history the root causes to our problems started, defining the real problem and designing a solution. The point of *Culturequake* covering so much ground is that people need something that they can hold in their hands that gives the complete picture—that brings all of the scattered ideas together.

A new vision and models of a better way to live will create a shift from a culture of *taking* to a culture of *restoration*—from dominion to peace and abundance.

PART I

Human History

1. The History We Were Taught

History matters—if you do not understand it, you cannot plan for a brighter future. To thrive in the future we need to know how things came to be this way, what affect our culture is having in the world and what has worked well in the past so we can apply it to the way we live today.

The history you were taught in school was a lie; we will correct it. This may give you a sense of relief knowing that the problem is not humanity but rather our culture. Through history we will find the hope for our children's future.

How we got to where we are today is a fascinating two-part story. The first part represents 99.7 percent of all human history. It took humanity about three million years to spread across the world and to reach a population of just four million. The second part starts with the birth of our culture 10,000 years ago with the agricultural revolution.[1]

Human history is one of overcoming the limits to growth and the environmental consequences of doing so. Each time we reached the limits of our environment, we used our ingenuity to overcome those limits. Our larger brain size enabled language, social cooperation and a series of technological breakthroughs. These breakthroughs enabled human population repeatedly to take over more of the earth's carrying capacity—resources that had previously been used by other species.

Our most recent breakthrough, global industrialization, has had spectacular results. However, we are currently using a very different method than in the past to exceed limits to growth. This

14

latest technique is a onetime drawdown of renewable and nonrenewable resources.[2]

BECOMING HUMAN

The story of how prehuman primates became Homo sapiens starts long after we came to walk on two legs and began to lose our hair. We were two-legged and hairless for hundreds of thousands of years before we became truly human. Becoming human includes storytelling, language, sense of time and an awareness of the sacred.

Nonhuman primates make their living by foraging, but that does not take much communication. A band of primates can settle in and begin foraging without any planning, coordination, cooperation or allotment of tasks. They just move in, and every body starts munching. But this behavior does not work for hunting. You just cannot move in and everybody starts hunting. In hunting teamwork is what pays off. For primates, hunting teamwork is not genetically wired in the way it is with wolves or hyenas. With primates, hunting teamwork can only work through communication.[3]

Not just any communication was necessary. A special kind of communication or language that enabled storytelling was needed. Look at the ground. This is where storytelling began. There is not a child anywhere in the world, in any culture of the world, that does not want to hear a story. There may not be a single storytelling gene, but it is a genetic characteristic of humans. Early human hunters who were able to organize events into stories were more successful than hunters who weren't. This success translated directly into reproductive success and better representation in the gene pool.

Another element was necessary to make storytelling an effective hunting skill, a sense of time. This is where the temporal structure of the universe began to be imprinted on the human brain. If you have tracks in the ground in front of you, they are here in the present, but they won't make any sense until we recognize them as traces of past events. They would be meaningless to any other species, because no other species would be able to read them as traces of the past. A dog can track a scent, but it does so in the present.

Think of how effective a sense of time would be to a hunter. If one day you were tracking an animal and after a few hundred yards you saw a mouse track cross over the animal track, you would give up the chase because you know from experience that mice are nocturnal and that the animal track is at least 12 hours old. The animal you are after is long gone.

Take the sense of time even further as an important trait of becoming human. Take time not only into the past, but now into the future. The future is inescapably the domain of the gods and of the sacred.

Early in humanity's history there was one universal religion—animism. Early humans shared the same experience and believed all life and natural objects to be sacred. When early humans began the hunt, they were walking into the sacred. They were walking into the future. They had crossed the border and had become Homo   sapiens.

EARLY TECHNOLOGY BREAKTHROUGHS

We take cooking for granted. However, this was a huge technological breakthrough. About two to three million years ago, our hunting and gathering prehuman relatives discovered that instead of avoiding fire, you could use it to warm yourself, ward off predators and for cooking. Fire made more foods digestible. Foods that had previously been inedible to humans could now be eaten, and thus enlarging humanity's carrying capacity.[4]

Prehumans also started to use simple stone and bone tools. Importantly, they learned to teach their children these techniques so they would not have to be reinvented each generation. This period lasted several hundred thousand years.

After 80,000 to 120,000 generations of human hunter-gatherers, their biological and cultural response to their surroundings had given rise to a descendent population with essentially the same physical traits as men and women today. Thus about 35,000 B.C., the humans on earth had evolved to our own species, Homo sapiens. A population of about four million was living by hunting and gathering. From the slow attainment of this number, we can be reasonably sure that this was about the maximum number the earth could support in the manner in which they were living.

About 35,000 B.C., two discoveries were made that further enlarged the earth's carrying capacity for humans. First, someone discovered that a spear could be thrown harder and farther if the thrower effectively lengthened his arm by fitting the end of the spear into a socket in the end of a handheld stick. Someone else invented a way of propelling mini spears, or arrows, not only faster, but also in a manner that enabled line-of-site aiming, by fitting the notched ends to a cord tied to the two ends of a springy stick. Using tools like the spear-thrower and the bow and arrow made humans more proficient hunters, and more of the earth's animals become food for humans.

With these technological discoveries, human population increased in a little over 1,000 generations from about four million to about eight million. Still, the slow rate of growth only increased tribe size by less than 1/10 of one percent during one generation.

Note the time scale. Prehumans have been around for as long as three million years. This is 99.7 percent of all human history. Our history courses teach us that nothing much happened during pre-history. However, our early relatives had developed an evolutionarily successful culture. They survived, adapted and continued to evolve. Their testimony to success is the fact that we are here today.

THE AGRICULTURAL REVOLUTION

Another technological breakthrough about 10,000 years ago enlarged the earth's human carrying capacity more than ever before. Somewhere in the fertile crescent, some of the people who gathered wild seeds to eat or for grinding into flour observed that seeds spilled on moist earth sprouted into plants and grew at least as well as those in the wild. These plants would bear a new conveniently harvestable crop of seeds. Homo sapiens went on to develop this discovery into techniques for plant cultivation that made the greatest change in our species' relation to the web of life to date.

By the beginning of the agricultural revolution human population had reached the huge, for that time, number of about 10 million. Agriculture enabled some nomadic hunter-gatherers to overcome the scarcity of once-abundant plants and game by staying in one place. These tribes now obtained their food from a newly, human-managed portion of the ecosystem that was previously used by other species as well. Other tribes intensified their nomadic way of life. They migrated out of their ancestral homes in Africa and the

Middle East and populated other areas of the game-rich world.[5]

This was a very big moment; it was the biggest in human history up to this point. Humanity was free of the limitations of the hunting-gathering life that had kept humans in check for three million years. With agriculture, those limitations vanished, and man's rise was meteoric. This big moment was the birth of our present day Taker culture.[6]

The degree to which agriculture increased human carrying capacity is shown by astonishing population growth, from 10 million to 800 million people by 1750. Today's population explosion to seven billion is merely the most recent episode in the process that began almost 10,000 years ago.

LAYING THE FOUNDATION OF CIVILIZATION

The climate when humanity first began farming was moderate. Rainfall of 15 to 30 inches a year was just the right amount of rain and sunshine to make farming relatively easy. Humanity planted its crop of emmer, spelt, barley, millet and wheat and simply waited to harvest it. This laid the foundation for modern civilization by enabling the farmer to stay in one place, and to grow a surplus of food.

We do not know where, when, or how farmers first learned the art and science of irrigation. Probably it was in some of the small valleys that were flooded annually. Possibly it was in the valleys of large rivers that overflowed regularly, such as the Nile, Euphrates and Indus. Humanity learned the art of irrigation long before we learned to write and read, probably before we had any form of stable government over a large area, and before we carried on extensive trade. In other words, we were irrigation farmers many centuries before we were living in civilized communities.

Most historians agree that the first civilizations were developed in three regions: the Nile Valley, Mesopotamia and the Indus Valley. All these valleys shared three common features: 1) the soil was fertile, 2) the water supply was dependable, mainly because irrigation was used and 3) the soil did not wash away because the land was relatively level and the rainfall was scant. All three of these conditions were important, but the third was most important.

The fertile soils and dependable water supply enabled farmers to produce large surpluses of food and insured a continuity of the food supply. Many people were freed to become artisans, indulge in trade and practice the civilizing arts. The stability of the land made it possible for farmers to farm the same land for many generations. This gave people an opportunity to settle down and build permanent homes. They were able to develop relatively stable governments and fairly stable channels of trade and commerce. This meant that they were eventually able to build cities.

THE BRONZE AND IRON AGES

Starting in about 4000 B.C., accelerating cultural development enabled the division of labor, which augmented stone and bone tools with metal tools. From then on, the growth of human organization would be an increasingly important factor in Homo sapiens' dominance over the natural environment.

Innovations continued to increase human carrying capacity. Around 3000 B.C., man started cultivating larger tracts of land than before with the help of animal-pulled plows. Slaves may have also pulled smaller plows. The new technology did not initially raise human carrying capacity as drastically as previous innovations, because some of the land had to be used to feed the animals.

About 1000 B.C., iron tools began to supplement and replace those made of bronze. For example, Roman swords were made of steel. Between the Bronze Age and the birth of Christ, the cumulative effect of these innovations expanded human population from about 86 million to about 300 million. Remember, it took three million years for human population to reach just four million.

FIREARMS AND DISCOVERY OF THE NEW WORLD

Then a different breakthrough occurred. Early in the fourteenth century, firearms were invented. They were hardly portable, but were immediately put to military use. They did not have a significant effect on carrying capacity, but they did change the nature of warfare and eventually changed political organization.

It took just three generations to develop portable firearms. These did have more of a direct effect enlarging human carrying capacity by increasing human ability to harvest meat. In the following sixteen generations, there was an above average increase in human population. This was not so much the result of an increased ability to gather food, as it was from the one time discovery of whole new of continents.

The cumulative effects of human population increases over the past three million years were significant. The portion of the world exposed to these technological breakthroughs was getting to be rather fully occupied by humans. The tools and knowledge developed by the most advanced humans was enabling them to leave the land and venture more daringly onto the sea. Less than a century after the invention of portable firearms, Europeans would discover lands not previously known to exist.

Firearms did not enlarge the planet. However, the superiority of weapons enabled the Europeans to take possession of whole new continents whose prior inhabitants were still living at the hunter-gatherer or early agricultural level. This increased human carrying capacity through the expansion of territory available to Europeans and their agriculture. William Catton called the centuries that followed the expansion of European man's habitat the Age of Exuberance in his 1982 book *Overshoot*.[7] During this period, people had largely forgotten that Europe had once been saturated with human population. Columbus's discovery of the new world increased the habitat available from 24 to 120 acres per European.

THE INDUSTRIAL REVOLUTION

The industrial revolution began in England as a response to vanishing trees and the substitution of abundant coal. The use of coal raised practical problems of earthmoving, mine construction, water pumping, transport and controlled combustion. These problems were solved relatively quickly, resulting in concentrations of labor around mines and mills. The process elevated technology and commerce to a prominent position in human society.[8]

This age of limitless opportunity, however, further accelerated population growth. In the two centuries between 1650 and 1850, human population doubled. In only 80 more years, it doubled again. The next doubling took only 45 years. As people became more numerous, the New World quickly filled up. In North America land per person shrank to a mere 11 acres. This was less than half the

space available in Europe before Columbus set sa
supports almost seven billion people, more than
ulation existing before the agricultural revolutio

Most of the people fortunate enough to live
read their good fortune. The seemingly limitle
which had to be of a limited duration, appeare
manent. The people of the Age of Exuberance looked back on
dismal lives of their forebears and pitied them for their changeless-
ness notions of the world.

As the gap between land and population closed, the world reen-
tered a period of population pressure, which resembled the Old
World of pre-Columbus times. There were so many more people, all
parts of the world were in touch with each other, per capita impact on
the biosphere had become amplified by technology, and depletion of
the earth's non-renewable resources was already far advanced. People
of this post-exuberant world had inherited expectations of perpetually
expansive human life from the Age of Exuberance.

TAKEOVER LEADS TO DRAWDOWN

European humans increased their biological carrying capacity by
displacing the lower density hunter-gatherer population of the New
World. This increased density of the humans diverted part of the
earth's biosphere previously supporting other species. Only once
could the technologically more advanced humans take over a second hemisphere to relieve the population pressure caused by a
filled up hemisphere.

Takeover gave way to a drawdown of natural resources. Industrialization in the 19th and 20th centuries first used coal and then
oil. Agricultural systems were also converted to fossil fuel energy.
This greatly increased yields through the use of machinery and fossil fuel based fertilizers. The most recent temporary extension of
carrying capacity has occurred because of a one-time use of nonrenewable resources. In a way, we are back to square one. Industrialization has committed us to hunting for and gathering nonrenewable natural deposits.

GROWTH ACCELERATION

on growth was further accelerated by breakthroughs in med-
echnology. In 1865 the practice of antiseptic surgery began.
ater breakthroughs included: hygienic practices, vaccination,
antibiotics, public health programs and computerized imaging.

This opened a whole new era of reduced death rates and drastically increased birth rates. Healthier people had more babies and
lived longer. Large family sizes that in the past would have led to stable or slow population growth through loss, are now further reducing
population doubling time. Reduction in the death rate in a population
will lead to disaster if the birth rate remains uncontrolled.[9] Thus, in
the seven generations since 1800, world population quadrupled, and
mankind has come to a precarious situation.

THE GREAT TURNING

David Korten's book *The Great Turning* is inspiring and shares sim-
ilarities to some of the thought and values of this book.

Korten describes The Great Turning as the present transition
from the industrial-growth society to a life-sustaining society. It iden-
tifies the shift from a self-destroying economy to one in harmony with
the earth. It unites and includes all the actions being taken to honor
and preserve life on earth. It is the third revolution to free us from the
agricultural and industrial first and second revolutions.

Of course, most people involved in this transition do not call it the
Great Turning. They do not need that name in order to fight for survival and to fashion the foundations for a better future.

The Great Turning is like a lens through which we can perceive
the extent to which it is happening. This lens reveals developments
that are ignored or distorted by the mainstream corporate media. In
the words of Gil Scott-Heron, "the revolution will not be televised." It
is hardly in the interests of billion-dollar industries, or the government
that serves them, that we should know how they are being challenged
and supplanted by grassroots initiatives.

It is important to review the three dimensions of this transition to
see the Great Turning in action and to recognize our part in it. While
presented as first, second, or third, they are not to be taken as sequen-
tial or ranked in importance.

The first dimension includes all the efforts underway to slow down
the destruction being wrought by the industrial-growth society.

These range from petitioning for species protection, to soup kitchens for homeless families, to civil disobedience against weapons makers, polluters, clear cutting and other depredations. Often discouraging and even dangerous, work in this dimension buys time. Saving some lives, some ecosystems, some species and some of the gene pool for future generations is a necessary part of the Great Turning. But even if every battle in this dimension were won, it would not be enough. A life-sustaining society requires new forms and structures.

The arising of these new forms constitutes the second dimension. Here we see the emergence of more sustainable alternatives, from solar panels to farmers markets, from land trusts to cohousing, perma-culture and local currencies. At no other time in human history have so many new ways of doing things appeared in so short a time. Many of them—as in health, animal husbandry and pest management reclaim old, traditional practices.

Yet, as promising as they are, these forms and structures cannot survive without deeply rooted values to nourish them. This is the third dimension of the Great Turning: a shift in consciousness. Both personal and collective, both cognitive and spiritual, this shift comes through many avenues. It is ignited by new sciences such as ecology and inspired by ancient traditions. It also arises out of grief for our world. This grief reveals the lies of the old notions of the isolated, competitive self. It reveals our full partnership in the web of life.

Today these three rivers—concern for our world, scientific break-throughs and ancestral teachings—flow together. From the conflu-ence of these rivers we awaken to what we once knew: we are alive on a living earth, source of all we are and know. Despite centuries of mechanistic conditioning, we want to name this world as sacred.

Whether they come through Gaia theory, systems theory, chaos theory, or through animism, shamanic practices, or the Goddess, such insights and experiences are necessary to free us from the grip of the industrial-growth society. They offer nobler goals and deeper pleasures. They redefine our wealth and our worth, liberating us from the compulsions to consume and control.[10]

2. Our Real History

You might read the previous chapter's version of the birth of our culture in any textbook. However, this is not the whole story of what happened in the Fertile Crescent 10,000 years ago. Several pieces of our culture's history are missing. As pieces are added, the image becomes clear.

Humanity evolved over millions of years to live much closer to the earth than we do now. That way of living was discarded when our culture was born.

Daniel Quinn in his teaching series *Ishmael, The Story of B,* and *My Ishmael,* offers several revelations based on modern paleontology about our history and the shaping of our culture. Quinn created a vocabulary for people of our culture being Takers and people of all other cultures being Leavers. Leavers, in Quinn's books, means native or indigenous peoples who live in harmony with the earth. However, I believe a future interpretation of Leaver may be expanded to include modern people who leave their industrial Taker culture; they simply walk away. This avoids having to use the heavily loaded terms of civilized and primitive.[1]

I have tried to summarize over 1,000 pages from five of Quinn's books into just a few here. I believe they will change how you see the world.

TAKER AGRICULTURAL REVOLUTION

The following statement on which we base the foundation of modern culture is a lie. It has spawned countless tragedies and puts limits on what we can understand about ourselves and what has happened during the course of human history: *Around 10,000 years ago people gave up the hunter-gatherer life and settled down in favor of agriculture.* See if you can find errors.

The date is right. The hunter-gatherer or forager part is right. The settled down or stayed in one place part is right enough. For someone from our Taker culture, it is hard to find the lies. It is repeated in all of our textbooks. Read it again.

The statement misleads in two profoundly important ways. First, it wasn't all people who did this, it was the people of our culture, one culture out of tens of thousands of cultures. The lie is that our actions are humanity's actions. The lie is that we are humanity itself, that our history is human history. The truth is that 10,000 years ago one people gave up the hunting-gathering life and settled down to become farmers. The other 99 percent went on exactly as before. The second lie is implying that agriculture is basically just one thing, the way foraging essentially is. There are many forms of agriculture.

Here is a more accurate version presented by Daniel Quinn: Many different styles of agriculture were in use all over the world 10,000 years ago, when our particular style of agriculture emerged in the Near East. This style, our style, Quinn calls totalitarian agriculture, because it subordinates all other life-forms to the relentless, single-minded production of human food. Fueled by the enormous food surpluses generated uniquely by this style of agriculture, rapid population growth occurred among its practitioners, followed by an equally rapid geographical expansion that obliterated other lifestyles including those based on other styles of agriculture. This expansion and obliteration of lifestyles continued without pause during the millennia that followed, eventually reaching the New World in the fifteenth century and continuing to the present in remote areas of Africa, Australia, New Guinea and South America.[2]

If you view human history as a time line, the Taker culture is a branch off the main line back about 10,000 years ago. The agricultural revolution was not a single event in time. It just spread, and has been spreading ever since.

Humanity did not take an evolutionary step from Homo hunter-gatherer to Homo farmer. First, homo hunter-gatherer did not become extinct. Second, hunter-gatherers and farmers do not belong to different species. They are biologically indistinguishable. The difference between them is strictly cultural. Bring up a hunter-gatherer's baby among farmers and he will be a farmer. Bring up a farmer's baby among hunter-gatherers and she will be a hunter-gatherer.[3]

THE FALL AND THE TREE OF KNOWLEDGE

When you look at a historical atlas with a shaded area between the Tigris and Euphrates representing the origin of the agricultural revolution, it can be deceiving. The early agriculturalists appear to be in an empty world. A better representation would be to surround the shaded Taker area with dots indicating all of the surrounding nonagricultural Leaver tribes that coexisted 10,000 years ago.[4]

The land of *The Fall* lays within the Fertile Crescent and was surrounded by non-totalitarian agriculturists. At the beginning of the agricultural revolution, the early Takers, the founders of our present culture, were unknown, isolated and unimportant.

If you flip the historical atlas ahead four thousand years, you will see that the Takers have expanded to include all of Asia Minor, and all the land to the north and east as far as the Caspian Sea and the Persian Gulf with Mesopotamia at the center. This would extend as far as the entrance to the Arabian peninsula, which was inhabited by the Semites.

The Semites were not eyewitnesses to the events known as The Fall. Those events happened hundreds of miles north of the Semites, among an entirely different people. According to the map, they were the Caucasians. However, the Semites were witnesses in 4500 B.C. to an event in their own front yard—the expansion of the Takers.

In four thousand years, the agricultural revolution had spread across Asia Minor to the west and to the mountains in the north and east. In the south, they were blocked by the Semites. The Semites were not agriculturalists, they were herders or pastoralists.

For an eyewitness account of what happened at the border between the Takers' culture and the Semites, we turn to the bible's story of Cain and Abel in chapter four of Genesis.

Now Abel kept flocks and Cain worked the soil. In the course of time Cain brought some of the fruits of the soil as an offering to the Lord. But Abel brought fat portions from one of the first-born of his flock. The Lord looked with favor on Abel and his offering but on

Cain he did not look with favor. So Cain was very angry and his face was downcast...

Now Cain said to his brother Abel, "Let's go out to the field." And while they were in the field, Cain attacked his brother Abel and killed him.

Then the Lord said to Cain, "Where is your brother Abel?"

"I don't know," he replied. "Am I my brother's keeper?"

The Lord said, "What have you done? Listen! Your brother's blood cries out to me from the ground."[5]

The tillers of the soil, Cain, were watering the fields with the blood of Semitic herders, Abel. What was happening there was what has always happened along the borders of Taker expansion: The Leavers were being killed off so that more land could be put under cultivation. Here at the border that separates tillers of the soil from Semitic herders, Cain and Abel confront each other.

It has always been a mystery as to why God accepted Abel and his offering and rejected Cain and his offering. This explains it. With this story, the Semites were telling their children, "God is on our side. He loves us herders but hates those murderous tillers of the soil from the north."

Also, if the tillers of the soil from the north were Caucasians, then the mark of Cain is our own white face.

But the Lord said to him, "Not so; if anyone kills Cain, he will suffer vengeance seven times over." Then the Lord put a mark on Cain so that no one who found him would kill him. So Cain went out from the Lord's presence and lived in the land of Nod, east of Eden.[6]

The story makes sense if the mark was given to Cain as a warning to others—leave this man alone. This is a dangerous man, one who exacts a sevenfold vengeance. Certainly a lot of people all over the world have learned that it doesn't pay to oppose people with white faces.

The Semites looked at the people they were fighting and said, "My God, how did they get this way? What's wrong with our brothers from the north? Why are they doing this to us? What's going on here is something wholly new. These aren't raiding parties. They are saying *we* have to die. They're saying, 'Abel has to be wiped out.'"

"Nobody has ever lived this way before. They're not just saying that 'we have to die.' They're saying that '*everything* has to die.'

They're saying, 'lions, you're dead.' They're saying, 'wolves, we've had it with you too. You're out of here.' They're saying, 'Nobody eats but us. All this food belongs to us and no one else can have any without permission.' "

If you read the Bible as a story from our own Taker cultural ancestors' perspective, it is incomprehensible. The Bible never comments on why the tree of the knowledge of good and evil should have been forbidden to Adam. It only begins to make sense when you realize that it originated among the enemies of our cultural ancestors.

That's it! They're acting as if they were gods. They're acting as if they eat at the gods' own tree of wisdom, as though they were as wise as the gods and could send life and death wherever they please. Yes, that's it. These people found the gods' own tree of wisdom and stole some of its fruit.

These are accursed people! When the gods found out what they'd done, they said, 'You wretched people, that's it for you! We're not taking care of you any more. You're out. We banish you from the garden. From now on, instead of living on our bounty, you can wrest your food from the ground by the sweat of your brows.' That's how these accursed tillers of the soil came to be hunting us down and watering the fields with our blood.

How does Eve fit in? According to Biblical notes, her name means *living* or *life*.[7] It does not mean woman. The authors of the story of The Fall made it clear that Adam's temptation wasn't sex or lust. Adam was tempted by *Life*. This is from the perspective of nonagricultural people, a people for whom population control is always a critical problem.

Adam named his wife Eve because she would become the mother of all the living.[8]

The herding people were being pushed into the desert by agriculturalists from the north. The agriculturalists wanted to put the herders' land under cultivation to increase food production to support an expanded population.

Adam and Eve spent three million years in the garden, living on the bounty of the gods, and their growth was modest. But when Eve presented Adam with the knowledge of good and evil and of who should live and who should die, Adam decided that he could create a bounty of his own. This meant he said yes to Life and to growth without limit. When Adam accepted the fruit of that tree, he succumbed to the temptation to live without limit and so the person who offered him that fruit is named Life or Living as told in Genesis.

Whenever a Taker couple talk about how wonderful it would be to have a big family, they are reenacting this scene beside the Tree of Knowledge of Good and Evil. They're saying in effect, "It is our right to apportion life on this planet as we please. Why stop at two children? We can have five or six. All we have to do is plow under another few hundred acres, and who cares if a dozen species disappear as a result?"

OBTAINING NATURAL RESOURCES WAS THE MOTIVE FOR TAKER EXPANSION

The pattern was set when the first Taker clan or tribe decided that their neighbors had better grazing, farming, fishing, or hunting grounds. It has continued through the ages and the future does not look any brighter.

The mass Taker expansion over the face of virtually the entire earth has mainly been to obtain natural resources. Regardless of whether you call such migrations colonization, conquest, or emigration, the objectives were much the same. The migrants were not merely seeking a change in scenery. Sometimes they were fleeing before an enemy who had dispossessed them. More often they were trying to dispossess a neighbor who had richer land or more wealth.

Once the pattern was set, Takers started overrunning Takers. When barbarians overran civilized communities, they were usually seeking the wealth that the more civilized societies had extracted from nature, and they usually thought of it as conquest. For example, the barbarous Aryans who invaded the civilized Indus Valley around 1700 B.C. simply called a war "a desire for more cattle." The Hyksos conquered Egypt and the Kassites overran Mesopotamia about the same time because they desired the rich cultivated fields and cities of the Egyptians and Babylonians. The Achaeans and Dorians overran Greece and Crete some six or eight centuries later because they desired the rich booty of the civilized Minoans and Mycenaeans. The Assyrians, and later Medes and Persians, moved into Mesopotamia for similar reasons. The Goths, Franks, Vandals, and others had similar motives for occupying the Roman Empire during the fifth century A.D., just as the Huns and Mongols had their own motives for overrunning Southwest Asia and Eastern and Central Europe during the Middle Ages. These are just a few of the more familiar examples. Countless others can be found by reading a few pages of almost any book on ancient history.[9]

The record of civilized peoples is even worse than that of barbarians, mainly because they had better weapons. The civilized societies, however, were seeking land and raw materials. They generally called it colonization when they took land away from Leaver peoples, although sometimes they frankly called it conquest. Regardless of what they called it, the results were much the same. Again, you can find the history books filled with the gory details.

Historians point out that most wars and colonization occurred because someone wanted more land. But seldom do they note that the conquerors or colonizers had despoiled their own land, creating the need to take that of their neighbors.

Most writers of current history recognize that the strong and wealthy nations of today are those with abundant natural resources. But too often they forget that most of the poor and weak nations of today once had abundant resources. Most of the poor peoples of the earth are poor mainly because their ancestors and conquerors wasted the natural resources upon which present generations must live.[10]

THE GREAT FORGETTING

Our cultural mythology that we inherit from our parents and pass on to our children, is squarely built on a *Great Forgetting* that occurred during the formative millennia of our civilization. Neolithic farming communes turned into villages, villages turned into towns and towns were gathered into kingdoms. What was forgotten during this time was the fact that there had been several million years when none of it was going on—a time when human life was sustained by hunting and gathering rather than by agriculture and animal husbandry. It was a time when villages, towns and kingdoms were undreamed of, a time when no one made a living as a potter or a basket maker or a metal worker, a time when trade was an informal and occasional thing, a time when commerce was unimaginable as a means of livelihood.

The memory of having been separate tribes didn't vanish in a single generation, but neither did it plausibly survive for more than four or five, maybe even ten generations, and this is only two centuries. At the end of a thousand years, the descendants of the original tribes would not even remember that such a thing as tribal life had ever existed. It is hard to imagine how this forgetting could have been avoided since it would have been necessary to hold on to the memory of our hunting-gathering past for 5,000 years before anyone would have had the means of making a written record of it.

By the time anyone was ready to write the human story, the foundation events of our culture were ancient history, but this did not make them unimaginable. Extrapolating backwards, there was a time when kingdoms did not exist, when towns got smaller and disappeared, and the population got smaller and smaller. Maybe that is just how things start. Maybe at the beginning of the world there was one man and one woman. Who at this point knew any better? Our cultural ancestors knew nothing about the agricultural revolution. As far as they knew, humans came into existence farming, just as deer come into existence browsing. As they saw it, agriculture and civilization were just as innately human as thought or speech. Our hunter-gatherer past was not just forgotten, it was unimaginable. The Great Forgetting was unknowingly woven into the fabric of the teachings of the foundation thinkers of our culture: Herodotus, Confucius, Abraham, Anaximander, Pythagoras, Socrates and many others.[11]

The destruction of tribal law, peace keeping strategies like *Erratic Retaliator* and hunting and gathering methods could not have happened gradually, over hundreds or thousands of years. It had to begin immediately, at the site of the very first Taker encroachment. Tribal law and Erratic Retaliator strategies were barricades that had to come down right at the outset. Whatever the Leavers' real tribal names were, they had to disappear as entities. Like the American Indians, willingly or unwillingly they exchanged tribal independence for Taker power.[12]

Our culture has made the human historical horizon too short. An accurate horizon is three million years. If you consider human history to have started with The Fall and the agricultural revolution, you are ignoring 99.7 percent of all human history.

That is a long time, but Leaver peoples are always conscious of having a tradition that goes back to very ancient times. We Takers have no such consciousness. We are a relatively new culture with each generation more thoroughly cut off from the past than the one that came before.

THE GREAT REMEMBERING

Paleontology exposed the Great Forgetting. It did so by making it unarguably clear that humanity had been around long before the planting of the first crop and the beginning of civilization. Paleontology made untenable the idea that humanity, agriculture and civilization all began at the same time. History and archaeology shows that agriculture and civilization are just a few thousand years old—paleontology puts the dawn of human history as several *million* years old. Paleontology shows that people could not possibly have been born as an agriculturist and civilization-builder. Early people were foragers and homeless nomads. Acknowledgement of this rich and lengthy period of human history was erased by the Great Forgetting.

It is hard to imagine what the foundation thinkers of our culture would have written if they had known that people had lived perfectly well on this planet for millions of years without agriculture or civilization. Our intellectual history would have been unthinkably different from what we find in our libraries today.

But amazingly, when the scientists and philosphers of the eighteenth, nineteenth and twentieth centuries were finally compelled to admit that the entire structure of thought in our culture had been built on a profoundly important error, absolutely nothing happened.[13]

When the existence of preagricultural societies became undeniable in the nineteenth century, the thinkers of our culture didn't care to disturb the wisdom of the ancients, so the study of preagricultural peoples became the study of nobody. They knew they could not get away with nonhistory, so they called the study *prehistory*. It is rather like prewater. Prewater is the stuff fish lived in before there was water, and prehistory is the period people lived in before there was history.

They revised their story this way: Man may not have been born as agriculturalists and civilization builders, but that has always been their destiny. In other words, the early people of the fiction known as prehistory came into our cultural awareness as a sort of a very, very slow starter.

Consider the customary designation of prehistory peoples as Stone Age; this nomenclature was chosen by people who did not doubt for a moment that stones were as important to these ancestors as printing presses and automobiles were to the people of the nineteenth century. Visit a modern Stone Age culture in New Guinea or Brazil, and you will see that stones are about as central to their lives as plastic is to ours. Calling them Stone Age people makes no better sense than calling us Plastic Age people.[14]

MOTHER CULTURE

We have been listening to Mother Culture since the day of our birth. Mother Culture speaks to us through the voice of our parents, who likewise have been listening to her voice from the day of their birth. She speaks to us through cartoon characters, through news programs, through school teachers, neighbors and politicians. We have heard her through popular music, movies, advertising, speeches, sermons, legends and jokes. We have read her thoughts in newspaper articles, textbooks, best selling books and on the Internet.[15]

It is kind of a low murmuring song that is in our ears from birth, heard so constantly throughout our lives that it is never consciously heard at all. The easiest way to start to see Mother Culture from the outside is to imagine that you are watching a movie and everything you hear, such as the news, is fake.

Most of the information you receive is from an entity that is trying to perpetuate itself. Schools educate you to become a member of the culture. The news perpetuates the government and corporations. Advertising is to make you feel dissatisfied with what you have so you consume more in order to perpetuate the economy.

The first chapter of this book *Human History* was Mother Culture's version of how we came to be the way we are. In this chapter *Takers and Leavers* I have tried to show you our history from another point of view. There are two fundamentally different human cultures: what we call civilized or Taker people, and what we call primitive, tribal, or Leaver people. Tribal people still exist today as hunter-gatherer aboriginal people in the outback of Australia or as the Huli of Papua New Guinea, or the Macuna Indians of eastern Columbia.

Every culture has its own particular nurturing and sustaining educational mother. The ideas being nurtured in you are very different from those nurtured in tribal peoples who are still living the way their ancestors lived more than 10,000 years ago.[16]

Most people have at least once had the experience of being a captive in our culture. We feel pressured to get an education, to get a job, to get married, to pay a mortgage, to consume and to act along acceptable social norms. We feel a responsibility to take our place in the story our culture is enacting in the world. Those who refuse to take their place do not get fed.

Mother Culture teaches us that this is the way it should be. Except for a few thousand savages scattered here and there, all people of the earth are now enacting this story. This is the story humanity was born to carry out, to veer from it is to resign from the human race itself. Taking our role in this tragic story, putting our shoulder to the grindstone and as a reward, we are fed. There is no way out except in death.[17] During the last two centuries every remaining Leaver people in North America was given a choice: to be exterminated or to accept imprisonment in the Taker cultural prison. To take our minds off the boredom, futility of our lives and long hours of work, we have been given one large cultural industry: to consume the world.

CULTURAL MEMES

Memes are to cultures what genes are to our bodies. Memes are the stories, beliefs and visions that perpetuate a culture from generation to generation. A culture is a collection of individual humans like cells in our body. You and everyone you know, contain a complete set of memes, which are the conceptual building plans for our culture. For more detail about memes, read Richard Dawkins's book *The Selfish Gene*. Dawkins coined the word *meme*, which rhymes with theme, to refer to what he perceived to be the cultural equivalent of the gene.[18]

Memes replicate themselves in the "meme pool" of our culture. They leap from mind to mind through Mother Culture the way genes leap from body to body. Each culture is a collection of individuals, and each individual has in his or her head a complete set of values, concepts, rules and preferences, that taken together, constitute the building plans for that particular culture.

The most important Taker culture meme began 10,000 years ago when the people of our culture took the power of the gods, of life and death over the world, into their own hands. The choice the gods make is good for one creature and evil for another. If the fox goes out to hunt and the gods send it a rabbit, then this is good for the fox but evil for the rabbit. If the fox goes out another day to hunt and god does not send it a rabbit, then this is evil for the fox and good for the rabbit. Adam was not the progenitor of our race, he was the progenitor of our culture.

The Takers, however, are not as wise as the gods. The gods ruled the world for billions of years, and they were doing just fine. After just a few thousand years of human rule, the blink of an eye in geologic scale, the world is approaching death. The authors of the story of The Fall predicted that if The Takers did not give up the knowledge of good and evil, they would die.[19] It looks like they knew what they were talking about.

The authors of Genesis described eating from the tree of the knowledge of good and evil as a matter of changed minds. What they saw being born in their neighbors was not a new lifestyle but a new mind-set, a mind-set that made us out to be as wise as the gods, that made the world out to be a piece of human property, a mind-set that gave us the power of life and death over the world. They believed that this new way of perceiving humanity's place in the world would be the death of Adam, and current events are proving them right.[20]

Early Semitic witnesses to our cultural beginnings saw that their neighbors had eaten some memes from the tree of wisdom. They said, "The meme of the knowledge of good and evil is benign to the gods, but deadly to humans." Their prediction was accurate, but it did not come true immediately. The memes that made us the rulers of the world did not have a lethal effect ten thousand years ago, or five thousand years ago, or even two thousand years ago. Their deadliness didn't become evident until the last century, when technological breakthroughs turned us into killing machines of the natural order. It is a matter of life and death that we rid ourselves of these memes—and it can be done.[21] The Maya and Olmec did it. They simply walked away from their cities when they lost belief in their culture's story. Take a deep breath—read this paragraph again.

Memes will play a very important role later in solving our

deepest problems for the long-term. The root cause of humanity's problems turn out to be our culture's memes and not human nature.

TAKER CULTURAL MYTHOLOGY

Meme: Man Is Separate From Nature

This meme sounds pretty harmless. You can hear it and think to yourself, "Uh huh, yeah, so?" It's pretty simple too. Here it is: humanity is separate from nature. Humans belong to an order of being that is separate from the rest of the community of life. There are people and then there is nature. There are humans and then there is the backdrop of the human drama.

The belief that humanity is separate from nature is the most dangerous idea ever conceived because it allows for mass extinction—even our own. This arrogant attitude is far more dangerous than our nuclear weapons, more dangerous than biological warfare and more dangerous than all the pollutants we pump into the air, the water and the land.[22]

Meme: The World Was Made For Man

The premise of the Taker story grew out of the Taker experience, from the way the people of our culture made a living, which was, after all, by conquering and ruling the natural world. The practice of totalitarian agriculture over thousands of years gave them the meme that the world had actually been made for them, and they had been made to conquer and rule it.[23] It is the consequence of the idea that the world was created for humanity—that the world *belongs* to people.

That is what has been happening for the last 10,000 years: people have been doing whatever they please with the world. Because the whole thing belongs to people anyway, Takers began to imagine that they were fulfilling human destiny.

The unfortunate result of Taker culture's destiny to conquer and rule the world, and this is what we have almost done, is that this may be our undoing. Humanity's conquest has devastated the world. And in spite of all our mastery, we still do not have the mastery to repair the devastation we have caused. We are just primates who have stumbled onto consciousness. Humanity is no better abile to rule the world than it does to create a galaxy.

We have poured our poisons into the world as though it were a bottomless pit. We have consumed irreplaceable resources as though they would never run out. It is hard to imagine how the world could survive another century of this abuse. It is a problem our children will have to solve, or their children.[24]

The story that our species alone should be fruitful and multiply regardless of the consequences and that we have dominion over other species is used as justification for our separation from the earth and for committing mass extinction. And let's be honest, mass extinction is mass species genocide committed by rolling down the aisles with our shopping carts and by expanding our population.

Humanity has taken this meme one step further as our population races past seven billion and increases competition for scarce natural resources. The resulting meme is: Get yours while you can. This is reflected in attitudes such as: Everybody does it, if we don't do it somebody else will, and it is still legal anyway. These are coming to be viewed as survival rationalizations. Greed-based cultural values are becoming more lethal and are what is killing the earth and her inhabitants. It is not humanity that is killing the earth. It's the consequences of acting out the Taker story told to us by Mother Culture since our birth. It is this story that must be changed.[25]

Meme: There is One Right Way To Live

To justify our conquest of the world we need a meme that tells us that there is one right way to live and that the right way is our Taker culture. This justifies our forcing everyone else in the world to live the way we do. Having a different way to live that works well will not do. This is a crushing culture with no empathy.

Takers also need certain knowledge of this one right way to live. However, this creates a circular reference. Since there really is no one, universal, right way to live, there can be no certain knowledge. The solution to this is to have the prophets to tell us how to live. We need Moses and Jesus and Muhammad and Confucius and Buddha to tell us how to live.

Take the case of abortion. We can argue about it for a thousand years, but there is never going to be an argument powerful enough to end the argument, because every argument has a counter argument. So it is impossible to know what we should do. That is why we need prophets. The prophets know and they tell us.

If Takers are going to be certain that they are living the one right way, they also need laws. So now here comes Hammurabi and Solon saying, "these my children are laws. Laws are things that tell you the one right way to live."[26]

The interesting thing is that the Leaver peoples do not need prophets to tell them how to live. They do not need prophets because they have a different meme: there is no one right way to live. So, they do not need someone to tell them how to live. It is that simple. Taker culture would say it is no surprise that savages have no prophets. God did not really get interested in mankind until those nice white Neolithic farmers came along.[27]

People imagine that it would be wonderful if all seven billion of us started living a new way tomorrow. It's our deep-rooted meme that there absolutely must be some one right way for everyone to live.

Here is how an ecologist would think. Macaws have a good life, but their habitats would fail if all birds lived like macaws. Giraffes have a good life, but their habitats would fail if all mammals lived like giraffes. Beavers have a good life, but their habitats would fail if all rodents lived like beavers.

Diversity, not uniformity, is what works. Our problem is not that people are necessarily living in a bad way but rather that we are all living the same way. The earth can accommodate many people living in wasteful and polluting ways, but it cannot accommodate *all* of us living that way.[28]

Meme: Civilization Must Continue

There is a meme about civilization that is implicit: Civilization is humanity's ultimate invention and can never be surpassed. This gives rise to a corollary meme: Civilization must continue at any cost and must not be abandoned. There cannot possibly be any superior invention. If we were to abandon civilization, then we would be finished.

Here is how the story goes. Once upon a time life evolved on a certain planet, bringing forth many different animal communities: packs, pods, flocks, troops, gaggles, herds and so on. Our species developed a unique community organization called a tribe. Tribalism worked well for them for millions of years, but there came a time when they decided to experiment with a new organization called civilization that was hierarchal rather than tribal.

This marked the break between humanity's evolutionarily developed tribal community and the birth of civilization or modern society. Society is the exclusive province of humans. What distinguishes a human society from an animal community is the existence of social institutions. Animal communities are relatively fixed over time. By contrast, human societies are structured around highly mutable ideological institutions, be they tribal, slave, feudal, or capitalist.[29] Culture, which we will discuss in detail later, is the beliefs, stories and customs that perpetuate a given human social organization.

Before long, a small group at the top of the hierarchy were living in luxury, enjoying leisure and having the best of everything. A larger group of people below them lived very well and had nothing to complain about. But the largest class, the masses living at the bottom of the social hierarchy lived like slaves, struggling just to survive.

"This isn't working," the masses said. "The tribal way was better. We should return to that way."

But the ruler of the hierarchy told them, "We've put that primitive life behind us forever. We can't go back to it."

"If we can't go back," the masses said, "then let's go forward on to something different."

"That can't be done," the ruler said, "because nothing different is possible. Nothing can be beyond civilization. Civilization is a final unsurpassable invention. It is the end of history."

But no invention is ever unsurpassable. The steam engine was surpassed by the gas engine. The radio was surpassed by television. The calculator was surpassed by the computer. Why should civilization be any different?"

"I don't know why it's different," the ruler said, "It just is."
But the masses didn't believe this.[30]

Meme: Growing All Your Own Food Is Best

The meme "Growing all your own food is best" entered our culture at its birth about 10,000 years ago. We would not have full-time farmers unless we believed it was the best way to live. The founders of our culture did not just fall into a lifestyle of total dependence on agriculture, they had to whip themselves into it, and the whip they used was this meme.

It is easy to imagine that growing all of your own food represents an inevitable development and the path of least resistance for people trying to make a living, but in fact it represents the path of *greatest* resistance. A hunter-gatherer who needs 2,000 calories a day to live has to expend only 400 calories to get them, because that's the rate hunting and gathering pays off, 1 calorie for work gets you 5 calories of food. By contrast, a farmer who needs 2,000 calories a day to live has to expend 1,000 calories to get them, because that's the rate at which farming pays off, 1 calorie of work gets you 2 calories of food.

For a food hungry person to trade hunting-gathering for farming is like a money hungry person trading a job that pays five dollars an hour for one that pays two dollars an hour. It makes no sense, and the hungrier you are, the less sense it makes.[31] For more information about how early humans made a living, read *Stone Age Economics* by Marshall Sahlins.

The problem we have now is that there are almost seven billion people in the world and so many species and habitats have already been destroyed. There are too many of us to go back to the hunter-gatherer lifestyle. Industrial agriculture is not a long-term option either because of its dependence on fossil fuel and continued soil depletion.

The agricultural revolution did not come about as a response to famine. Starving people do not plant crops any more than drowning people build life rafts. The only people who can afford to wait for crops to grow are people who already have food. Famine, far from being banished by agriculture, is actually a by-product of agriculture and is never found apart from it. Travel to the most inhospitable desert of Australia during the most horrendous drought, and you won't find a single starving aborigine.[32]

Growing all of your own food makes life more toilsome and less secure. Farmers 10,000 years ago and today are pushed along by the meme that growing all your food is best.

WE ARE EXPERIENCING THE BEGINNINGS
OF CULTURAL COLLAPSE

The belief that technological society is forever going to bring us a better world is starting to fall open to grave doubts. The industrial revolution is about a century old and clearly has not lived up to its promise of providing greater human contentment, fulfillment, health, security, or peace.[33] Human problems such as poverty, hunger and disease are all on the rise and the ecosystems that sustain us are in drastic decline.

Rachel Carson was the first to present a substantive challenge to the motivating vision of our culture. *Silent Spring*, published in 1962, shattered for all time our cultural faith that the world was capable of repairing any damage we made to it, that the natural world and god himself would bale us out and always be on our side. The facts in *Silent Spring* plainly contradicted all these ideas. DDT, something presumably beneficial to humanity, was not being tolerated by nature. One of the reasons *Silent Spring* may have been so compelling is that Rachel Carson was dying of breast cancer while she was writing the book.

Since then many people have uncovered other examples of undesirable side effects of human activities that have shattered our cultural faith in humanity's ability to improved upon nature. Another seminal book with equally disturbing conclusions written 34 years after *Silent Spring* is Theo Colborn's, *Our Stolen Future*. Colborn's team reviews the dangers to human health from chemically produced estrogens and their long-term persistence in the environment.

In our present numbers and enacting our present story, our culture is having a lethal impact upon the world. Lakes are dying, seas are dying, forests are dying, the land is dying, for reasons directly traceable to our activities.[34]

The scientific theories advanced to explain these things are, for the most part, well known. But you also hear, for example, that the human race is fatally flawed, or the human race is a sort of planetary disease that Gaia will eventually shake off, that insatiable capitalist greed or technology is to blame, or that parents or schools are to blame.

Remedies to correct what's gone wrong are usually expressed in this form: All we have to do is . . . something. Elect the right party. Get rid of the leader. Handcuff the liberals. Handcuff the conservatives. Write stricter laws. Give longer prison sentences. Meditate. Pray the Rosary. Raise consciousness. Evolve to some new plane of existence.

Daniel Quinn has proposed a another theory to explain what is going wrong. This is not a minor variation. I believe it is something entirely new in intellectual history. Here it is: We are experiencing cultural collapse. Similar to the collapse that was experienced by the Plains Indians when their way of life was destroyed and they were herded onto reservations. It doesn't matter that the particular circumstances of the collapse were different for them than they are for us. For both of us, in just a few decades, shocking new realities invalidated our vision of the world and made nonsense of the destiny that we had always been following. The song we have been singing since the beginning of our culture is suddenly dying in our throats.

The outcome may be the same for both of us: Things fall apart. Order and purpose are replaced by chaos and bewilderment. People become listless, violent, they seek spiritual redemption, take to drugs and resort to crime. The matrix that once held the tribe in place is shattered; laws, customs and institutions fall into disuse and disrespect. It may be 20 or 200 years until the full effect is felt but we can no longer believe that the world was made for humanity alone and that people were made to rule it.[35]

I believe that today's children will feel the greatest loss of belief in our cultural mythology. Adults today grew up with the color TV, men landing on the moon, the end of the cold war and personal computers. Kids today grow up with resource wars, global warming, mass extinction, water depletion, privatization of the commons and peak oil.

GOOD NEWS, WE ARE NOT HUMANITY

Here is the good news: Our culture is not humanity. These five words can change your life. They are a summary of all that was forgotten during the Great Forgetting. We forgot that we are only a single culture and came to think of ourselves as humanity itself. Humanity lived very well on the earth for three million years before the Great Forgetting. It is important to teach this to our children to give them hope for the future. It is not human nature that has brought us here, it is our culture.

The intellectual and spiritual foundations of our Taker culture were established by people who believed that we *are* humanity itself: Thucydides, Socrates, Plato, Aristotle, Ssu-ma Ch'ien, Gautama Buddha, Confucius, Moses, Jesus, St Paul, Muhammad, Avicenna, Thomas Aquinas, Copernicus, Galileo and Descartes all believed it.

It would be bad news if we were, in fact, humanity. If we were all of the terrible things we say about humanity would be true. If we were humanity, all our destructiveness would not belong to one misguided culture, but to humanity itself. If we were humanity itself, then the fact that our culture is doomed would mean that humanity itself is doomed, and that would be very bad news indeed.

But we are not humanity. We are simply one culture out of hundreds of thousands that have lived their vision on this planet and sung their song, and that is wonderful news, even for us.[36]

PART II

Why Civilization Cannot be Fixed

3. Population Explosion

If you were a newly married couple at the start of the agricultural revolution, the number of your descendants living today would have grown to the size of a town with a population of 1,200 people. That is a 600 times increase or a total of nine population doublings.[1]

In 1650, the world's population had a doubling time of 240 years. By 1900, the doubling time was 100 years. When Donella Meadows published *The Limits To Growth* in 1972, there were fewer than four billion people in the world. Today there are more than six billion. If you plot human population over the last three million years, the line would look fairly flat for 99.7 percent of the length, and then it would shoot strait up like a backwards L.

Another area of exponential growth has been the world economy. From 1930 to 2000, the money value of world industrial output grew by a factor of 14. This is an average doubling time of 19 years.[2]

Exponential growth is like compound interest. It builds each subsequent growth on top of the previous growth leading to ever-faster increase. This makes populations double more rapidly than it seems possible.

If the annual rate of increase is 2 percent, the doubling time would be 35 years. If you added 20 people per thousand per year to the population, it would take 50 years to double. But the doubling time is actually much shorter because populations grow at compound interest rates.

GROWTH PROJECTIONS

Taking the median United Nations (UN) projection, world population will grow to nine billion by 2050. This is an increase of 47 percent between 2000 and 2050—95 percent of this growth will be in cities.[3]

There has been a massive acceleration in growth of cities over the last century. At the turn of the century, roughly 5.5 percent of the world's population lived in cities with populations of over 100,000. Between 1950 and 1995, the number of million-plus cities in the developed world more than doubled, from 49 to 112. In that same period, however, the number of million-plus cities in the developing world rose by a factor of six, from 34 to 213. The UN estimates that rural numbers will remain virtually steady from now on, but urban populations will continue to explode. By how much is open to debate; the UN estimates that by 2025 more than five billion people, 61 percent of the projected population, will live in cities.[4]

This raises the question of how economically and socially secure a rapidly growing city of 10 million will be, if climate change, increasing resource competition, dwindling supplies, or civil and social upheaval threaten distant sources of food, water, energy and other critical resources?

What is becoming clear is that the risk of an eventual collapse from environmental degradation caused by rising populations is real and growing. The scientific and satellite measurements are incontrovertible: "business as usual" will kill us. A new atlas published by the U.N. Environmental Program called *One Planet Many People* documents the environmental changes being caused by humanity.

Although public policy makers are still not facing it, practically everyone else is paying close attention to the possibility of overshoot and collapse. By the 1990s, *Limits to Growth* had sold nine million copies in twenty-nine languages. In 2004 a third volume, *Limits To Growth: The 30-Year Update*, revisited the argument, showing how the critics had been wrong. Able to draw on better and updated data, the authors now say that with its all-out commitment to growth, humanity is walking on thin ice and may soon be past the point of preventing the ice from breaking. Unlimited growth cannot continue and a new, ecologically sound way of life must be discovered for our culture to survive.[5]

GROWTH CAUSES

The Food Race

People are not exempt from the biological rules that govern other species. Famine, for example, is not unique to humans. When the population of any species outstrips its food resources, that population declines until it is once again in balance with its carrying capacity.

Mother Culture dictates that humans should be exempt from that rule. When she finds a population that has outstripped its resources, she rushes in with food instead of birth control, to be sure there will be even more people to starve in the next generation. The population is never allowed to decline to the point where it can be supported by its own carrying capacity. Famine becomes a chronic feature of our existence.

We Takers have appointed ourselves as divine rulers of the world. Mother Culture says, "I will not let them starve, I will not let the drought come, I will not let the river flood. It is the gods who let these things happen, not us." If we do not manage world population now, we will have a much bigger problem in the very near future.

Let's call this the food race. The phenomenon is this: "every increase in food production to feed an increased population is answered by another increase in population."

We need to take a step back from the problem in order to see it in a global perspective. At present there are six billion on earth, and, though millions are starving, we are producing enough food to feed seven billion. Because we are producing enough food for seven billion, it is a biological certainty that in a few years there will be seven billion. By that time we will be producing enough food for eight billion, even though millions will still be starving, which again means that in a few years there will be eight billion. In order to get off this treadmill, we must realize that increasing food production does not feed our hungry; it only fuels our population explosion.[6]

Our food race is rapidly converting our planet's biomass into human mass. We clear a piece of land of wildlife and a vibrant ecosystem and replant it with human crops. What had previously supported hundreds of thousands of species is now converted into cropland strictly for human food. Now all the productivity of what had previously been sustenance for all of nature's creatures is being turned into human mass—literally into human flesh. Every day, all over the world, biodiversity is disappearing as more and more of our planet's biomass is being turned into human mass. This is what the food race is about.[7]

Human overpopulation is not a social problem. Our population explosion is a biological problem. If we continue a policy that is fatal for other species, it will be fatal to us as well. We cannot make an evolutionarily unsuccessful strategy successful simply because we are human. Nature will not make an exception just for us.[8]

Taker Story Prevents Population Control

Mother Culture talks out of both sides of her mouth on this issue. When you raise the question of the population explosion, she replies global population control, but when you raise the issue of famine, she replies increased food production. As it happens, increased food production is an annual event and global population control is an event that never happens at all.

Have you seen the ads for sending food to starving peoples around the world? Have you ever seen ads for sending contraceptives? Within our culture there has never been a serious attempt at global population control. There never will be such an attempt as long as we are enacting a story that says the gods made the world for people alone. As long as we have that meme, Mother Culture will demand increased food production today, and promise population control tomorrow.[9]

Failure of Family Planning

Religious efforts to increase their own membership or work indirectly to prevent effective birth control make this situation worse. The Catholic Church, for example, sanctions only the rhythm method of birth control. Unfortunately, people who practice this method of birth control commonly become parents. Even under the most carefully controlled conditions, women using this technique run a 15 percent risk of pregnancy each year they use it. With the pill, the rate is less than one percent. Of course, the failure rate of the rhythm method is much higher, about 25 percent.

Family planning alone is inadequate in the field of population control. The things that make family planning acceptable are the very things that make it ineffective. By stressing the right of parents to have any number of children they want, it evades the basic question of population policy, which is how to give societies the number of children they need. By offering only the means for couples to control fertility, it neglects the means for societies to do so. Family planning as it stands now means that if we are going to multiply like rabbits, we should do it on purpose. One couple may plan to have three children; another couple may plan six. In both cases they are a cause of the population problem, not a solution to it.[10]

Denial

The world's environmental movement has a blind spot. While it addresses a wide range of issues related to militarism, inequity, environmental degradation and social injustice, it cannot comfortably speak to resource and population issues. That is because movement leaders are vulnerable to political incentives and constraints that prevent them from coming to grips with the most fundamental facts about our species-wide ecological dilemma.

The population issue is also problematic from a human rights perspective, because no one has come up with a way of significantly reducing human population over the next few decades without resorting to a method that would compromise what many regard as the most sacred of human rights—the right to reproduce. So, for the sake of solidarity and mutual support, the organizations tend to downplay their differences. But this requires that environmental organizations refrain from speaking frankly about the central problem which is exponential population growth.[11]

DOUBLE STANDARD WITH ALL OTHER LIFE

Not content with presiding over the biggest extinction for 65 million years, human beings have been quick to drive back any rival mammals with aspirations to multiply. These range from harp seals in Canada—some 325,000 clubbed to death every spring—to bears in the US and elephants in Africa. In the UK meanwhile, the list of species potentially targeted for culling is ever longer: ruddy ducks, foxes, badgers, red deer, grey squirrels, wild boar.

There's an irony here for those with eyes to see. The black bear hunt in New Jersey last year was licensed because the state's bear population had reached an estimated 2,000–3,000, Norway gave permission for a cull of five wolves out of a national population estimated at twenty. The UK population of wild boar, which were nearly hunted to extinction in the Middle Ages, is put at several hundred.

Now compare those figures with the equivalent human populations. New Jersey's is 8.7 million, Norway's 4.6 million, the UK's over 60 million. All are growing, all are composed of individuals with a planetary impact several orders of magnitude greater than any bear, wolf or seal. Yet while the projected growth of the world's human population by 40 percent over the next four decades scarcely registers on the political seismograph, a few hundred wild boar are enough to get us calling for the marksmen.[12]

EFFECTIVE POPULATION CONTROL

Tribalism

Human beings lived sustainably on the earth for millions of years with a stable population. The key was tribalism. How do tribes control their populations, if not by cannibalism, infanticide, rampant disease, or high levels of infant mortality? While our culture assumes these are their methods of population control, this is not the case. In fact, populations in modern developing nations, even Mexico, have higher rates of infectious disease, infant mortality, suicide, murder, malnutrition and hunger than any known indigenous tribal group ever studied. Yet tribal populations tend to remain relatively stable. How do they do it?[13]

The key difference is the Leaver story: humanity belongs to the earth. Since the earth does not belong to people alone, Leaver communities did not violate the natural *law of limited competition* and endeavor to expand themselves over the world.

Take, for example, the effect of the simple law of tribal integrity and boundaries. Around each of the Leaver peoples was a boundary that was definitely not imaginary, a cultural boundary. If the Navajo started feeling crowded, they could not say to themselves, "Well, the Hopi have a lot of wide open space. Lets go over there and be Hopi." Such a thing would have been unthinkable to them.

New Yorkers can solve their population problems by becoming Arizonans, but the Navajo could not solve their population problems by becoming Hopi. If you crossed over into Hopi territory, they did not give you a form to fill out, they may kill you. That worked very well. That gave people a powerful incentive to limit their populations.[14]

Fertility is also a function of available food supplies. We know that animal populations will grow to the capacity their food supply allows. When the food supply drops below an optimum level, the endocrine system is triggered to reduce sperm count or motility, or the viability of ova, or even to release fewer hormones and pheromones that stimulate a desire for sex. It should be noted that some tribal peoples were agriculturalists, but they also had a limited territory and thus an incentive to control their population.

Exercise also reduces population growth. In a study published in 1997, it was found that 57 percent of women who were cross-country runners had amenorrhea, a condition in which menstruation stops its normal cycle and a woman is temporarily infertile. Amenorrhea is viewed as a disease by modern medicine, which attempts to treat it by returning menstrual regularity with the addition of estrogen and other hormones. In a natural environment it may have been part of a delicate mechanism to balance tribal populations. If more than half of all women on the planet for the past five hundred years had been infertile, taking turns as their levels of exercise changed in response to the need to help gather and hunt food during lean times, we might not have the population explosion we are now experiencing.

Tribal people have a sophisticated knowledge of how to use indiginious plants and fungi to their advantage in solving problems of everyday life. For example, tribal people had been using penicillin for thousands of years before its discovery by modern scientists. They had been using the Pacific yew tree to treat breast cancer for five thousand years before the discovery of Taxol in the plant in the 1990's. Similarly, many plants are now known to contain compounds that directly affect estrogen or other hormonal functions in both women and men. The chaste tree was used for thousands of years in Europe to reduce men's sex drive. Other herbs, such as tansy and rue, are such effective morning after drugs that they were commonly described as such in medical textbooks up until the early years of the twentieth century. Tribal people with an advanced knowledge of natural pharmacology use their knowledge to control their fertility.

Another custom that reduces tribal population growth is breast-feeding. It is common for tribal women to breast-feed their children for as many as three to five years. During this time, the mother's body produces hormones that inhibit menstruation and fertility, presumably to prevent the woman's body from being stressed by breast-feeding and growing a fetus at the same time.

Yet another factor which helped control the population of early human societies is that in most tribal cultures, women hold positions of status and power equal to that of men. In those societies women would have more of a say in their reproductive processes, when and how to have sex, when and how to use birth control and so on. In modern times, as women have become increasingly empowered in the United States and Europe over the past 50 years, there has been a corresponding drop in population growth there.

However they do it, though, tribal populations are stable in a way that reflects the available carrying capacity of their environment. Like healthy tissues in the body, they take what they need and nothing more. It works as if by magic, except it is a magic that also works for every other species of plants or animals in nature.

End The Food Race

The answer to our demographic dilemma is clear: we must abandon the myth that we can sustain infinite growth on a finite planet. We cannot grow our way out of the corner we are painting ourselves into. More food just makes the problem worse. We could mow down the entire planet and terrace the mountains to maximize human food production, but is that the beautiful livable world we want to bequeath to our children?

The earlier arms race could only be ended in one of two ways, either by catastrophe or by the participants walking away from it. Luckily, the second of these happened. The Soviets called it quits, and there was no catastrophe.

The race between food and population is the same. It can be ended by catastrophe, when simply too much of our plant's bio-mass is tied up in our human creations causing ecological collapse, but it does not have to end that way. It can end the way the arms race ended, by people walking away from it. There can be no final triumph of food over population. This is because every single win made on the side of food is answered by a win on the side of population. It has to be that way, it always has been that way, and we can see that it is never going to stop being that way.[15]

OPTIMUM POPULATION

Fundamental changes in our culture are going to be required to preserve any semblance of the world we know. Those changes need to be within natural limits. Even though we would like to dominate nature, we will never win.

What are the limits imposed by nature? We do not know exactly. Finding out will involve complex questions of energy sources, food production, and finding space for other species on earth to reach for their own evolutionary fulfillment. The greatness of a culture is not measured by what it takes, but by what it chooses to leave behind.

A reasonable human population is one that does not degrade the capacity of earth's systems to sustain all species in natural patterns of abundance and distribution, and to maintain fully functional ecological and evolutionary processes.[16]

The causes of environmental degradation today are easily followed to the source. Too many cars, too many factories, too much detergent, too much pesticide, multiplying contrails, inadequate sewage treatment plants, too little clean water, too much carbon dioxide all can be traced easily to too many people.

Paul Ehrlich in *The Population Bomb* suggested a population of .5 to one billion could be sustained in reasonable comfort with no environmental crisis.[17] It is as much a question of per capita consumption as it is of population. If everyone wants to have more, then there would have to be fewer of us making demands on the natural environment.

A mere century of stability may provide enough time to investigate most technological leads and to make some cultural adjustments. Our big problem for the next century is to bring the population under control, then to reduce it far enough below overshoot to pay back the ecological debt that we are now accumulating.[18]

However, for the species we push into extinction everyday, there is no way for us to ever pay them back.

It would take just 100 years to reduce human population to one billion if, on average, we had one-child families. In 2100, the human population could be only one billion instead of the projected nine or 10 billion. Humanity could then average six-acre footprints and still leave 80 percent of the earth's biosphere to the wild. This is a solution that does not assume humans dominate nature, and it is a solution with no losers.[19] By any measure that leaves space enough for wild nature to flourish. We have already greatly surpassed the earth's carrying capacity, and thus the truly smart growth would be negative growth.

4. Overshooting Carrying Capacity

Since 1983, humanity has overshot the earth's carrying capacity. What does that mean? Human population has grown to a size that is now consuming renewable natural resources faster than the earth can regenerate them. This process is called drawdown. It also includes nonrenewable resources such as oil and minerals.

Carrying capacity is the population size at a given per capita rate of consumption that its environment can support over the long-term. A population can overshoot carrying capacity, or biocapacity, for a while by drawing down renewable resources. But, if population is not quickly reduced below carrying capacity to enable the earth's life-support system to regenerate and pay back the ecological debt, the population will collapse when the natural resources are depleted. This is something like a farmer eating his seed corn to make it through the winter. In the spring he will have nothing left to plant and he will starve.

DRAWDOWN

Drawdown has been by far the most successful strategy to increase the human carrying capacity of the planet, and the degree of that success can be gauged in a single statistic, namely that of the world population growth since the beginning of the industrial revolution. The human population did not reach one billion until about 1820; in the less than two centuries since then, it has increased six-fold.

This is a rate of growth unprecedented in human history.

The exploitation of fossil fuels created so much new carrying capacity, and so quickly, that much of that new capacity could be translated into increased wealth and a higher standard of living for a small but significant portion of the world's population. Previously, a parasitic increase of the standard of living for a wealthy few kings, nobles and lords nearly always entailed a lessening of the standard of living of far more numerous serfs and peasants. Now, with so much energy being liberated from fossil fuels the standard of living could be improved for large numbers of people, at least to a certain extent. Even though the majority of the world's population shared but little in this bonanza and continued to be exploited for cheap labor, virtually everyone shared in the expectation that the benefits of fuel-fed industrialism could eventually be spread to all. This expectation led in turn to a partial relaxation of the class-based tensions that had plagued complex societies since their beginnings.[1]

The danger of the drawdown strategy is our increasing dependency on energy resources that are being depleted within historically short time frames. There are now somewhere between two and five billion humans alive who probably would not exist but for fossil fuels. Thus if the availability of these fuels were to decline significantly without our having found effective replacements to maintain all their life-sustaining benefits, then the global human carrying capacity would plummet even below its pre-industrial levels. When the flow of fuels begins to diminish, everyone will actually be worse off than they would have been had those fuels never been discovered because our pre-industrial survival skills will have been lost and there will be an intense competition for food and water among members of the now unsupportable population.[2]

OVERSHOOT TODAY

The World Wide Fund for Nature's (WWF) Living Planet Report 2004 indicates that the human global ecological footprint now exceeds the earth's sustainable carrying capacity by about 20 percent. Our global ecological footprint would require two or three earths to be sustainable over the long run rather than the one we actually have to live on. It bears mentioning that the American ecological footprint is ten times its world share of resources.[3] This overshoot depletes the earth's natural capital, and is therefore possible only for a limited number of people and for a limited period of time.

Ecosystems are suffering, and the global climate is changing. The further we continue down this road of unsustainable consumption and exploitation, the more difficult it will become to protect the biodiversity that remains. The WWF report also noted that 40 percent of species of the natural world have been lost since 1970 alone.[4] At this rate there may only be humans, cows, chickens, cats, dogs and a few stragglers left on the planet by 2100. We have a moral responsibility to leave the world for our children and other forms of life in good health. But right now we are on the wrong road and we know better.

Western Nations With Stable Populations Are In Overshoot

Even European countries with stable populations, such as Norway, Germany and Italy, are currently overshooting their carrying capacity. These countries are already overpopulated. First, they are overpopulated by the simple criterion that they are not able to produce enough food to feed themselves. Second, they are overpopulated because they must import more materials and energy than they produce to maintain their economies. They are also overpopulated because they have exceeded the capacity of their environments to dispose of their wastes.[5]

Even though western European per capita consumption of energy is lower than that of the United States, these nation-states exist in relative peace and prosperity only because they are able to exploit nonrenewable fossil fuels that one day will be exhausted. Although they may be stable at the moment, all city-states dependent on oil and unlimited growth on a finite planet are inherently unstable because of the cultural stories upon which they are based.[6]

Ecological Debt

A WWF Living Planet Report explored four possible ecological footprint scenarios from about 2002 to 2120 to measure the consequences of possible societal choices. An ecological footprint is the total human consumption relative to the earth's carrying capacity (CC). An infinite slow growth path is contrasted with three paths that would eliminate overshoot and return humanity back to living within the earth's biological carrying capacity. These three paths compare a soft landing and different speeds of collapse back to a sustainable level of human consumption. The slow growth path will inevitably result in a hard crash to a sustainable level far below the original earth's carrying capacity.

Path Name	of Target Earth Carrying Capacity	Year CC Achieved collapse	Accumulated Ecological Debt
Slow Growth◊			40 planet-years
Path One*	50 percent	2030	3.5
Path Two	67	2050	6.0
Path Three†	88	2100	20.0

◊ Between 1983 and 2001, humanity accumulated 1.5 planet-years of ecological debt. In this Slow Growth scenario, this ecological debt rises to more than 40 planet-years by 2050 and then continues to accumulate until collapse.

* Soft Landing path proposed by biologist E. O. Wilson in 2002

† Suggestion put forward by the Brundtland Commission in 1987 that the remaining 12 percent be available for wild species. Considering we are just one of 30 million species on earth, and dropping rapidly, leaving only 12 percent of the earth's total carrying capacity does not seem too generous.

The paths differ in the extent to which human demand exceeds the earth's carrying capacity and the number of years in which overshoot continues. Adding up the annual global deficits provides a measure of accumulated ecological debt. Ecological debt can also be looked at as the total drawdown of renewable natural resources caused by overshoot. One planet-year is the total productive carrying capacity of the earth for one year.[7]

Assessing Risk

Forests are productive ecosystems with a large biomass stock. Each year immature forests accumulate about 2 percent of the biomass of a mature forest, making the ecological assets in a mature forest equal to 50 years of production. If the entire carrying capacity of the planet were forest, the maximum possible one-time depletion would be 50 planet-years.

However, most ecosystem types have less stock available than forests and are depleted more rapidly if overused. In addition, assuming full substitutability amount among types of ecological assets underestimates the severity of overshoot, since overuse of one type may lead to depletion and degradation of that particular asset, even if overall demand does not indicate a global overshoot. Furthermore, irreversible damage to ecosystems may occur as a result of ecosystem loss. Fifty planet-years may, therefore, be a high estimate of what the biosphere can tolerate.

This comparison helps to interpret the risk associated with each of the four paths. The 50 percent path in the WWF report, for example is economically risky in that it requires large investments now, but ecologically the least risky as it minimizes ecological debt. On the other hand, the 88 percent path requires smaller financial investment up front, but runs the risk of seriously compromising the ability of the biosphere to meet humanity's demands.[8]

This risk assessment is just from a human point of view. It ignores the millions of species that we will push into extinction during overshoot and even when we are taking more than our fair share before overshoot.

LIMITS TO GROWTH

There are limits to how far exponential population and economic growth can continue on a planet with an ecosystem that is finite, non-growing, and materially closed. Limits to growth include both the material and energy that are extracted from the earth, and the capacity of the planet to absorb the pollutants that are generated as those materials and energy are used.

The most obvious limit on food production is land. Millions of acres of cultivated land are being degraded by processes such as soil erosion and salinisation, while the cultivated area remains roughly constant. Higher yields have compensated somewhat for this loss, but yields cannot increase indefinitely. Per capita grain production peaked in 1985 and has been trending down slowly ever since.

Another limit to food production is water. In many countries, both developing and developed, current water use is often not sustainable. In an increasing number of the world's watersheds, limits have already been reached. In the U.S., the Midwestern Ogallala aquifer is over-drawn by 12 cubic kilometers each year. Its depletion has so far caused 2.46 million acres of farmland to be taken out of cultivation.

Another renewable resource is forests, which moderate climate, build soils, control floods and harbor many plant, animal and micro organism species. But today, only one-fifth of the planet's original mature forest cover remains in large tracts of undisturbed natural forests. From 1990 to 2000, the U.N. Food and Agriculture Organization (FAO) reports that more than 370 million acres of forest cover, an area the size of Mexico, was converted to other uses. If the loss of 49 million acres of forest per year, typical in the 1990s, continues to increase at 2 percent per year, the unprotected forest will be gone before the end of the century.[9]

Why Technology and Markets Alone Cannot Solve Limits

The authors of *Limits To Growth* created the World3 overshoot computer simulation. It revealed that in a complex, finite world, if you remove or raise one limit and go on growing, you encounter another limit. Especially if the growth is exponential, the next limit will show up surprisingly soon. There are layers of limits. In an increasingly linked global economy, a society under duress anywhere in the world sends out shock waves that are felt everywhere. Furthermore, globalization enhances the likelihood that those parts of the world involved in active trade with each other will reach many of their limits more or less simultaneously.

A second lesson from the World3 simulation is that the more suc-cessfully society puts off its limits through economic and technologi-cal innovations, the more likely it is to run into several of these limits at the same time.

In most World3 runs, the world system does not totally run out of land, food, resources, or pollution control. What it runs out of is the ability to cope. Determinants of the ability to cope include: peo-ple and their motivation, political attention, financial risk, capacity to develop and implement new technologies, capacity of the media and leaders to remain focused on the main problems, voter consensus, and the degree to which people anticipate problems.

People can process and handle just so much. When problems arise exponentially and in multitudes, problems that could normally be handled one by one can overwhelm the ability to cope. Exponential growth is insidious because it shortens the time for effective action. It loads stress on the system faster and faster, until coping mechanisms that have been adequate with slower rates of change finally begin to fail. Lesser-developed countries will fail first because they will have 95 percent of the population growth, but have fewer resources.[10] This may cause a domino effect from lesser to more developed countries.

There are three other reasons why technology and market mechanisms, that otherwise function well, cannot solve the problems generated by a society driving toward interconnected limits at an exponential rate. First, markets and technologies are merely tools that serve the goals, the ethics and the time horizons of the society as a whole. If a society's implicit goals are to exploit nature, enrich the elite and ignore long-term consequences, then that society will develop technologies and markets that destroy the environment, widen the gap between the rich and the poor and optimize for short-term gains. In short, that society develops technologies and markets that hasten a collapse instead of preventing it.

The second reason for the vulnerability of technology is that adjustment mechanisms have costs. These costs tend to rise exponentially as limits are approached. For example, it is fairly inexpensive to remove almost 50 percent of auto nitrogen oxide emissions. There is a rising, but still affordable, cost for removing almost 80 percent. But then there is a limit, a threshold, beyond which costs of further removals rise enormously.

Pollution abatement curves will always have the same basic shape. There are fundamental physical reasons why abatement costs soar as 100 percent abatement, that is zero emissions, is approached. It may be affordable to cut pollutants per car in half, but if the number of cars then doubles, pollutants per car have to be cut in half again just to keep the same air quality. Two doublings will require 75 percent pollution abatement. Three doublings will require 87.5 percent.

At some point it stops being true that growth will allow an economy to become rich enough to afford pollution control. In fact, growth takes an economy up a nonlinear cost curve to the point where further abatement becomes unaffordable.[11]

This is particularly clear when one turns to South Korea, one country that has come to symbolize the miracle of rapid economic growth. Close examination of the Korean experience shows the danger of confusing sustainable economic growth and sustainable development. Air pollution in Seoul is among the highest in the world. A study in the 1980's concluded that 67 percent of the rain falling on that city contained levels of acid hazardous to human health. Sulfur dioxide emissions in Seoul have been found to be five times that of Taipei and eight times that of Tokyo, two cities well known for heavy air pollution. In 1989, the government discovered that water at ten purification plants contained heavy metals such as cadmium, iron and manganese at twice the official tolerance levels. Korea has one of the highest rates of occupational-related illnesses in the world, with 2.66 out of every 11 persons suffering from occupational-related illnesses, compared to 0.70 in Taiwan, 0.93 in Singapore and 0.61 in Japan.[12]

The third reason technology and the market cannot automatically solve these problems is that they operate through feedback loops with information distortions and delays. Delays in market and technology responses can be much longer than expected. Technology-market feedback loops are themselves sources of overshoot, oscillation and instability. One example of instability is the fluctuation in oil prices today and during the decades after 1973.

Denial

In the twilight of the age of exuberance the idea that there might be limits to growth is still impossible to imagine for many people. Limits are politically unmentionable and economically unthinkable. Our culture tends to deny the possibility of limits by placing a profound faith in the power of technology, the workings of a free market, and the growth of the economy as the solution to all problems, even the problems created by growth.

"Twenty years ago some spoke of limits to growth. But today, we now know that growth is the engine of change. Growth is the friend of the environment." President George H. W. Bush, 1992.

The solution to infinite growth on a finite planet may be found in Herman Daly's book *Beyond Growth: The Economics of Sustainable Development*. Daly explores steady state economics.

Part of the problem is that the damage being done is largely invisible. Most people, especially Americans, do not see what is happening because the costs have been externalized somewhere else, the poverty is somewhere else, the hunger is somewhere else, and the media does not shine a spotlight on it. When you build a new house, the builder gets the lumber from the lumberyard; you do not get to see the clearcut forest. When you buy a new computer, you do not see the thousands of pounds of waste created per pound of electronics. When you look at a Midwestern farm field, you cannot see the topsoil that used to be there nor the forest or the prairie. They are simply gone.

TEMPORARY EXTENSIONS TO CARRYING CAPACITY

We and our immediate ancestors have lived through an age of exuberant growth overshooting permanent carrying capacity without knowing what we were doing. The past four centuries of magnificent progress were made possible by two non-repeatable events: (1) discovery of a second hemisphere, and (2) development of ways to exploit the planet's store of ancient sunlight in the form of fossil fuels.

The resulting opportunities for economic and demographic exuberance convinced people that it was natural for the future to always be better than the past. For a while that belief was a workable story for our lives and institutions. But now that the New World has become as populated as the Old World, and now that resource depletion is becoming unmistakable, the future will be different from what we expected.[13]

The ruthless displacement of unwanted plants and animals was part of the takeover process by which American pioneers inflicted European agriculture on the New World. Nature's tendency is to turn farms into wilderness; our culture's tendency during the past 10,000 years has been to turn wilderness into farms. The Europeans who came to the New World did not just fight the native inhabitants; they also fought succession, thereby claiming far more of the New World's carrying capacity strictly for Homo sapiens than the Indians had.

People alive today are more numerous than our preagricultural ancestors and depend for their existence on humanity's continued success in converting a climax ecosystem, or wilderness, with minimum but permanent human carrying capacity, into a less mature stage with greatly enlarged but precarious human carrying capacit.

A climax ecosystem has more inherent stability through biodiversity than a farm does, but it will not feed as many people because much of its production is being consumed by other species.

As we have seen, the drawdown method increases human carrying capacity on a strictly temporary basis. We have assumed so far that the takeover method yields permanent increments in carrying capacity. But now, relating this method to succession, we can see the gains are precarious at best. It is like a dike or a levee, requiring constant maintenance and perpetual improvement, to hold back the ever rising floodwaters of succession.[14]

COLLAPSE

Can the growth of population and physical capital continue forever? The answer is no. Growth in population and capital increase the human ecological footprint unless there is a successful effort to avoid such an increase. It is theoretically possible to reduce the per capita ecological footprint through technology or other means quickly enough to allow continued growth in population and industrial capital. But based on our culture's recent track record and the fact that population growth will eventually overwhelm technology gains, this probably will not be achieved. Evidence from around the world today shows that a sufficient reduction is not taking place. The ecological footprint is growing. Instead of a Marshall Plan to reduce our footprint and impacts such as CO_2 emissions and soil loss, we have a war for oil.

Once the footprint has grown beyond the sustainable level, as it has, it must eventually come down either through a semi-managed process or through the work of nature. There is no question about whether growth in the ecological footprint will stop, the only questions are when and by what means.[15] There is no magic recipe for avoiding a collapse when overshoot has already happened.[16]

Population growth will eventually cease and decline, either because the birth rates fall farther or because death rates begin to rise or both. World fertility rates were projected to drop from 4.5 births per woman from 1970-1975 to 2.7 births from 2000-2005.[17] However, a birth rate of 2.7 still leads to a population of over 20 billion by 2100.[18] It would take a birth rate of 1.0 to get population down to an optimal level of 1 billion by 2100, allowing us to return a fair share of the earth to other species.[19]

Population will have a forced decrease because the alternative of reducing per capita consumption appears unlikely. The less-developed countries cannot get much poorer and many want to attain a wasteful Western lifestyle. The over-developed nations have made consumption a kind of religion, and unless forced to, will not be be letting go of their cultural story anytime soon.

Soft or Hard Landing?

The U.S. Census Bureau currently predicts word population to peak in 2042 at nine billion. After that, the three soft landing paths described in the WWF report showing reductions to 50 percent, 67 percent, or 88 percent of the earth's carrying capacity peak in about 2005, 2015 and 2025 respectively. They return from overshoot to one planet's carrying capacity and start paying off their ecological debt in 2015, 2030 and 2075 respectively. The 50 percent path is out for now because we have not even begun to invest in the necessary technologies and structural changes to reduce our ecological footprint. The slow growth path would precipitate a rapid population crash once its peak is reached. The following chapters on energy, agriculture, the environment and the economy will reveal more.

Delay Reduces Future Carrying Capacity

Waiting to introduce fundamental change reduces the options for humanity's long-term future. The longer the world takes to reduce its ecological footprint, the lower the population and material standard that will be ultimately supportable.[20] In other words, when we overshoot the carrying capacity of our environment, we damage the future productivity of our habitat, causing its future carrying capacity to be less than it was originally.[21]

Here is an example from the animal kingdom. In 1944, 29 reindeer were introduced onto St. Matthew Island in the Bering Sea. The island has an area of 128 square miles and is well suited to support them. In 1957, 1,350 of them were counted. By 1963, the herd had increased to 6,000. Estimates of reindeer carrying capacity for land and climate similar to St. Mathews Island vary between 13 and 18 head per square mile, making the carrying capacity of this habitat between 1,600 and 2,300 reindeer. The 1963 population was thus at least 2.6 times what the island could permanently support. At least 3,700 of the living reindeer in 1963 were overshoot. This did not mean, however, that when that many had died off, the population would stabilize at the island's carrying capacity. Overshoot leads to habitat damage, so the collapse population stabilized below its original level. The bloated overgrazing herd stole from its own posterity. In 1966, only three years after the peak number was reached, there were just 42 reindeer left on St. Mathew Island.

₀LIMITS TO GROWTH₁ FRAMEWORK NOT ENOUGH

A key problem with how the limits to growth debate is framed is that it refers to future events. The possibility of a growth-caused ecological crisis is always set for tomorrow. Limits to growth literature falls into this trap of future-oriented thinking such as "humanity is close to limits," or "hazardous times are just ahead," or "we may soon see such and such."

From an ecological present day view this approach is self-defeating. Tomorrow is a slippery idea. It never comes, so it essentially refers to nothing. When today arrives it is not a catastrophe, it is simply a world that is increasingly poorer than it was yesterday. Directing attention toward future possible disasters can subtly shape how the present is experienced. As long as the test for an ecological crisis is in the future, we cannot see that we are immersed in it here and now, which is the only place change can happen.

Also, since our lives are relatively short, our time scale of reference is short. If we could see the world from our grandparent's lives to ours, we would see enormous changes in our world. But since we only get one relatively short life, we will have to try a little harder in this one to see the crises of today.

Over time wild Nature's original service might become massively tweaked and substituted by support services engineered for people alone. While the latter world would be an ecological wasteland by any comparison to the former, it might be capable of sustaining human beings, perhaps even in large numbers. So, as the limits to growth debate keeps circling around an upcoming collision with carrying capacity limits, what we are seeing is the unfolding of a slow motion decline that is ending the natural world not with a bang but a whimper.

In short, the limits to growth framework is inadequate to address the central crisis of our day: (1) because mass extinction could conceivably come to pass without jeopardizing the survival of the human species; (2) because people might be materially sustained by a technologically managed world made to yield services and products required for human life. At a population of nine billion, the destruction of the natural areas of the world may be complete, and the only ecosystems left would be under human cultivation.

The question is not whether a colonized world is viable but rather who wants to live in such a world? Presented with a portrait of a planet devoid of natural ecosystems, wildlife and wilderness, people might awaken to the bleak world now unfolding.

If biophilia is born to the human soul, as E.O. Wilson has eloquently maintained, then devastating the biosphere is tantamount to the betrayal of love. Such is the treason at the heart of the biodiversity crisis. One has to be as clear and precise as possible about the consequences of the human order under construction: in this emerging reality it may not be our survival and well being that are primarily on the line, but everybody else's as well.[22]

5. Culture's Hunger, War, Inequality, and Distress

The hunger, poverty, war, inequity and distress suffered by most of the people in the world is almost invisible to those who live in western countries. You could say Mother Culture does not like to show us her dirty laundry. We do not see them on the nightly news for the most part nor read about them in the daily paper.

Try to go to bed hungry tonight; 800 million people will. Have you ever walked across a landfill or visited a sewage treatment plant? How about living near one or on top of one? Veterans who read this know something about war. But for most of us, war is something we know only by watching television. We see generals talking about precision guided bombs, but don't see the doctors explaining the effects on a child's body when the bomb explodes.

This chapter is a meager attempt to explain what is happening in the overpopulated world. Photographer Sebastiao Salgado has published two stunning books, *Workers* and *Migrations*, which show the plight of these people in graphic images.

HUNGER

Of the 800 million who go to bed hungry each night, 300 million are children. More than 90 percent of these children suffer long-term malnutrition and micronutrient deficiencies.

Every 3.6 seconds, another person dies of starvation, the large majority of whom are children under the age of five. Six million children die each year from malnutrition before their fifth birthday.[1]

The food race cannot be won. Every increase in food production to feed an increased population is answered by another increase in population. We will never have *enough* food. The solution is not more food, but a return to a way of life in which people belong to the earth, not that the earth belongs to humanity. When a culture belongs to the earth, it lives within its carrying capacity; there is enough food for all.

The price of losing the food race every year, year after year, from 1968 to 1996 were 250 million people dying of starvation—250 million in just the last few decades alone![2]

In the United States, the land of plenty and the breadbasket of the world, hunger is growing. The number of hungry families in the U.S. has increased for five consecutive years now from 10.5 million families in 1999 to 12.6 million in 2003. The U.S. Conference of Mayors reported that emergency requests for food assistance in the U.S. had increased by 14 percent in 2006.

Our competitive culture not only concentrates wealth, which we will talk in detail about later, but it also concentrates food in the hands of a few. A few people in the world can choose which supermarket they will drive their SUV to, then choosing from a seemingly endless variety of available foods. What the SUV-driving mom does not see is how globalization has forced the majority of small farmers worldwide to give up their self-sufficient farms and move to city slums. Or if they stay on the farm, how their government, Monsanto and Cargill force them to grow genetically modified crops for export to pay crushing third-world debt. When debt relief does come, as it has in 2005, it is only in exchange for strict structural adjustments that increase corporate access and control.

So, instead of feeding their families, they feed our families. More than 50 countries that had food self-sufficiency in the 1930s were net importers of food by the 1980s.[3]

Can things get any worse? Probably. Through the miracle of globalization, the wealthy nations have grabbed the lion's share of the world's protein. Through the export of cash crops, we take more protein from starving nations than we return to them. What is worse, we feed a great deal of the protein we import to our pets and to our farm animals. Originally, the world belonged to humanity and all other forms of life, but now most of it belongs to rich people alone.

Let's finish by super sizing. Because mother culture has us believe that the world belongs to humanity alone, we take more than we need.

While millions starve, we die from eating too much. Obesity now kills 330,000 North Americans a year and will soon pass tobacco as the leading preventable cause of sickness and death.[4] Obesity and physical inactivity cost the state of California alone $21.7 billion a year in the form of rising medical care costs, workers' compensation rates and lost productivity.[5]

Morgan Spurlock's *Super Size Me* is an award-winning documentary film on the subject.

POVERTY

Our Taker culture has had 10,000 years to end poverty, fairly distribute wealth, ensure individual, family and community security, live within the earth's carrying capacity and respect all other species. However, it has failed miserably.

According to the federal government poverty guidelines, to live in poverty in the U.S. means to live on less than $26 a day. Under this definition, there are 35.9 million poor people in the United States, nearly one out of every eight citizens.

It takes nothing away from the daily challenges faced by poor people in America to look beyond our shores at the awful, breathtaking expanse of global poverty. In many countries around the world, $26 a day is a distant dream. Over 1.1 billion of the world's people live on less than one dollar a day. Not one dollar a day, *less* than one dollar a day. That is nearly one out of every six people on earth.

Since 1990, the number of people living on less than $2 per day increased by about 40 percent to just over 2.7 billion. Even though the percentage of people living on less than $2 per day dropped during the period, the sheer numbers of people in poverty grew, as population growth overwhelmed all progress.[6] Fifty four nations experienced declines in per capita gross domestic product (GDP) for more than a decade during the period 1990-2001.[7]

Moreover, in the current system, economic growth generally occurs in the already rich countries and flows disproportionately to the richest people within those countries. According to the United Nations Development Program, the 20 percent of the world's people who lived in the wealthiest nations had 30 times the per capita income of the poorest 20 percent of nations. By 1995, the average income ratio between the richest and poorest had increased from 30:1 to 82:1.

Only eight percent of the world's people own a car. Hundreds of millions of people live in inadequate houses or have no shelter at all, much less refrigerators. Social arrangements common in many cultures systematically reward the privileged, and it is easier for rich populations to save, invest and multiply their capital.[8]

SANITATION

Poor sanitation goes hand in hand with poverty. More than 2.6 billion people, over 40 percent of the world's population, do not have basic sanitation, and more than one billion people still use unsafe drinking water. Four out of every 10 people in the world do not have access even to a simple latrine.[9]

Here is a story about living poverty by Thom Hartman from *The Last Hours of Ancient Sunlight*:

"When I was in the Philippines in 1985, Father Ben Carreon, an activist priest and the author of a popular column for the *Manila Times*, took me to one of that city's huge garbage dumps. The smell was awful, the air thick with insects, as mountains of rotted garbage stretched off into the distance.

We stood in the hot afternoon sun, and Father Ben said, 'Look carefully at the piles of garbage.'

I squinted in the bright light, looking at the distant piles, and noticed something. 'They're moving!' I said.

'No, it's children on them that are moving,' he said. 'Thousands of them. Their families live all around here, and the children spend their days scavenging for garbage that the family can eat.'

Father Ben's response to his discovery years ago that there were armies of children living among the garbage dumps was to begin a scholarship program to put the 'garbage dump kids' through grade school and high school. Hundreds have graduated from high school and dozens from college as a result of his efforts. 'Still, it's only a drop in the sea,' he said to me a few years after we first met. 'The task is enormous.' "[10]

INEQUITY

Consider three equities that our Taker culture has lost: equality between generations, between people and between species.

Inter-generational Equality

I believe it is a fundamental human right to be born into a world that is not already over crowded.

When my grandfather was born, in 1898, there were 1.6 billion people. On my father's birth date in 1927, there were two billion. When I was born, in 1962, global population had risen to 2.9 billion. Now, 100 years after my grandfather's birth, we have added another 4.4 billion people. During the same time period the percent of fallow and wild land dropped from 67 percent surplus to 20 percent overshoot. In the 150 years since the industrial revolution began, we have doubled the population four times and doubled the global economy 20 times.

A journey back 60,000 generations to the Rift Valley in what is now northeast Africa—a period of 1.5 million years—shows the relatively small human settlements that left the bulk of earth's space wild.

Intergenerational equality can be summed up as simply passing the land and life on to the next generation with out degradation. How intensively did you use the earth's resources? Did you leave a buffer, as in wetlands, forests and fallow fields, so the unborn generations would be assured wild and productive diversity? The earth produces a tremendous amount of life each year. Currently, humanity takes 20 percent more than nature produces, thus drawing down the earth's capital. Might it be wise to scale back our annual take to help the overworked systems rebound? We can either err on the side of caution or gamble with our children's future.[11]

Inter-human Equality

It is difficult to speculate just how equitable earlier societies actually were, but we can glean insights from historical records and contemporary egalitarian communities. For example, Russell Thornton's book, *American Indian Holocaust and Survival*, estimated that in 1492, 1.8 million people lived in what is now called the United States. If we divide the biologically productive area of the continent's 1.79 billion acres by 1.8 million people, each person had 1,000 acres of productive land, and we know their ecological footprints were a fraction of ours. Anthropologist Richard Robbins wrote of native North Americans, "Since there was little occupational specialization and little difference in individual wealth or possessions, relations were of an egalitarian nature." Other written accounts offer support for this statement.

The Spanish priest, Bartholomew de las Casas, who accompanied Columbus on his initial journey, wrote in his journal about the Arawak of the Bahaman Islands: "They lived in large communal bell-shaped buildings, housing up to 600 people at one time...made of very strong wood and roofed with palm leaves... They lacked all manners of commerce, neither buying nor selling, and rely exclusively on their natural environment for maintenance. They are extremely generous with their possessions and by the same token covet the possessions of their friends and expect the same degree of liberality... Endless testimonies ... prove the mild and pacific temperament of the natives ... But our work was to exasperate, ravage, kill, mangle and destroy."[12]

Inter-species Equality

Humanity's current overshoot leaves ever less room for the 30 million other species on earth. In fact, it leaves so little, that humanity is single-handedly causing the greatest mass extinction since the age of the dinosaurs.

If we are only one species, should that not mean we leave the rest of the species 80 or 90 percent of the earth? This takes us back to an optimal human population of .5 to one billion or less. The earth does not belong to humanity, humanity belongs to the earth.

POPULATION GROWTH OVERWHELMS ALL GAINS

Whatever your cause, it will be a lost cause without population control.
   —paul ehrlich

I believe Paul Ehrlich's statement is very true. Exponential population growth will eventually overwhelm all efforts to create a sustainable society. Improve auto fuel efficiency by half but double the number of cars, and you are back to where you started. Increase food production and more people will eat it up. Preserve open space here, development will occur some place else. Cut greenhouse gas emissions in half, but double population and all of the gains are wiped out.

Those on the left like to claim sustainability is just a matter of redistributing wealth. However, Sandy Irvine writes, "Studies in Guatemala, for example, show that the benefits of land redistribution would disappear within a generation simply because of population growth."[13]

The Millennium Ecosystem Assessment Synthesis Report released in March 2005 reveals that approximately 60 percent of the ecosystem services that support life, such as fresh water, capture fisheries, air and water regulation, and the regulation of regional climate, natural hazards and pests are being degraded or used unsustainably. Scientists warn that the harmful consequences of this degradation could grow significantly worse in the next 50 years.

The report, which was conducted by 1,300 experts from 95 countries noted that, "Any progress achieved in addressing the goals of poverty and hunger eradication, improved health, and environmental protection is unlikely to be sustained if most of the ecosystem services on which humanity relies continue to be degraded." This 2005 report specifically states that the ongoing degradation of ecosystem services is a roadblock to the Millennium Development Goals agreed to by the world leaders at the United Nations in 2000.[14]

A finite planet cannot sustain an infinite growth.

WAR

Our Taker culture has done away with the peace keeper law of limited competition. We now make war. Before our culture, Leaver people practiced the erratic retaliator strategy, which kept the peace and ensured cultural diversity. This natural law of limited competition worked well for humanity for three million years.

As long as our Taker culture believes that the earth was made for people alone and humanity had the right to conquer and rule over it, war will never end—never.

Over the last century, wars have claimed 175 million lives.[15] Technology has shifted civilians into the crosshairs. At the turn of the century 90 percent of all war casualties were among military personnel. That has changed with today's remote-controlled, high tech weaponry, which kills more efficiently and protects soldiers from direct combat. The widespread proliferation of remote weaponry,

has reversed the proportion: 90 percent of the dead in wars worldwide are now civilians. Over 20 million people have died in wars
since World War II. Of those 82 identifiable wars, 79 were internal
civil wars which hit civilians hardest.

Here are some facts to show how important war has become:
The U.S. now spends more on the military than all other nations
combined. We outspend our nearest competitors, China and Russia by 10 to 1. If you take out the social security trust fund from the
general fund and add in veteran's benefits and related debt, military
spending is over a third of the entire federal budget. We spend 10
times more on the military than on K-12 education.

DISTRESS [9] THE BOILING OF OUR TAKER CULTURE

Daniel Quinn in *The Story of B* wrote the best description that I
have read of the complete failure of modern culture. He describes
through history how increasing population creates stress in the
form of war, crime, famine, plague, revolt and finally, the need for
salvation. The following is the history that Mother Culture did not
teach you in school. The purpose is to show that our Taker culture
cannot be *fixed* and that we must rediscover the life story that
humanity belongs to the earth.

Signs of distress: 5000-3000 B.C.

Our Taker culture was getting crowded and overworked, overgrazed land was becoming less and less productive. There were
more people, and they were competing for dwindling resources.

The water is beginning to heat up under our caldron. Remember what we're looking for: signs of distress. What happens when
more people begin competing for less? They start fighting. But of
course they do not fight at random. The town butcher does not battle the town baker; the town tailor does not battle the town shoemaker. No, the town's butcher, baker, tailor, and shoemaker get
together to battle some other town's butcher, baker, tailor, and
shoemaker.

This was the beginning of the age of war that has continued to
the present. We need to see the war-making machinery for what it
is. I don't mean mechanical machinery: the chariots, catapults, siege

machines and so on. I mean the political machinery. Butchers, bakers, tailors and shoemakers don't organize themselves into armies. They need warlords, kings, princes and emperors to do it for them.

Starting around five thousand years ago, the first states began to form for the purpose of armed defense and aggression. It's during this period that we see the standing army forged as the monarch's sword of power. Without a standing army, a king is just a windbag in fancy clothes. But with a standing army, a king can impose his will on his enemies and engrave his name in history. Think about it. The only names we have from this period are the names of conquering kings. No scientists, no philosophers, no historians, no prophets—just conquerors. For the first time in human history, the important people are the people with armies.

After this point the military and its needs became the chief stimulus for technological advancement and foreign conquest. Soldiers needed better armor, better swords, better chariots, better bows and arrows, better scaling machines, better rams, better artillery, better guns, better tanks, better planes, better bombs, better nerve gas and better rockets. At this early stage of modern human culture no one saw technology in the service of warfare as a sign that something bad was going on. They thought it was an improvement.

Signs of distress: 3000-1400 B.C.

The fire burned on under the cauldron of our culture, and the next doubling of our population took only 1,600 years. There were a 100 million humans now, at 1400 B.C., probably 90 percent of them being members of our Modern culture. The Near East hadn't been big enough for us for a long time. Totalitarian agriculture had moved northward and eastward into Russia and India and China, northward and westward into Asia Minor and Europe. Other kinds of agriculture which had once been practiced in these lands were displaced by our way of agriculture.

The wars of the previous age were piddling affairs compared with the wars of this age. This is the Bronze Age! Real weapons, real armor. There were vast standing armies, supported by unbelievable imperial wealth.

Unlike the effects of war, other signs of distress are not cast in bronze or chiseled in stone. Nonetheless, there is at least one sign that can be read in the historical evidence: crime was emerging as a major problem.

You may be unimpressed with this news. Crime? Crime is universal among humans, isn't it? No, actually it isn't. Misbehavior, yes. Unpleasant behavior, disruptive behavior, yes. People can always be counted on to fall in love with the wrong person or to lose their tempers or to be stupid or greedy or vengeful. Crime is something else. By today's definition crime does not exist among tribal peoples. This isn't because they are nicer people than we are, it's because they are organized in a different way. We will discuss this in detail later.

Suffice to say that durning this period, crime appeared in society. Notice that crime made its appearance at the beginning of the age of literacy. As soon as people started to write, they started writing laws; this is because writing enabled them to do something they had not been able to do before. Writing enabled them to define in exact, fixed terms the behaviors they wanted to regulate, punish and suppress.

Signs of distress: 1400-0 B.C.

The fire burned on under the cauldron of our culture, and the next doubling of our population took only 1,400 years. There were 200 million humans now, at the beginning of our "Common Era," 95 percent or more of them belonging to our Taker culture, East and West.

It was an era of political and military adventurism. Hammurabi made himself master of all Mesopotamia. Sesostris III of Egypt invaded Palestine and Syria. Assyria's Tiglath Pileser I extended his rule to the shores of the Mediterranean. Egyptian pharaoh Sheshonk overran Palestine. Tiglath Pileser III conquered Syria, Palestine, Israel and Babylon. Babylon's Second Nebuchadnezzar took Jerusalem and Tyre. Cyrus the Great extended his reach across the whole of the *civilized* west, and two centuries later Alexander the Great made the same imperial reach.

It was also an era of civil revolt and assassination. The reign of Assyria's Shalmaneser ended in revolution. A revolt in Chalcidice against Athenian rule marked the beginning of the 20-year-long conflict known as the Peloponnesian War. A few years later

Mitylene, in Lesbos, also revolted. Spartans, Achaeans and Arcadians organized a rebellion against Macedonian rule. A revolt in Egypt brought Ptolemy III home from his military campaign in Syria. Philip of Macedon was assassinated, as was Darius III of Persia, Seleucus III Soter, the Carthaginian general Hasdrubel, social reformer Tiberius Sempronius Gracchus, the Seleucid king Antiochus VIII, Chinese emperor Wong Mong, and Roman emperors Claudius and Domitian.

But these weren't the only new signs of stress which appeared durning this age. Counterfeiting, coinage debasement, catastrophic inflation—all those nasty tricks became common. Famine was an ongoing reality throughout the civilized world. Plague appeared, ever symptomatic of overcrowding and poor sanitation. In 429 B.C. plague carried off as much as two thirds of the population of Athens.

Slavery became a huge, international business, and of course remains so even today. At the midpoint of the fifth century B.C. every third or fourth person in Athens was a slave. When Carthage fell to Rome in 146 B.C., 50,000 of the survivors were sold as slaves. In 132 B.C. some 70,000 Roman slaves rebelled; when the revolt was put down, 20,000 were crucified.

Other signs of distress appeared during this period that were expressed in an entirely new way. For the first time in history, people sensed that something was fundamentally wrong. People felt empty, as though their lives were not amounting to anything. They began wondering if this is all there was to life, or was there something more—something better than their daily suffering. For the first time people began listening to religious teachers who promised salvation. Judaism, Brahmanism, Hinduism and Buddhism all came into being during this period.

Religion in some form had been in existence in our culture for thousands of years, but it had never been centered around the idea of salvation. Earlier animism had cherished the fire of life in the meadow. People would pray to the spirits of nature for successful crops, hunting expeditions, rain, personal well being and so forth. Other later religions had been state religions, part of the apparatus of sovereignty and governance, as is apparent from their temples, built for royal ceremonies, not for popular public devotions.

Signs of distress: 0-1200 A.D.

The fire burned on under the cauldron of our culture, and the next doubling of our population would take only 1,200 years. There would be 400 million humans at the end of it, 98 percent of them belonging to our culture, East and West. War, plague, famine, political corruption, civil unrest, crime and economic instability were fixtures of our cultural life and would remain so.

Salvationist religions had been entrenched in the East for centuries when this period began, but the great empires of the West still saluted its dozens of talismanic deities, from Aeolus to Zephyrus. Nonetheless the ordinary people of those empires—the slaves, the conquered, the peasants, the unenfranchised masses— were ready when the first great salvationist religion of the West arrived on its doorstep. It was easy for them to envision humankind as innately flawed and to envision themselves as sinners in need of rescue from eternal damnation. They were eager to despise the world and to dream of a blissful afterlife in which the poor and the humble of this world would be exalted over the proud and the powerful.

The fire burned unwaveringly under the cauldron of our culture, but people everywhere now had salvationist religions to show them how to understand and cope with the suffering of everyday life. Adherents tend to concentrate on the differences between these religions, but let's look for a moment at the points they have in common: The human condition is what it is, and no amount of effort on your part can change that; it is not within your power to save your people, your friends, your parents, your children or your spouse. You can carry the word to others and they can carry the word to you, but there is one person, and only one, you can save, and that's you. The message is essentially the same, whether it's Buddhism, Hinduism, Judaism, Christianity or Islam. Salvation is of course the most wonderful thing one can achieve in life and even offers eternal bliss in the afterlife.

This became the new vision of what really counts in the world.

Signs of distress: 1200-1700

It was quite a vision—but of course the fire burned on under the cauldron of our culture, and the next doubling of our population would take only 500 years. There would be 800 million humans at the end of it, 99 percent of them belonging to our culture, East and West. It's the age of bubonic plague, the Mongol Horde and the Inquisition. The first known madhouse was established and the first debtor's prison was opened in London.

Farm laborers revolt in France in 1251 and 1358, textile workers revolt in Flanders in 1280; Wat Tyler's rebellion reduces England to anarchy in 1381 as workers of all kinds unite to demand an end to exploitation; workers riot in plague and famine-racked Japan in 1428, and again in 1461; Russia's serfs rise in revolt in 1671 and 1672; Bohemia's serfs revolt eight years later. The Black Death arrives to devastate Europe in the middle of the fourteenth century and returns periodically for the next two centuries, carrying off tens of thousands with every outbreak; in two years alone in the seventeenth century it will kill a million people in northern Italy.

Millions will die as famine strikes Japan in 1232, Germany and Italy in 1258, England in 1294 and 1555, all of Western Europe in 1315, Lisbon in 1569, Italy in 1591, Austria in 1596, Russia in 1603, Denmark in 1650, Bengal in 1669, Japan in 1674.

Syphilis and typhus make their appearance in Europe. Ergotism, a fungus food poisoning, becomes endemic in Germany killing thousands. An unknown sweating sickness visits and revisits England killing tens of thousands. Smallpox, typhus and diphtheria epidemics carry off thousands more.

Inquisitors develop a novel technique to combat heresy and witchcraft, torturing suspects until they implicate others, who are tortured until they implicate others. The slave trade flourishes as millions of Africans are transported to the New World. This is not to mention ongoing war, political corruption and crime, which continue unabated and reach new heights.

Christianity becomes the first global salvationist religion, penetrating the Far East and the New World. At the same time it fractures. The first schism is fiercely resisted, but after that, disintegration becomes commonplace.

These human catastrophes are all reactions to overcrowding—too many people competing for too few resources, eating rotten food, drinking fouled water, watching their families starve, watching their families fall to the plague.

Signs of distress: 1700-1900

The fire burned on under the cauldron of our culture, and the next doubling of our population would take only 200 years. There would be 1.5 billion humans at the end of it, all but .5 percent of them belonging to our culture, East and West.

It would be a period in which, for the first time, religious prophets would attract followers simply by predicting the imminent end of the world; in which the opium trade would become a big international business sponsored by the East India Company and protected by British warships; in which Australia, New Guinea, India, Indochina and Africa would be claimed or carved up as colonies by the major powers of Europe; in which millions of indigenous people all over the world would be wiped out by diseases brought by Europeans—measles, pellagra, whooping cough, smallpox, cholera—with millions more herded onto reservations or killed outright to make room for white expansion.

This isn't to say that native peoples alone were suffering—60 million Europeans died of smallpox in the eighteenth century alone. Tens of millions died in cholera epidemics. This is not to mention the dozens of fatal appearances of plague, typhus, yellow fever, scarlet fever and influenza. Anyone who doubts the integral connection between agriculture and famine need only examine the historical record of this period: crop failure and famine, crop failure and famine, again and again all over the civilized world. The numbers are staggering: 10 million starved to death in Bengal, 1769, two million in Ireland and Russia in 1845 and 1846, and nearly 15 million in China and India from 1876 to 1879. In France, Germany, Italy, Britain, Japan and elsewhere, tens of thousands, hundreds of thousands died in other famines too numerous to mention.

As the cities became more crowded, human anguish reached heights that would have been unimaginable in previous ages, with hundreds of millions inhabiting slums of inconceivable squalor, prey to disease borne by rats and contaminated water, without education or means of betterment. Crime flourished as never before and was generally punished by public maiming, branding, flogging, or death; imprisonment as an alternate form of punishment developed only late in the period. Mental illness also flourished—madness, derangement, whatever you choose to call it. No one knew what to do with lunatics; they were typically incarcerated alongside criminals, chained to the walls, flogged and forgotten.

Economic instability remained high, and its consequences were felt more widely than ever before. Three years of economic chaos in France led directly to the 1789 revolution that claimed some 400,000 victims burned, shot, drowned or guillotined. Periodic market collapses and depressions wiped out hundreds of thousands of businesses and reduced millions to starvation.

The age also ushered in the industrial revolution, but this did not bring ease and prosperity to the masses as promised; rather it brought heartless exploitation with women and small children working 10, 12, and more hours a day for starvation wages in sweatshops, factories and mines. In 1787 it was estimated that French workers labored as much as 16 hours a day and spent 60 percent of their wages on a diet consisting of little more than bread and water. In the middle of the nineteenth century the British Parliament finally limited children's workdays to 10 hours. Hopeless and frustrated, people everywhere became rebellious. Governments everywhere answered with systematic repression, brutality and tyranny. General uprisings, peasant uprisings, colonial uprisings, slave uprisings, worker uprisings—there were hundreds. East and West, twins of a common birth, it was the age of revolutions. Tens of millions of people died in them.

The wolf and the wild boar were deliberately exterminated in Europe during this period. The great auk of Edley Island, near Iceland, was hunted to extinction for its feathers in 1844, becoming the first species to be wiped out for purely commercial purposes. In North America, in order to facilitate railway construction and undermine the food base of hostile native populations, professional hunters destroyed the bison herds, wiping out as many as three million in a single year. Only a thousand were left by 1893.

In this age, people no longer went to war to defend their religious beliefs. They still had them, still clung to them, but more pressing material concerns made religious differences seem less important. The consolations of religion are one thing, but food, jobs, fair wages, decent living and working conditions, freedom from oppression, and some faint hope of social and economic betterment are another.

The hopes that had been invested in religion during former ages were now being invested in revolution and political reform instead. The promise of "pie in the sky when you die" was no longer enough to make the misery of life in the cauldron endurable. In 1843 the young Karl Marx called religion "the opiate of the people." From the greater distance of another century and a half, however, it's clear that religion was in fact no longer very effective as a narcotic.

Signs of distress: 1900-1960

The fire burned on under the cauldron of our culture, and the next doubling of our population would take only 60 years. There would be three billion humans at the end of it, all but perhaps .2 of a percent of them belonging to our culture, East and West.

Is the cauldron boiling yet, do you think? Does the first global economic collapse, beginning in 1929, look like a sign of distress to you? Do two cataclysmic world wars look like signs of distress to you? Stand off a few thousand miles and watch from outer space as 65 million people are slaughtered on battlefields or blasted to bits in bombing strikes, as another 100 million count themselves lucky to escape merely blinded, maimed, or crippled. We are talking about a number of people equal to the entire human population in the Golden Age of classical Greece. The water is hot. Our culture is boiling.

Signs of distress: 1960-1996

The next doubling of our population occurred in only 36 years, bringing us to the present moment, when there are almost seven billion humans on this planet, all but a few scattered millions belonging to our culture, East and West.

And then came us: 1960 to the present.

For some decades now the water has been boiling around our culture. Now even the life-sustaining biosphere of our home planet is beginning to collapse. We have started a war for oil that will not end in our lifetimes. We are looking at cultural collapse and ecological suicide. The point of all this is that modern culture cannot be *fixed.* Every *revolution* just accelerates the destructive process.

There is great hope. It however does not lie in a technological singularity or revolution that will save us, but in merging what has worked well for the average person for millions of years with what we have today. This may become an act of faith that if we let go nature will catch us—she has for the last three million years. Remember too that nature alone is not catching us; we are all catching each other.

6. Civilization Destroys Ecosystems

Within every civilization are the seeds of its own demise. Civilization degrades its natural environment and that destruction leads to the decline and collapse of the civilization. In 1955, Tom Dale and Vernon Gill Carter, both highly experienced ecologists, published *Topsoil and Civilization*. The overview section of their book plays an influential part in this chapter. It is about the link between civilization and the natural environment.

SOIL BUILDING

The process of natural selection has led plants and animals to support the soil building process. Plant species could not long survive on sloping hillsides unless they helped check soil erosion. Animal species could not survive for long unless they tended to support the continued growth of plants and soil. If a species of plant or animal did evolve which led to the degradation of the soil, it usually destroyed itself before destroying its primary source of food.

For about 350 million years the growth of soil and land-based flora and fauna continued. The quantity, complexity, diversity of soil, plant and animal life increased. Earth upheavals, broad climatic changes and other natural phenomena caused destruction of both soil and life in many regions at times. But over the earth as a whole, the soil-building process went on, and with it the evolution of plants and animals to higher forms and greater abundance continued.[1]

CIVILIZATION DEGRADES THE ENVIRONMENT

With the advent of civilized society, about 10,000 years ago, the soil-building process was reversed in most areas where we have resided; the quantity and quality of soil and the amount of life the soil supported all began to decline. Superior tools and intelligence enabled human society to domesticate or destroy a great part of the plant and animal life around us. But more important, improved tools and techniques helped us to destroy the productivity of the soil that supported life. People's intelligence and versatility made it possible for us to do something no other animal had ever been able to do before—greatly alter the environment and still survive and multiply.

Civilized society was nearly always able to become master of the environment, at least temporarily. Our chief troubles came from our delusions that our temporary mastership would be permanent. We thought of ourselves as rulers of the world, while failing to understand fully the laws of nature.

People, whether civilized or savage, are children of nature—not its master. Our actions must conform to natural law if we are to maintain dominance over our environment. When we try to circumvent the laws of nature, we usually destroy the natural environment that sustains us. And when our environment deteriorates rapidly, civilization declines and often disappears entirely.

Dale and Carter summarized it this way: "Civilized man has marched across the face of the earth and left deserts in his footprints." This statement may be somewhat of an exaggeration, but it is not without foundation. Civilization has despoiled most of the lands on which we have lived on for very long. This is the main reason why people of progressive civilizations have moved from place to place. It has been a chief cause for the decline of civilizations in older settled regions. It has been a dominant factor in determining the trends of modern history.

The writers of history have seldom noted the importance of land use. They seem not to have recognized that the destinies of most empires and civilizations were determined largely by the way the land was used. While recognizing the influence of environment on history, they fail to note that people changed and usually despoiled the environment.

Historical records of the last 10,000 years show that with only a few exceptions, great civilizations were not able to continue in one area for more than 30 to 70 generations, 800 to 2,000 years. There were three notable exceptions: the Nile Valley, Mesopotamia and the Indus Valley where annual flooding gradually adds soil through silt. After a few centuries of growth and progress in a favorable environment, the civilizations declined, perished or were forced to move to new land. The average life span was 40 to 60 generations, 1,000 to 1,500 years. In most cases, the more brilliant the civilization, the shorter was its existence. These civilizations declined in the same geographical areas that had nurtured them, mainly because man himself despoiled or ruined the environments that helped develop his civilizations.

How did civilized man despoil his favorable environment? He did it mainly by depleting or destroying the natural resources. He cut down or burned most of the usable timber from the forested hillsides and valleys. He overgrazed and denuded the grasslands that fed his livestock. He killed the wildlife and much of the fish and other water life. He permitted erosion to rob his farmland of its productive topsoil. He allowed eroded soil to clog the streams and fill reservoirs, irrigation canals and harbors with silt. In many cases, he used or wasted most of the easily mined metals and other needed minerals. Then the civilization declined or died amidst the desolation of his own creation or he moved to new land. There have been from 10 to 30 different civilizations that have followed this road to ruin, the number depending on how the civilizations are classified.

Man seldom created a complete desert from a formerly fertile land. Sometimes the damaged land reverted to jungle. Usually, enough soil and vegetation was left to support a meager population of semi-nomadic herdsmen or peasant farmers. In some cases, there was still enough natural vitality left to support a moderate city population. But never has he left enough of the basic natural resources to sustain a progressive and dynamic civilization.[2]

ENVIRONMENTAL DEGRADATION CAUSES THE
DECLINE OF CIVILIZATION

Civilization spread from the irrigated valleys to other areas. In most cases, these other areas did not have the conditions that provided the sustained fertility of the Nile Valley, Mesopotamia and the

Indus Valley. The soil was fertile, but much of the land was sloping, and water for the crops came from capricious rain. When the rains came, they often washed fertile topsoil from the sloping grain fields. People deforested hillsides, and overgrazed grasslands. The land was often ruined for farming in just a few generations. When this happened, the people had to move to a new land or eke out their existence on the newly impoverished land. These civilizations declined or perished within a few centuries.

Across Asia and parts of Europe and North Africa, one can find vast areas which formerly sustained great civilizations and are now among the most backward areas of the world. You need not search to find such areas: just call the roll of the ancients, and then look at the lands they lived on, as they are today. You will soon see what was meant that human civilization has left a desert in its footprints as it moved from place to place across the earth.

Look at western Iran, where the Medes and the Persians prospered; look at northern Iraq, the former home of the Assyrians; look at Syria, Lebanon, Palestine, Algeria, and Tunisia, which once supported proud civilizations. Or take Crete, Greece, Italy, Sicily, China and Asia Minor as examples; these are the lands from which our western civilization arose.

Let us not put the blame for the barrenness of these areas on the conquering hordes that repeatedly overran them. True, those conquerors often sacked and razed the cities, burned the villages and slaughtered or drove off the people who populated them. But as long as the soil and other resources remained fertile, the cities were usually rebuilt.

The rise and fall of most of the ancients can be described in one paragraph because the pattern is much the same for all.

Most of the progressive and dynamic civilizations of humanity started on new land, on land that had not been the center of a former civilization. Each civilization flourished and grew for a few centuries on the land that gave it birth. The people who evolved it became more and more civilized during this period of growth. Then they found that their native land would no longer support them, so they began to conquer and take the land of some of their neighbors. With the new land thus acquired, they held their gains for a few more centuries. After they reached their limits of conquest, their civilization began to decline. Eventually the surrounding barbarians engulfed it and a dark age ensued. After that, a new civilization arose on new land among some of the semicivilized barbarians. Then the pattern was repeated.

This is the basic pattern for the rise, growth and decline of past empires and civilizations. Of course the details vary, some of them were conquered by the semicivilized barbarians they had subdued and taught. Others were overwhelmed by raiding hordes from outside their sphere of influence. Some were conquered by more virile civilized peoples. Usually political corruption and economic maladjustment hastened thier demise. Often, religion, moral decay or poor leadership played a role in the decline. But, with few exceptions, the decline did not come until they had despoiled the land that gave them food and supported them during their growth.[3]

The Cedars of Lebanon

The Epic of Gilgamesh is the earliest recorded story of downstream siltation and desertification caused by the destruction of forestlands. Lebanon went from more than 90 percent forest, the famous Cedars of Lebanon, to less than seven percent over a 1,500-year period, causing downwind rainfall to decrease by 80 percent. Trees and their roots, after all, are an important part of the water cycle. As a result, millions of acres of land in the Fertile Crescent area turned to desert or scrubland, and remain relatively barren to this day.

The staple food of the Mesopotamians was barley, but after several hundred years of continuous barley growing using irrigation, the land became exhausted. The soil developed such high levels of salt, carried in by the irrigation water, that it would no longer grow crops. Because the forests were gone, wood had become such a precious commodity that it was equal in value to some gems and mineral ores. Neighboring countries were conquered for their wood supplies, as well as to get new fertile land to grow barley. Vast areas of timberland along the Euphrates and Tigris rivers were cut bare, increasing siltation of the irrigation canals and cropland and further decreasing downwind rainfall.

As a result of this ecological destruction more than 5,000 years ago the climate became more arid. Widespread famine ensued. The collapse of the last Mesopotamian empire occurred around 4,000 years ago. The records they left behind show that only at the very end of their empire did they realize how they had destroyed their precious source of food and fuel by razing their forests and despoiling the rest of their environment. Although things looked good for a while, they did not realize it was not sustainable. It worked only as long as they had other people's land to conquer. Once they ran out of neighbors, their decline was sudden and devastating.[4]

Greece

The collapse of the Mesopotamian empire paved the way for the rise of Greece as a worldwide empire in the late Bronze Age. Between 1500 B.C. and 200 B.C., the Greeks adopted widespread agricultural practices similar to the Mesopotamians' system which led to a sudden jump in food production. As a result, by the thirteenth century B.C., Greek population growth began. They also used tens of thousands of acres of forest wood to feed the bronze furnaces for which they were famous.

The decline of Greek civilization is linked to their population eventually outstripping their available fuel and wood. By 600 B.C., most of Greece was an environmental wasteland. Denuded hillsides eroded casuing silt to choke the rivers. Cropland lost its productivity due to accumulated irrigation salts and nutrient exhaustion. A bounty was offered to farmers to grow olive trees on the hillsides. The desperate Greeks found that only olive trees could grow on the fragile, steep slopes and help slow erosion. But it was too late. As Plato writes in his *Cririas*, "What now remains compared with what then existed is like the skeleton of a sick man, all the fat and soft earth having wasted away, and only the bare framework of the land being left."

It has, indeed, happened before.

Rome

The collapse of Greece was followed by the rise of the Roman Empire. Rome had its own needs for wood. In early Rome, one could walk North Africa's coast from end to end without leaving the shade of trees. Now it is a desert. By 200 B.C., the forests of what we now call Italy were all but wiped out to meet the Roman needs for fuel and shelter, to warm the public baths, and to smelt metals. Large quantities of wood were necessary to smelt silver from ore, refine the metal, and

mint it into coins that were the basis of Rome's monetary system. So
when Italy's forests were exhausted around the first century A.D., the
repeated doublings in the cost of wood to smelt silver caused a monetary crisis, the first huge crack in the Roman Empire. [5]

The inevitable consequence of deforestation was much greater
soil erosion. The silt was carried into rivers, eventually clogging the
ports in the estuaries. The port of Paestum in southern Italy silted
up completely, and Ravenna lost all access to the sea. Ostia, the port
of Rome, only survived as a port because new docks were built.
Elsewhere, marshes developed around river mouths built with the
soil eroded from the hills. The Pontine marshes were created about
200 B.C., in an area which had supported 16 Volscian towns 400
years earlier.[6]

About the same time, the productivity of Roman croplands drastically declined because of siltation, salinization, soil exhaustion
and decreased rainfall from the loss of upwind forests. Subsequent
food shortages threatened the stability of the Roman Empire. This
led Rome's leaders to build a fleet of 60 wooden ships to conquer
the nearby Mediterranean countries, extending the empire in its last
days. They were desperately reaching out for minerals, food and
wood. Ultimately, Rome's watershed destruction, deforestation,
depleted soil and surging population led to widespread famine, and
eventual collapse of the entire empire.

Mayan

Deforestation caused the Mayan population to pull back from the
hills. From excavation of Mayan building foundations on the valley
floor, we see that they had become covered with sediment during the
eighth century, meaning that the hill slopes were becoming eroded
and probably leached of nutrients. The poor acidic hill soils that
were carried into the valley plains reduced agricultural yields. The
reason for the erosion of the hillsides is that the forests that formerly
covered them and protected their soil were cut down. Dated pollen
samples show that the pine forests originally covering the hilltops
were cleared and used as fuel.

Besides causing sediment in the valleys and depriving inhabitants of wood, the deforestation also caused a man-made drought in
the lowlands. As already mentioned, forests play a major role in the

water cycle. Deforestation results in lower rainfall. We will discuss this later in greater detail.

Hundreds of skeletons recovered from Copán archaeological sites have been studied for signs of disease and poor nutrition, such as porous bones and stress lines in the teeth. Those skeletal signs show that the health of Copán's inhabitants deteriorated from 650 to 850 A.D., among both the elite and commoners, though the health of commoners was worse.[7]

Anasazi

Climate historians have speculated that a similar pattern of expansion beyond the environment's carrying capacity may provide an explanation for the mysterious disappearance of southwestern Colorado's Anasazi civilization around the year 1280 A.D. This civilization occupied the spectacular cliff dwellings of Mesa Verde and surrounding areas. Reliable evidence indicates that its disappearance corresponded with a drought which, while severe, was not dissimilar from earlier droughts that the cliff dwellers successfully endured. According to the archaeological record, however, there were crucial differences this time around. The Anasazi had cut the juniper forests near their settlements such as Chaco canyon for building and fuel, and used irrigation for farming in an area with high salt content. The Anasazi population had also grown significantly just before its disappearance.

The lesson from the Anasazi experience for us is clear. Our global civilization, which, after the thousands of generations up to the end of World War II had reached a population of fewer than 2.5 billion people, may, by quadrupling in the space of a single lifetime, dramatically increase our vulnerability to the extreme climate changes that we ourselves are now setting in motion.[8]

CIVILIZATION IS LIMITED BY ITS NATURAL RESOURCES

Many people take the flow of surplus goods for granted. They think, "If a city grows, the farmers will automatically feed it." The reverse is more accurate. When the farms, forests, and grasslands produce a surplus, the cities automatically grow. When the farmers, herders, woodsmen, and other primary producers fail to produce a surplus, cities wither and die.

The factors that determine the amount of surplus produced by
the primary producers largely limit the status of any civilization.
These factors are fundamentals: the fertility and extent of arable
soil, the amount of rain infiltration into the soil, the extent and
reproductive success of forests, the quantity and quality of grasslands, the abundance of wildlife, fish, and water life, the supply of
usable water, and the abundance of fossil fuels, metals, construction
materials and other deposits in the earth's crust. These are the natural resources with which the primary producers work. The quantity and quality of these resources largely determine the amount of
surplus produced.

A common error has been to consider these resources as static.
The proponents of the standard formula, "capital plus labor plus
raw materials plus management multiplied by technology equals
production," have nearly always considered raw materials as a constant. But they are not constant. Soil fertility, usable water, forests,
grasslands, wildlife and other resources have not remained fixed in
any region. They have decreased in most areas occupied by civilization. In many of the older countries they have almost disappeared.
Their decrease has nearly always led to a decline in civilization.

These are not the only factors which determine the status of any
given civilization, but they largely determine its limits.[9]

OTHER FACTORS FOR DECLINE ARE SECONDARY

We know that the decline of past civilizations, or any given civilization, cannot be attributed to one specific cause. Civilized societies
lead a complicated existence, and their civilizations are complex
affairs. You cannot rightfully use the yardstick of spiritual, intellectual or biological development to accurately measure their progress.
Nor can you use any particular feature of physical environment as a
barometer to predict their rise and fall. But, one factor definitely
limits the status of any civilized society—the amount of surplus raw
materials produced by the primary producers.

The decline of any given civilization has been ascribed by historians to various causes or combinations of causes. Among the factors
most frequently mentioned are war, change of climate, moral decay,
political corruption, economic decline, deterioration of the race, and

poor leadership. These and many other factors have doubtless had significant influence on the decline of most civilizations. But it is doubtful that they were the primary causes for the permanent decline of civilization in any region.

So many civilizations have survived and advanced after repeated wars that it is not feasible to claim that such violence, in itself, is a primary cause for the decline of a civilization. Many of the great civilizing peoples, the Babylonians, Greeks and Romans, for example, were at war almost constantly throughout the period of their progressive growth.

It is true that most of the extinct civilizations succumbed at the time they lost wars and had their cities destroyed. It is also true that conquest caused a temporary decline of civilization in many regions. Such a decline was especially notable where the conquerors maintained their seats of government in distant lands and shipped most of the surplus production out of the conquered regions. But the decline of civilization because of war or conquest was never permanent in a region that still had the natural resources to rebuild cities and support a continuing civilization.

For example, in the Nile Valley and Mesopotamia, civilization was destroyed and dark ages ensued at least once, while temporary decline came several times as a result of conquest. But new, progressive civilizations were built in these regions after each period of decline as long as the resources to support civilization were still there.

War, especially large-scale war of the twentieth-century type, consumes natural resources at a rapid rate. It may temporarily prevent a people from practicing true conservation. In these ways, war contributes to resource destruction and the ultimate decline of civilization. But war has not always caused resource depletion. In some cases, it has actually led to conservation by limiting the population and preventing intensive use of the land. This happened to parts of the Near East during ancient times and to Western Europe in the Middle Ages. War may be an important contributing factor in the decline of civilization, but it has seldom been the basic cause for the permanent decline of civilization in any region.

"Moral decay" and "political corruption" have been prominent features of most declining civilizations. They have doubtless been important contributing factors in the decline of some. But they were largely the result rather than cause of decline.

Many civilizations have continued to progress long after moral decay and political corruption were obvious. Several of the European nations of early modern times furnish good examples. These social diseases have a way of curing themselves, if the physical environment remains productive. Sometimes the cure is affected through the conquest of the decadent people by a more virile people, and the civilization is perpetuated by the conquerors. That is what happened in North Africa with Rome's conquest of Carthage. It happened several times in Mesopotamia and in other regions.

"Economic decline" has also been apparent in declining civilizations. In some cases, an almost complete breakdown of the economic system preceded the final collapse. Again, it is doubtful that this was more of a cause than an effect. For example, material wealth was concentrated in the hands of a few while the masses were generally poverty stricken in most dying civilizations. But this condition developed to an alarming extent in some growing civilizations and was corrected. Revolution, taxes, or other means were found to redistribute the wealth, and civilization advanced to greater heights than before. This happened in Athens from the time of Solon to Cleisthenes, in the sixth century B.C., and it happened in most nations of Western Europe during the late Middle Ages and early modern times.

Of course, concentration of the land and other resources in the hands of a few may hasten resource destruction and thus contribute indirectly to the decline of civilization. There are also many other forms of economic maladjustment that may influence the ultimate decline of civilization, but these things are usually only contributing factors.

"Deterioration of the race" as a cause for the decline of civilization has little scientific basis. Random mating usually insures an average quality of population. Where deterioration seems to exist, it is usually the result of improper nourishment. This has frequently happened where the productivity of the soil deteriorated, or where overpopulation forced an inadequate diet. Most of the depleted lands or overpopulated regions of the present bear this out.

"Poor leadership" as a cause for decline of civilization has some plausibility. It might seriously affect the will to progress, lead to destructive wars, economic maladjustment or seriously affect the moral fiber of a people. Yet, because of the time element, it is questionable whether poor leadership has ever led to the demise of any great civilization. Take the Roman Empire, for example. When such incompetents as Caligula, Claudius, Nero, Galba, Otho and Vitellius were successive emperors for a period of thirty-two years, the civilization held its own, and the "silver age" of Rome followed.

Civilizations do not die in a few decades. Stupid, incompetent, or careless leaders seldom last long—competition usually takes care of that. It is true that poor leaders may retard civilization or cause a temporary decline, but in the long run they do not stop it from going up, and they do not cause permanent decline, provided other factors are favorable for advancement.

The purpose of this discussion is not to prove that these factors were of no consequence in the decline of past civilizations, but to show that they were not the fundamental causes of decline. The fundamental cause for the decline of a civilization was deterioration of the natural resource base on which civilization rested.[10]

DEGRADATION TODAY

Environmental problems are nothing new. However, with the expansion of our Taker culture to every corner of the globe, the exponential growth in the human population, the cultivation of wild areas, and the growth of industrialization, the scale and complexity of environmental problems has increased. The entire world now faces a series of interrelated crises caused by civilization's past actions: deforestation, soil erosion, desertification, salinization, loss of biodiversity, unequal distribution of food and wealth and increasing pollution.

Another challenge facing modern civilization is the sheer speed of change. If this book were to give a chronologically accurate account of human history, then of its 295 pages, 285 pages would be devoted to hunter-gatherer communities, one page to agricultural societies and just a line to modern industrial civilization.[11]

We are in a situation similar to this: Let's say bees stopped living in hives and did something else that caused their population to explode so much that they killed the flowers and forests they had depended on for food and climate stability. They had better get back to living in hives bringing with them only customs that do not interfere with what originally worked for them for millions of years.

Let's be clear. There is no way to reconcile our Taker culture with the earth. Its memes require dominion and destruction of the earth. Our Taker culture has had 10,000 years to succeed, yet it continues to make the situation worse as it expands. If our current civilization were going to find harmony with the earth, it would have done so long ago when its impact was much smaller.

There is nothing wrong with human settlement. Many varieties of settlement have worked sustainably for humanity for tens of thousands of years. However, human settlement cannot be above the ecological laws of nature. That is, people cannot be at population and consumption levels that require use of the earth from fence row to fence row strictly for human benefit. We cannot deprive other forms of life of their habitat. If we do that they will die—and so will we.

Today civilization has merged into one global industrial economy. Because of this globalization, the stakes are higher. If we despoil the site of this global civilization we will have no other place to go. There are no new fertile lands to conquer.

Anyone who has flown over America has seen that our control over arable land with farms and urban centers is just about complete. The resilience of the the earth is being drawn down from sea to shining sea. It is taking a remarkably short time, just a few generations, to sap the life out of this once abundant land. This not only is true for our natural resources but for our communities as well.

Taker culture *will* come to an end. Either by our walking away from it or by letting nature take its course. It will happen. We have overshot the earth's carrying capacity and the loan is coming due.

7. Ecosystems Collapse

It is difficult to see environmental degradation if you have lived in our exuberant culture all of your life and never had to depend on the wild for your livelihood. If you have lived in the city or suburbs, it appears that this is how things should be. Look out your window at home or from an airplane and you will see mile after mile of human-managed landscape.

We depend on this ecosystem to support our lives and the lives of future generations. Does it build soil or does it deplete the soil? Does it maintain fresh drinking water or does it pollute it? Does it support biodiversity for a resilient ecosystem or is it vulnerable because of monoculture? Does it maintain clean air or does it pollute the air as well?

As we have seen, a good place to look to see the consequences of our current resource management practices is past civilizations. Now let us look forward. Imagine most of our western forests clear cut to build more wood framed houses, to print more Sunday newspapers and make more copier paper. Imagine that largely as a result of deforestation the rain coming from the west to the Midwest has dropped by up to 80 percent and the Ogallala aquifer, which supports farmers from Texas to the Dakotas and 40 percent of U.S. grain production, is gone. Then, remember the cedars of Lebanon. We will bequeath to our children a new Midwest desert. If you live on the east or west coasts, I would be nervous—this is where much of your food comes from.

This book is mainly for those alive today who can still make

positive changes before it is too late. It is also for the unborn generations. Let's not leave deserts in our footsteps. I am also writing for all
the other voiceless species that have as much of a right to live for their
own sake as we do.

Here is a summary of what has been happening over the last few
years while we have been watching Mother Culture on television.

There were so many statistics that it was difficult to organize them
all. Ecosystems collapse has been broken into five chapters including
the previous chapter. This chapter provides an overview of current
degradation and briefly looks at two ecosystem indicators: water and
aquatic life. Separate chapters are dedicated to biodiversity crash, forest loss, and global warming.

SCALE AND RATE OF DEGRADATION

Our Taker culture has consumed more in the last century than in all
of previous human history combined.[1] The rate of destruction is
accelerating. Over the past 50 years, humans have changed ecosystems more rapidly and extensively than in any comparable period.
The result is that approximately 60 percent of the ecological systems are being degraded or are being used unsustainably.

Degradation of ecosystems often causes significant harm to
human wellbeing and represents a loss of natural wealth. The changes
being made also increase the likelihood of further abrupt and unpredictable changes which could have dire consequences.[2]

IRREPLACEABLE ECOSYSTEMS

The study of ecology is shifting to examine what the world would
look like if process, rather than matter, were the basis of reality. We
are starting to define a species in terms of its life process: something is
what it does. This notion of life-as-process might seem unusual in a
society in which the material is primary. But such a perception
informs our deepest understanding of life. For example, when a loved
one is simply a body, devoid of the capacity to care, respond or relate
ever again, we understand that they are gone even before they are
dead.[3]

Next we link the processes into cooperative relationships. Ecology is a science of relationships among the members of ecosystem

communities. Instead of seeing the world as a machine composed of elementary building blocks, scientists have discovered that the world is a network of inseparable patterns of relationships; the planet is a whole, living, self-regulating system.

This pattern of relationships sees the brain, the immune system, the bodily tissues and even each cell, as living cognitive systems. This replaces the view that the human body is simply a machine. The human body is one complex interrelated ecosystem.[4]

The earth's ecosystems are being frayed to the point where they are no longer resilient and able to withstand natural disturbances, setting the stage for unnatural disasters to occur more frequently. Imagine if suddenly, like the earth's ecosystems, 60 percent of your body's systems became degraded. Not just one, such as your kidneys, but 60 percent. By destroying forests, damming rivers, filling in wetlands and destabilizing the climate, we are unraveling the strands of a complex ecological safety net.[5]

Our ecosystem is irreplaceable. Many of the services we receive from living systems have no substitutes at any price, for example, oxygen production by green plants. This was demonstrated in 1991-1993, when the scientists operating the $200 million Biosphere 2 experiment in Arizona discovered that it was unable to maintain a balanced, life-supporting atmosphere for the eight people living inside. Biosphere 1, also known as earth, performs this task daily at no charge for almost seven billion people.[6]

STEWARDSHIP IS IMPOSSIBLE FOR HUMANITY

The human intellect is simply incapable of fully understanding let alone managing natural ecosystems. Nature is too complex. We have not even been able to save all of the pieces, as Aldo Leopold so eloquently said. Yet we are confidently acting as if we know enough to manipulate these ecosystems and predict what the outcome of this manipulation will be. We act like we know what is good for plant and animal species, humankind and wilderness. But do we?[7]

Stewardship implies that contemporary science can holistically understand natural ecosystems, and that people are willing and able to work together to keep the earth a fit and comfortable place for life. E. O. Wilson, in a moving article in the *New York Times*, reminds us that we are just carnivores that happened on intelligence. Does anyone believe that such animals prone to tribal genocide could, by using their limited intellect, change their natures and become wise and gentle gardeners, stewards, of all the natural life systems of our planet? It takes a lot of hubris even to think of us as stewards of the earth. In practice, few of us can take care even of our own bodies. I would sooner expect a goat to succeed as a gardener than expect humans to become stewards of the earth; something, which until we began to dismantle it, was our inheritance from 3.6 billion years of life on earth.[8]

EARTH IS GAIA

Gaia was first seen from space. James Lovelock in *The Ages of Gaia: A Biography of Our Living earth*, best expressed that combination of scientific insights and older tribal beliefs that assert that the earth is alive in the sense that it is a self-regulating and self-generating system.[9] Today, Pagans and others of earth-based spirituality see the earth as the one body of the Goddess.

The conditions that make life possible are balanced about such fine tolerances. Many of the earth's processes exist simply to preserve this equilibrium.

Organisms, including people, exist only as an inseparable part of our environment. We are in a continual process of exchange with all other animate and inanimate entities with whom we live. We are acted upon and acting, created and creating, shaped and shaping. The earth, and even the cosmos, is an infinite complex of interrelated events.[10]

HUMANITY AND GAIA

Gaia is our home. She[1] will care for our children when we are gone. Our culture has lost its soul. Western Shoshone educator Glenn Wasson said in *Newe Sogobia: The Western Shoshone People and Land*,

"In Indian terms there is no equation in dollars for the loss of a way of life. . . you cannot equate dollars to lives. The redmen are the last people on earth who speak on behalf of all living things. The bear, the deer, the sagebrush have no one else to speak for them. The animals and plants were put here by the Great Spirit before he put the humans here. . . . There is a story that the old people tell about the white man. That they are like children. They want this and that, they want everything they see, like it's their first time on earth. The white men have all these tools but they don't know how to use them properly. The white people try to equate national defense with human lives. There can never be an equation between the dollar bill and living things—the fish, the birds, the deer, the clean air, clean water. There is no way of comparing them. The white people have no love for this land. If we human beings persist in what we are doing, we will become like a bad cancer on Mother Earth. If we don't stop ourselves, something will stop us. We are destroying everything."[11]

The next vision is from Thom Hartman's book *The Prophets Way*,

"That night I awoke from a sound sleep and sat up in my bed. I was living in a small, rented room over a storefront across the street from Michigan State University, and there were people coming and going at all hours. I figured a noise in the hall had awakened me, but I could hear nothing.

Then, in the air a few feet in front of me, a globe materialized, slowly spinning, the size of a beach ball. I immediately recognized it as the earth, as seen from space. The blue oceans, green and brown land masses, and white patterns of clouds and storms. It was both real and not-real: like a hologram projected into the air.

As I watched, the land masses began to darken at various points. Small black pustules formed, like little blisters or cancers on the earth. The blue of the oceans became brown and muddy around these areas. The cancers slowly expanded, blackening the earth and cracking it in places, until they covered virtually all the land of the planet. The clouds turned a death-like yellow-gray, and the waters no longer sparkled blue but were a dull and putrid green-brown.

A thought came into my mind as if a voice were speaking to me: 'The earth is a living thing. It is infected.'

Then the earth shuddered as it spun. It jerked to one side, as if the spin were changing, and the blackened areas split open. The earth shuddered again, and the black areas cracked and shattered into fragments, falling off into the air around the image and vanishing. The earth was once again clear and clean, spinning gracefully, displaying oceans the color of lapis lazuli and land richly covered with green.

The voice in my mind said, 'The earth has healed itself.'

The image vanished and I lay back in my bed, realizing that the infection in my vision was humankind; the earth was as much a living organism as I was, a single and complete entity in its own right, perhaps even with its own unique consciousness, and it would respond to a toxic infection by throwing it off, as my body would shed a bacterial invasion or a scab.

I couldn't sleep, so I pulled out a Bible from the stack of books next to my bed. I flipped it open to a random page toward the end, and my eyes looked down at the words of the Book of Revelation (11:18): '. . . and I shall destroy them which destroy the earth.'

Stunned, I closed the Bible and put it on the bookshelf as if it were hot. I slept fitfully the rest of that night, knowing intuitively that every major change—be it in the world or in individual human life—was preceded by signs and markers. There are always warnings, and I'd just seen a vivid one."[12]

Lastly, Leonardo Boff passionately offered this in *Resurgence* magazine,

"Not only do the poor scream, but also the water, the animals, the forests, the soils: that is, the earth as our living super-organism, called Gaia. They scream because they are continuously attacked. They scream because their autonomy and intrinsic value are not recognized. They scream because they are threatened with extinction. Every day around ten [probably closer to 50 to 200] species of living beings disappear as a result of human aggressiveness in the contemporary industrial process."[13]

STEALING FROM OUR CHILDREN

Today we are stealing from our children. Many great authors, environmentalists, and even a few U.S. presidents have warned us of this sin. May we learn from their wisdom.

"We do not inherit the earth from our fathers, we are borrowing it from our children." These words by David Brower are inscribed in stone at the National Aquarium. Later in his book *Let The Mountains Talk, Let The Rivers Run*, he decided those words were too conservative and believed that we are not borrowing from our children, we are stealing from them—and it's not even considered to be a crime.

In the years since the industrial revolution, we humans have been partying pretty hard. We have ransacked most of the earth for resources. A small part of the world's population wound up with some nice goodies, but now we are eating the seed corn. We are living off the natural capital of the planet, the principal not the interest. The soil, the seas, the forests, the rivers, the atmosphere—everything is being spoiled. It was quite a binge, but the hangover is now upon us. It may be one we never get over.

To our unborn children, it will seem that we did, indeed, burn books to get light, burn furniture to run air-conditioning and burn arbors to warm ourselves. For a while it worked. We multiplied and subdued the earth. Our children may credit us for that, but they must also face the fact that the earth is not theirs to subdue, but rather to cherish. There is after all only one planet earth.[14]

Henry David Thoreau, in Journals, March 23, 1856 writes, "I seek acquaintance with nature—to know her moods and manners. Primitive nature is the most interesting to me. I take infinite pains to know all the phenomena of spring, for instance, thinking that I have here the entire poem. And then, to my chagrin, I learn that it is but an imperfect copy that I possess and have read, that my ancestors have torn out many of the first leaves and grandest passages, and mutilated it in many places. I should not like to think that some demigod had come before me and picked out some of the best of the stars. I wish to know an entire heaven and an entire earth."[15]

In a letter to James Madison, Thomas Jefferson warned of stealing from future generations, "The earth belongs in use to the living. . . no man can by natural right oblige the lands he occupies, or the persons who succeed him in that occupation, to the payment of debts contracted by him. For if he could, he might during his own life, eat up the use of the lands for several generations to come. . . then the earth would belong to the dead and not the living generation. . . . No generation can contract debts greater than may be paid during the course of its own existence."[16]

William Catton, in *Overshoot: The Ecological Basis of Revolutionary Change*, tells a story of a refugee community on the banks of the Volga River in 1921. An American newspaper correspondent had come to write about the Russian famine. Almost half the people in this community were already dead of starvation and the death rate was rising. Those still surviving had no real prospect for a prolonged life. In an adjacent field, a lone soldier was guarding a huge mound of sacks full of grain. The American newsman asked a white-bearded leader of the community why his people did not overpower this one guard, take the grain and relieve their hunger. The dignified old Russian explained that the sacks contained seed to be planted for the next growing season. "We do not steal from the future," he said.[17]

And finally, Wendell Berry adds in *The Gift of Good Land: Further Essays Cultural and Agricultural*, "That is the real foundation of our progress and our affluence. The reason that we are a rich nation is not that we have earned so much wealth—you cannot, by any honest means, earn or deserve so much. The reason is simply that we have learned, and become willing, to market and use up in our own time the birthright and livelihood of posterity."[18]

WATER

One American consumes roughly 117,000 gallons of water per year through direct and indirect consumption such as manufacturing and farming. If you add outputs generated overseas for products and services consumed here, that figure easily exceeds 140,000 gallons. It is equivalent to 109 tractor-trailer-sized truckloads for a family of four.[19]

While we in the U.S. consume water like there is no tomorrow, some 1.1 billion people still lack access to a community water supply and more than 2.6 billion lack access to modern water sanitation. In general, water scarcity affects roughly one to two billion people worldwide.[20]

My friend Jin Zidell has founded an inspiring around the world foot race called the Blue Planet Run to raise the level of awareness of the world's safe drinking water crisis; visit www.blueplanetrun.org.

Aquifer Depletion

We are coming to the end of plentiful water in the U.S. as well. Slowly replenished aquifers are more like oil wells. Consider, for example, the Ogallala Aquifer. It stretches from South Dakota to Texas, covering 174,000 square miles and holds enough water to fill Lake Huron.

The Ogallala Aquifer averages about 200 feet in depth, and during the 40 year period from 1940 to 1980 it dropped at a rate of 3 to 10 feet per year, losing as much as 100 feet in some parts of Texas. The recharge rate is so slow that much of the water being pumped out of the aquifer is more than 10,000 years old. Once it has been drained it will take 10,000 to 15,000 years to recharge.

Right now the amount of water being pumped out of the aquifer, both for residential use and for agriculture, is greater than the total flow of the Colorado River. At this rate the aquifer will pump dry, or at least get low enough to become unusable, sometime in the next 30 to 50 years.

Over 40 percent of the grain grown in the U.S. and about a third of the cotton is irrigated by the Ogallala. A quarter of all the feed grains exported by the United States are grown using its water. In total, over 14 million acres of cropland draw their sustenance from the aquifer-land that will become unproductive once it runs dry.[21]

Another example is an area that you might not expect to be running short of water, Florida. The massive Florida Aquifer is being depleted so rapidly by the state's growing population that they have begun injecting treated human sewage into it to try to recharge it before it runs dry. The hope is that the gravel in the aquifer will clean up the reclaimed water before the sewer from the state's toilets works it way back up to the drinking-water wells. In this case, 400 million gallons of municipally treated human waste are injected into the aquifer every day.

Unfortunately, according to the Environmental News Service, nobody knows yet if this scheme works. Will human viruses survive being pumped back up and chlorinated? How will the tons of unmetabolized drugs that go from Floridians' kidneys into toilets every day, drugs ranging from antibiotics to blood pressure medications, tranquilizers, to birth control, affect people when the drugs one day show up in Florida's drinking water? Nobody knows.[22]

The last example is from Mexico City. Built over a confined aquifer trapped in the upper layers of an extinct volcano, Mexico City has fallen 30 feet in the past century because of the grounds settling into sand once thick with water. The unevenness of the sinking has created havoc throughout the city, cracking ancient buildings, bursting over 40,000 water and sewer pipes a year and turning the city's once-flat rapid transit rail system into a roller coaster. A water pipe drilled into the aquifer at ground level in 1934 now hangs 26 feet in the air as the city has dropped around it. The city has had to invest in expensive pumping equipment to lift sewage to a level where it will drain through the city's sewer system that was once well underground.

Future water shortages will be at least as politically destabilizing and threatening to human and other life as are the oil shortages that are to come.[23]

When we take all of the water, there is not much left for the other species on earth. According to the United Nations' *Pilot Analysis of Global Ecosystems*, half of the world's wetlands have vanished in the past century.[24]

The Futility of Dams

Rivers are the essence of wildness. They can be managed, but not controlled. Water flowing downhill and reaching the ocean is something that cannot long be controlled by human beings. If you have a reservoir, and it silts up, as is currently happening in the West, the river will eventually roll over the top and take the dam out.

River people have a saying: "The river always wins." If people are still around in 500 years, they'll laugh at the fact that we tried to dam the Colorado River. You can modify it for a time, but you have to let the water through. Rivers are wild. They do their own thing. When the water comes down from the peaks, it is heading for the ocean. No matter how we try to manipulate it along the way, the basic process will continue. Ultimately the water will prevail.[25]

In Egypt, the Nile River had been doing just fine for millennia, replenishing life-giving nutrients during annual flooding. This made early agriculture possible and later fed an immense sardine fishery in the Mediterranean. Then Russia helped the Egyptians dam the Nile at Aswan to provide hydroelectric power. Today the sardines in the Mediterranean are gone, and Egypt's farmers are not very happy either. Instead of rich alluvial soil the Nile now offers soil loaded with crop-weakening salts. A parasite, schistosomiasis that lives in snails in the now warm irrigation ditches has infected three-quarters of the human population. We can be very clever, we humans, but sometimes not so smart.[26]

FISHERIES

We are also depleting many of the world's most important fisheries. Since 1950 the total annual catch worldwide has increased by 500 percent and is now assumed to be higher than the replenishment rate in most areas. A growing number of valuable food species are disappearing entirely.

In just 50 years, the global spread of industrial-scale commercial fishing has cut the ocean populations of large predatory fishes, such as blue marlin and cod, by about 90 percent.[27] The cod fishery, fished sustainably for five hundred years, has collapsed. The species is now on the brink of extinction.[28] They have become like the passenger pigeon. Fully, one-third of all fish species, compared with one-fourth of all mammal species, are threatened with extinction.[29]

The Canadian government is now brutally clubbing 325,000 harp seals to death per year in an attempt to bring the cod back. This is a futile attempt since harp seals actually eat the predators of the food that the cod eat. Cod numbers were much higher when there were more seals. See *Seal Wars* by Paul Watson.

The use of 30-mile-long, fine-mesh drift nets to "strip-mine" the oceans has recently, and rightly, provoked a great deal of public protest. But even without driftnets, fishing fleets throughout the world are making an all-out assault on the productivity of the oceans. According to a California fishing authority, Duane Garrett, the new technology means that fish no longer have a chance. "Virtually every species has its Thermopylae, a narrow stretch of ocean through which it migrates, or an ancient spawning ground, and with advanced sonar and spotter planes, they've all been discovered and are being exploited worldwide with neither mercy nor foresight." Particularly haunting are satellite photographs of the ocean east of New Zealand, taken at night, which show a necklace of light draped across the powerful current that races through the Cook Strait, separating the North Island and South Island. The spiraling current carries an astonishingly rich load of fish and squid. Its swirls and whorls are visible from space at night because the boats of Asian fishing fleets track the fish so accurately that the lights themselves precisely replicate the spirals of the current.[30]

Our ability to over fish oceans with 30-mile-long lines results in 20 million tons of annual bycatch—dead or entangled swordfish, turtles, dolphins, marlin and other fish that are discarded, pushed overboard, tossed back or definned for soup in the case of sharks. This bycatch that is thrown overboard is the equivalent of ten pounds of fish for every person on earth.[31]

Wild salmon are going the way of the cod too. There used to be 6,000 miles of good salmon streams in California's Central Valley. Now it is down to about 200. Sadly people are now arguing over how much water the endangered salmon should be allowed to be endangered in. Only eighty years ago there were no dams on the mighty Columbia River. Now there are many dams, and the salmon don't like it.

There are too many dams on the Snake River, as well as on the Frazier, the Sacramento, the Kalamath and the San Joaquin. Dams make it nearly impossible for the fish to return to their spawning grounds. Few salmon survive the arduous journey over the fish ladders in rivers with flows that are too low and water that is too warm. Once they hatch, the few young salmon must then swim miles through the slack water and survive the turbines which pump water for irrigation. If they make it to the ocean, they must contend with drift-netters on the high seas—the buffalo hunters of our time.[32] There are so few salmon left now that there was no commercial salmon fishing allowed off the coast of California and most of Oregon in 2008 and 2009.

Not only are we killing most of the fish in the ocean, we are actually killing the ocean itself. At a January 1999 meeting of the American Association for the Advancement of Science, researchers reported that there is a 7000-square-mile dead zone the size of New Jersey in the Gulf of Mexico leaving a huge area now devoid of fish, shrimp, and almost every other form of life except certain bacteria that prefer low-oxygen environments. The cause is the runoff from the 6.5 million metric tons of nitrogen fertilizer used on U.S. agricultural land every year. This nitrogen makes its way into thousands of waterways that drain into the Mississippi River and the Gulf.

While the dead zones in the Gulf of Mexico, Oregon and Washington are well studied because they are just off the coast of the United States, similar dead zones are appearing around the world, threatening fisheries and disturbing the ocean's ecosystem. Among other things these dead zones reduce the ocean's ability to sequester greenhouse gasses and contribute oxygen to the atmosphere.[33]

One last note about oceans—plastic is forever. When it breaks up into small pieces, plastic looks just like plankton. If Christopher Columbus left a plastic fork on the beach in 1492, it still would be there. The amount of plastic floating in the oceans is now six times that of actual plankton. The plastic along with its estrogen mimickers is entering the food chain in enormous quantities as fish and birds eat the plastic by accident. Visit www.oceanrevolution.org for more information about saving the oceans.

If you care about wild fisheries, watch these two movies from Patagonia: *DamNation* and *Artifishal*.

WASTE

Not only are Americans super-consumers, we are also super-wasters. Americans waste nearly one million pounds of materials per person per year. This figure includes: 3.3 trillion pounds of carbon in CO_2 gas emitted into the atmosphere, 19 billion pounds of polystyrene peanuts, 28 billion pounds of food discarded at home, 360 billion pounds of organic and inorganic chemicals used for manufacturing and processing, 710 billion pounds of hazardous waste generated by chemical production, and 3.7 trillion pounds of construction debris and 3.5 billion pounds of carpet.[34]

Each American generates about one ton of municipal landfill waste per year and about the same quantity of hazardous waste. Electronic devices represent less than 4 percent of total solid waste, but they make up 70 percent of all hazardous waste.[35] For every pound of electronics in your pocket or on your desk, approximately 8,000 pounds of waste is created somewhere in the world.[36]

Our cavalier attitude toward this problem is an indication of how hard it will be to solve. Even the words we use to describe our behavior reveal the pattern of self-deception. Take, for example, the word consumption, which implies an almost mechanical efficiency, suggesting that all traces of whatever we consume magically vanish after we use it. In fact, when we consume something, it doesn't go away at all. Rather, it is transformed into material of two very different kinds: something useful and the stuff left over, which we call waste. Moreover, anything we think of as useful becomes waste as soon as we are finished with it.[37] Away has even gone away.

Too many materials and too much energy are used to support

human activities. Easily 94 percent of what American industry uses up is waste. Only six percent of what we process winds up as products. Durable products are only one percent of what we process.

The contemporary automobile is also stunningly inefficient. Only 20 percent of the energy in the fuel is used to turn the wheels, while 80 percent is lost in the engine's heat and exhaust. Moreover, a full 95 percent of the energy that is used moves the car, and only five percent moves the driver. The overall efficiency in terms of the proportion of fuel energy used to move the driver is five percent of 20 percent—a mere one percent.[38]

Eliminating the very idea of waste is the key; instead, every material used should be reused somewhere else when we're finished with it. It should be raw material for some other process. That means not making or using toxic chemicals and it means using processes that mimic nature. Competitive pressures are already pushing businesses to start practicing biomimicry. If we could also take away hidden subsidies to waste, then the costs would drastically speed up the transition.[39]

To get a visual of the scale of our waste, see the work of photographer Chris Jordan at www.chrisjordan.com. Chris explains his work, "Exploring around our country's shipping ports and industrial yards, where the accumulated detritus of our consumption is exposed to view like eroded layers in the Grand Canyon, I find evidence of a slow-motion apocalypse in progress. I am appalled by these scenes, and yet also drawn into them with awe and fascination. The immense scale of our consumption can appear desolate, macabre, oddly comical and ironic, and even darkly beautiful; for me its consistent feature is a staggering complexity.

The pervasiveness of our consumerism holds a seductive kind of mob mentality. Collectively we are committing a vast and unsustainable act of taking, but we each are anonymous and no one is in charge or accountable for the consequences. I fear that in this process we are doing irreparable harm to our planet and to our individual spirits."

OUR STORY IS CAUSING ECOSYSTEM COLLAPSE

When the early European settlers fanned out across the American prairies and killed every buffalo they could find, the Native Americans watched in shock and horror at what they considered a senseless act of insanity. How could the settlers take the life of the plains?

How could they parcel up the flesh of Mother Earth? How could they be so crazy as to cut down every tree in sight? The settlers looked at the Indians and thought they were crazy to not take and eat all the buffalo they could. How could they have sat on this valuable resource for 10,000 years and not have used it? They had to be savages, uncivilized half-humans who didn't have the good sense to know how to use nature's bounty for the good of the human race.

For a while, this worked for the conquering "Americans." Just as Gilgamesh could cut down the cedars of Lebanon, just as the Greeks could destroy their own forests, just as Americans could strip half their topsoil from the land, the rapid consumption of "out there" to satisfy the needs of us "in here" worked for more than a few generations. No more, as we are seeing in the early warning system of the Third World.

Leaver cultures are older because they have survived for tens of thousands of years. The Leaver vision of the world says that humanity belongs to the earth. Leaver culture is proven to be evolutionarily successful.

In comparison, Taker culture is still an experiment, and every time a civilization has been attempted, Samaria, Rome, Greece, however great its grandeur, it has self-destructed. Taker cultures are built on a foundation that is spiritually barren.[40] Our story, that the world was made for humanity alone and humanity was destined to conquer it, is not working.

8. Mass Extinction

For all of our intellect and accomplishment, we do not seem to be able to prevent our culture from killing almost everything in its wake in the name of jobs and progress. Our Taker culture has become a great extermination machine. Globally, capitalism has become our default economic system because it is the most efficient at turning natural materials into something useful.

These pages bear witness to our culture's folly. Humanity lived in harmony with the 30 million other species on the planet for three to four million years. But now we have thrown that vibrant lifestyle away in favor of making more things to be thrown away.

Leaver culture is evolutionarily proven to enable humanity to be a member of a world filled with a diverse riot of life. Biodiversity is the cornerstone of the resilience of life on earth. This century is precisely the moment of culminating human-caused ecological crises, when the planet needs the full strength of its immune system resilience. But we are stripping away this resilience with our cities, suburbs, monoculture crops and plantation pulp forests. This is like giving a person AIDS just before you attack their health.

SCALE OF THE CATASTROPHE

Our great failure is the termination of the journey for so many of the most brilliant species of the web of life. Our Taker culture is making the greatest single setback to life's abundance and diversity since the first flickering of life almost four billion years ago. The labor and care

114

expended over billions of years and untold billions of experiments to bring fourth such a gorgeous world is all being negated within less than a century for what we consider *progress*. Our culture has literally gone mad—it has no empathy.[1]

One species, ours, is causing the earth's sixth mega extinction of species. The complete recovery, the reestablishment of previous species, will require tens of millions of years. As Edward O. Wilson warns, "these figures should give pause to anyone who believes that what *Homo sapiens* destroys, Nature will redeem. Maybe so, but not within any length of time that has any meaning for contemporary humanity."

As a result of global economic development, exponential population growth, urbanization, and careless use of natural resources, diverse habitats are threatened and the degradation of entire ecosystems is occurring. The widespread degradation of the natural landscape is at the core of the current biodiversity crash

RATE OF EXTINCTION IS ACCELERATING

The 2005 Millennium Ecosystem Assessment describes significant and irreversible changes to species diversity. The distribution of species on earth is becoming more homogeneous. Humans have increased the species extinction rate by as much as 1,000 times over the background rate typical over the planet's history. With a medium to high degree of certainty, 10 to 30 percent of mammal, bird, and amphibian species are currently threatened with extinction.[3] According to the Living Planet Report 2004, average trends in populations of terrestrial, freshwater and marine species worldwide has declined by about 40 percent from 1970 to 2000.[4]

The relationship between humanity and evolution has begun to reverse. Beginning 65 million years ago with the disappearance of the dinosaurs, the Cenozoic era has been characterized by the flourishing of a larger number and more varied life forms than during any previous era in the earth's 4.6 billion year history. Theologian Thomas Berry notes that because human civilization is destroying as many as half of all living species on earth during our lifetime, it is in effect bringing about the end of the Cenozoic era.[5]

Among the most widely cited figures estimating global habitat losses, there are some shocking and depressing conclusions—4,000 and 25,000 species per year are lost, which translates to 40 to 50 per day, or one to three species every hour! As you read this passage, another species has been lost. This far surpasses the rate of any of the other previous five mega extinctions.[6]

In other words, maintaining a population of six billion humans costs the earth 40 to 50 species a day. We are literally turning 40 to 50 species a day into human tissue. And this will go on every day, day after day until drastic changes are made.

Most people seem to believe that we are separate from nature and the rest of the living community. Since we are separate, it does not matter how many species we destroy since we are superior to them anyway.

It is conservatively estimated that our population will increase to nine billion by the end of the century. People seem to take this shocking piece of information very calmly. Most people do not realize that the extinction of other species will continue to increase as our human population increases—and probably exponentially.

This cataclysmic destruction, however, cannot be sustained. We are systematically destroying the biodiversity of the living community which supports ourselves. That is to say, we are systematically destroying the infrastructure that keeps us alive.

If there are still people living here in 200 years, they will know that humanity is not separate from the rest of the living community. They will know this as surely as we know that the earth revolves around the sun. If people go on thinking that we belong to a separate order of being apart from nature, there may not be people living on the earth in 200 years.[7]

HOW HUMANITY IS CAUSING THIS TO HAPPEN

In their urgency to convey the importance of species extinction, conservation biologists will appeal to sheer self-interest, trying to explain that human survival depends on the integrity of the global environment. The prospect of mass species extinction spells doom for humans too. Niles Eldredge asks: "Why not just let the sixth extinction runs its course? After all, evolution ultimately creates new species that become the players in newly rebuilt ecosystems. The answer is simple: New species evolve, and ecosystems are reassembled, only after the cause of disruption and extinction is removed or stabilized. In other words, *Homo sapiens* will have to cease acting as the cause of the sixth extinction whether through our own demise, or, preferably, through determined action, before evolutionary ecological recovery can begin. Our fate is inextricably linked to the fate of earth's species and ecosystems."[8]

Extinction expert David Wilcove and his colleagues list five human causes of extinction in the United States, in order of current importance:

1. Habitat destruction
2. Non-native or alien species
3. Pollution
4. Overexploitation
5. Disease.[9]

Habitat Destruction

We modify or transform natural habitat upon which species depend by burning land for agriculture, logging, grazing by domestic animals, preventing natural fire, damming rivers, diverting rivers through irrigation diversion, drying up springs and streams through groundwater depletion, eliminating keystone species like beaver and prairie dogs, whose activities create habitat for other species, and urban/suburban development. Furthermore, we fragment habitat, thereby disrupting necessary patterns of movement for many species, through the above activities and by building roads, clearing power line rights-of-way and driving vehicles.

Migrations require large undisturbed tracks of land. Migrations are seasonal treks that require movement away from a home area and back again. For instance, a mouse that moves from your house in winter to a shed in summer and then back again when the snow falls would fit the definition. For most people though, images of migration are usually of larger species such as grey whales moving from Mexican to Arctic waters and back, or even of diminutive Monarch butterflies wintering in Mexican highlands and summering far to the north. Though no exact threshold has been established for a long-distance migration, they typically cover many kilometers, often across a range of habitat types and political jurisdictions.

Many long-distance migrations have been truncated during the last 100-150 years. Worse, it has been estimated that some 95–99

percent have been entirely lost during recent times. Among the most
notable losses in the past 40 years are the vast treks of thousands of
springbok and perhaps a quarter-million wildebeest from the Kalahari, Karoo and Etosha pans of Botswana, South Africa and Namibia.
From Sudan, white-eared kob were possibly the longest migrators in
Africa, traversing up to 700 kilometers. They suffered during Sudan's
civil war and no longer navigate the marshes of the Sudd. In North
America, bison are well known for their population losses, but less
known is that none of their historic migration routes into and out of
Yellowstone Park still exist. For pronghorn and elk, conservative estimates suggest that even within the 60,000-square-kilometer Greater
Yellowstone Ecosystem, some 80 percent and 60 percent of their
respective migration routes are gone. This is relevant because the
Greater Yellowstone Ecosystem is touted as one of the most intact
temperate systems in the world. Given the magnitude of losses there,
the losses must be higher elsewhere.[10]

The migration of the porcupine caribou is currently intact, but it
would be threatened if the Alaska National Wildlife Refuge were
opened to oil drilling in the sensitive caribou calving grounds. A
beautiful and award winning film about the threat to the caribou is
Being Caribou. Karsten and Leanne Heuer document the migration.
They trek with the caribou all the way from the caribou's winter
home in Canada, to calving in the Alaska National Wildlife Refuge,
and back. Visit www.beingcaribou.com.

Non-native Species

As humans have spread into new land, we have brought with us disruptive alien species that are generally well adapted to human activity
and disturbance. These species often out compete native species, in
part because the predators and diseases they evolved with in their
habitat are left behind. The invaders include plants and animals introduced both deliberately and accidentally.

Non-native species include predators such as cats, rats and pigs
and competitors such as starlings, tamarisk and zebra mussels. Alfred
Crosby of the University of Texas offered an early and insightful look
at exotic species invasions in *Ecological Imperialism: The Biological
Expansion of Europe, 900-1900*. He showed that temperate regions of
the world in North America, South America, Australia, and New

Zealand have become "Neo-Europes" with the arrival of European colonists and their domestic crops, livestock, weeds, worms, diseases and pests.

Pollution

Pollution, whether localized or global, acid rain or green-house gases, can poison the waters and soils that are habitat for sensitive species, or leach away needed nutrients. Global warming and atmospheric ozone depletion, major threats to life forms worldwide, are caused largely by air pollution. The magnitude of chemicals and waste discharged into the air, water and land is significant and growing. [11]

Overexploitation

In the previous chapter we discussed the exhaustion of marine fisheries as one clear example of humanity's over-exploitation of other species. Lets now look back in history to when people first arrived in North America.

The overkill theory for why the horses, camels, elephants, sloths, glyptodonts, tapirs, peccaries, long-horned bison and giant tortoises disappeared at the end of the Pleistocene is now widely accepted. The ripple effects of overkill—extinction by starvation, exacerbated by hunting—is now the accepted explanation for the simultaneous or somewhat later extinctions of the continent's great native carnivores: dire wolf, sabertooth cats, American lion, cheetah and the biggest mammalian land carnivore of all time, Arctodus, the short-faced bear. People caused the overkill. Thirteen thousand years ago is the time we may come to look upon as the beginning of the end of the Cenozoic era, when spear-wielding humans entered North America and over hunted to extinction most of the continent's large mammals which had evolved without predation from intelligent, socially organized humans.[12]

A more recent example is the passenger pigeon, once the most abundant bird in North America. In the early 1800's there were billions of passenger pigeons. They darkened the sky as they flew. When they landed, branches sighed and sometimes broke. For millions of years, the forests and skies bore the weight of passenger pigeons, yet it took fewer than a hundred years for people to decimate their population. Americans shot passenger pigeons for food, for fun and even out of boredom. By the 1890s, there were not enough passenger pigeons to form the massive aggregations that likely triggered them to breed. The birds that remained did not lay eggs and then either died or were shot. In 1899, a fourteen-year-old boy in Ohio killed the last known wild passenger pigeon.[13]

Disease

As humans have spread around the world, we have brought exotic diseases with us. An exotic disease caused the loss of the American chestnut in the wild. In the American Midwest, Dutch Elm Disease has nearly decimated the stately elm. The black-footed ferret was nearly wiped out by canine distemper. Human population density is creating new pandemics. Without a vaccine, the future threat is that the genes which make COVID-19 contagious combine with a virus like MERS which is 35 percent fatal.

LESSONS FOR HUMANITY

Perhaps our willingness to overlook the passing of the Rocky Mountain locust will be a matter of blissful ignorance, for if we understood the story of its extinction, our complacency would be most disturbing. The *Guinness Book of World Records* reported a swarm of over ten billion insects in 1875 which is disconcertingly similar to the current human population. The simplest and most unambiguous lesson that we can learn from the Rocky Mountain locust is that numerical abundance does not assure future survival. Having reached almost seven billion people already, we need only look to the Rocky Mountain locusts that blackened the skies of North America or the enormous numbers of bison that dotted vast tracts of the West to realize that our future as a species is no brighter for our quantity.

One might optimistically contend that we are the ultimate generalists, capable of rapidly adapting to an immense range of environmental challenges and occupying new habitats. However, the Rocky Mountain locust might quietly remind us that it consumed no fewer than 50 kinds of plants from more than a dozen families, as well as leather, laundry and sheep wool when hunger demanded. The overwhelming majority of human caloric intake on the other hand is derived from just three plant species—corn, wheat and rice—which are all members of a single family. Moreover, if the body size of the Rocky Mountain locust was increased to that of a human, it would be capable of traveling 36,000 miles, about the same distance that our ancestors traveled in the process of circumnavigating and eventually colonizing the planet. It appears that being a highly mobile generalist is no assurance against extinction.

BEARING WITNESS TO EXTINCTION

Mitchell Thomashow in *Bringing the Biosphere Home* wrote this moving passage about bearing witness to extinction:

"Whoever observes the natural world is also likely to notice threats to biodiversity. In contemplating biodiversity, you acknowledge the inevitability of extinction. An informed observer understands that extinction and speciation run their course with or without humanity, but when humanity serves as an agent of mass extinction, one has to deal with an awesome responsibility. Your actions, taken as a whole, in ways that you cannot completely understand, have long-lasting impacts, on the order of tens of millions of years.

Who bears witness to extinction? Who feels the emptiness, the sadness, and the incomprehensible sense of loss when the last individual of a species expires? Typically there are no human witnesses. This enhances the mysterious, existential quality of the idea of extinction. You may viscerally observe the decline or demise of a species to which you have the privilege of relative proximity. But knowledge of extinction is mainly gained abstractly, by reading accounts of species losses around the world, or by grappling with the cold, stark mathematics of extinction statistics and extrapolations. The final act almost always occurs without human witness." Consider Edward O. Wilson's poignant commentary:

"Extinction is the most obscure and local of all biological processes. We don't see the last butterfly of its species snatched from the air by a bird or the last orchid of a certain kind killed by the collapse of its supporting tree in some distant mountain forest. We hear that a certain animal or plant is on the edge, perhaps already gone. We return to the last known locality to search, and when no individuals are encountered there year after year we pronounce the species extinct. But hope lingers on. Someone flying a light plane over Louisiana swamps thinks he sees a few ivory-billed woodpeckers start up and glide back down into the foliage . . . but it is probably all fantasy."

This profound and forlorn passage captures the paradox of extinction. Only those who develop intimate knowledge of a species can bear witness to its loss. With intimacy one cultivates an appreciation for the life history of a species, its unique ecology and behavior providing the details for its description in the Great Encyclopedia of Life. What you don't know about, you may never miss. It takes courage to search for the last of its kind.

Most species pass away unnoticed. Many go extinct before they are ever named or identified by human taxonomists. Does that make their loss any less significant? Why should any one species matter more than another? Why should a species be mourned—because of sentimentality, because it represents the end of evolutionary possibility or perhaps because it is a statement about the human condition?

So the fate of species is both the measure of biodiversity and a barometer of human destiny. Many fine ecologists, ethicists, theologians and all manner of environmental thinkers have written superb rationales for promoting biodiversity—with reasons ranging from the economic and biological to the aesthetic and spiritual.

But Thomashow emphasizes the importance of bearing witness to extinction. One most appreciates life in the shadow of death. To observe the destruction of any ecological habitat or to perceive a threat to its integrity is a reminder of the fragility of biodiversity—how thousands of years of ecological and evolutionary history can be dispatched in a moment with a bulldozer or an application of herbicide or ammonium phosphate. It can happen even before you have a chance to figure out what is going on. Habitats and species disappear overnight.[14]

CULTURAL DIVERSITY LOSS

Biodiversity hot spots occur in areas where cultural diversity also persists. There is, for example, a direct correspondence between the prevalence of biodiversity, the long-term coexistence of diverse cultures, and the presence of multiple languages. Of the nine countries in which 60 percent of the world's remaining 6,500 languages are spoken, five of them are also centers of mega diversity for flora and fauna:

Mexico, Brazil, Indonesia, Zaire and Australia.

Geographer David Harmon has made lists of the 25 countries harboring the greatest number of endemic wildlife species within their boundaries and of the 25 countries where the greatest number of endemic languages are spoken. These two lists have 16 countries in common. It is fair to say that wherever many cultures have coexisted within the same region, biodiversity has also survived. Wherever empires have spread to suppress other cultures' languages and land-tenure traditions, the loss of biodiversity has been dramatic.[15]

From an entirely different quarter, Steven Pinker, a linguist, describes the global extinction of indigenous languages. Approximately 3,600 to 5,400 languages may well be lost in the next century, what amounts to 90 percent of the world's total. What is the significance of this for biodiversity studies? Despite the best attempts of conservation biologists and ecologists to collect natural history data, the most important knowledge regarding natural history is locked in the languages of indigenous peoples who study proximate species over dozens of generations. As the language is lost, so is the tradition of direct, visceral ecological and evolutionary learning. Languages are a species of sorts and their extinction is inextricably linked to the loss of biodiversity and ancient cultural knowledge.[16]

ALTARS OF EXTINCTION

There are no easy answers, no simple to do list. But the choices we make today, individually and collectively, will have a profound impact on the direction life will take in the coming millennia and far beyond. Finding our way to wise courses of action will require that we open ourselves to the spiritual dimension of the extinction crisis, allowing ourselves to love that which is dying as well as that which lives on, extending our circle of community to include all that lives and all that has left this world, feeling the fragile beauty as well as the resilience of the life force as it pulses through us all, mourning the passing of a lost species as we would a friend, a family member, a beloved.

Mary E. Gomes and Allen Kanner have created altars of extinction, memorials to those who have passed. The altars are associated with no particular creed or religion, allowing each person to find her or his own heartfelt response. At the center of many of their exhibits stands the altar to unknown extinctions. Let us enter it now:

A black curtain hangs from ceiling to floor. Take a rock from the basket outside the curtain and walk inside, where you find a dark well. Look into the well. You cannot see the bottom. Drop the rock in. Feel the weight of it leave your hand, and wait as it sinks slowly to the bottom of the dark pool. Feel the loss, the mystery. Another species gone, another form of life extinguished. Who has left this world already? So often, no one knows. Most extinctions go unwitnessed by humans. Those that are named are simply the edges of a great unraveling. So you come here with a humble and open heart, taking this moment to say good-bye.[17]

SAVE THE WORLD [8] WHAT DO WE MEAN?

Humanity will probably survive; we have a knack for adaptability. The question is under what conditions and what will happen to the other 30 million species with whom we share this beautiful home? When we say, "save the world," we mean save our brother and sister species. We mean save today's biodiversity. We mean make sure there is room for all others to follow their own destiny. We mean giving back much of what we have taken. We mean living in harmony with the earth as we have for millions of years. We can do it. The fact that we are here proves it.

WHAT DO WE TELL OUR CHILDREN?

As the reality of this age of widespread extinctions enters human consciousness, we may collectively enter a teachable moment in our cultural consciousness. As our understanding deepens, we begin to re-discover the principles of living in harmony with the earth.

We know the hour is late. Much of our inheritance already has been lost. Far more will be needlessly squandered before we have any hope of consolidating an ecological renaissance. We also know that we may not succeed. The forces of destruction may overwhelm our bravest efforts. But the question of whether we will succeed is not the deepest question for us. The questions we must ask ourselves are how do we choose to live during this Age of Extinctions and what do we tell our children?[18]

9. Forest Loss and Ecological Services

Global forest health is one of the key indicators of the earth's overall health. Forests act as the earth's lungs, circulate fresh water, and are home to nature's rich treasury of biodiversity. Today, our Taker culture is rapidly cutting the forests down and so sawing off the branch we are standing on. During our children's lifetime, or perhaps ours, the branch will be cut through. Based on our culture's track record, and judging by the rate we are going, it is unlikely we will be able to stop in time.

This chapter explains how forests support life on earth. The forest is more than an assembly of plant and animal species. Rather it is a single living organism with differing cells, organs, circulatory system and other functions. Can the orchid exist without the tree that supports it, or the wasp that fertilizes it? Can the forest extend its borders and occupy grasslands without the pigeon that carries its berries away so the seeds germinate and grow elsewhere?

WE CANNOT LIVE WITHOUT FORESTS

When we cut forests, we must pay the consequences in drought, a decrease in water holding capacity, nutrient loss and erosion. Unwise or corrupt governments do not take these costs into consideration, and deforestation has therefore impoverished many nations. The U.S. government has recently announced grants totaling $4.1 million for businesses to find even more uses for woody biomass from national forests. This would rob the forest of the raw materials it needs for decomposition and its long-term fertility.

We should not be deceived by the propaganda that says, for every tree cut down, another tree is planted. The exchange of a 50g seedling for a forest giant of 50-100 tons is like the offer of a mouse for an elephant. It would take 4,000-8,000 tree seedlings to replace the atmospheric benefit of one mature tree. No new reforestation can replace an old forest in ecosystem value, and even this lip service is omitted in clearcut forestry practiced throughout the world.

Trees are, for the earth, the ultimate translators and moderators of incoming energy. Within the forest canopy, the vast energies of sunlight, wind and precipitation are being modified for life and growth. Trees not only build, but also conserve the soil, shielding it from the impact of raindrops and the desiccation of wind and sunlight. If we could only understand what a tree does for us, how beneficial it is to life on earth, we would, as many tribes have done, revere all trees as brothers and sisters.

Without trees, we cannot inhabit the earth. Without trees the land turns to deserts and the climate to drought. Without trees, the atmosphere will change and life support systems will fail.[1]

LET IT RAIN

A Story About an Oak Tree

This ecology of an oak tree told by Toby Hemenway in *Gaia's Garden: A Guide To Home-Scale Permaculture* captured me when I first read it. It educates and fills the heart at the same time:

"It's dawn. The first rays of sunlight strike the canopy of the oak, but most of the energy in these beams is consumed in evaporating dew on the leaves. Only after the leaves are dry does the sunlight warm the air within the tree. Above the oak, however, the air has begun to heat, and a cloud of just-awakened insects swirls here. Below the canopy, it's still too chilly for insects to venture. The insects roil in a narrow band, sharply defining the layer of warm air above the tree. Together the sun and the oak have created insect habitat, and with it, a place for birds, who quickly swoop to feast on the swarm of bugs.

In the cool shade of this tree, snow remains late into the spring, long after unprotected snow has melted. Soil near the tree stays moist, watering both the oak and nearby plantings, and helping to keep a nearby creek flowing. Early miners in the West frequently reported creeks disappearing once they'd cut nearby forests for mine timbers.

Soon the sun warms the humid, night-chilled air within the tree. The entrapped air dries, its moisture escaping to the sky to help form clouds. This lost moisture is quickly replaced by the transpiring leaves, which pump water up from roots and exhale it through puffy-lipped pores in the leaves called stomata. Groundwater, whether polluted or clean, is filtered by the tree and exits through the leaves as pure water. So trees are excellent water purifiers, and active ones. A full-grown tree can transpire 2,000 gallons of water on a hot, dry day. But this moisture doesn't just go away—it soon returns as rain: Up to half of the rainfall over forested land comes from the trees themselves, the rest arrives as evaporation from bodies of water. Cut the trees, and the rain disappears.

Sun striking the leaves ignites the engines of photosynthesis, and from these green factories, oxygen streams into the air. But more benefits exist. To build sugars and the other carbon-based molecules that provide fuel and structure for the tree, the leaves remove carbon dioxide from the air. This is how trees help reduce the level of greenhouse gases.

As the leaves absorb sunlight and warm the air within the tree, this hot, moist air rises and mixes with the drier, cool air above. Convection currents begin to churn, and morning breezes begin. So trees help create cooling winds.

But closer to the ground, trees block the wind. The oak's upper branches toss in the morning breeze, while down below the air is still. The tree has captured the energetic movement of the air and converted it into its own motion. Where does this energy go? Some scientists think that captured wind energy is converted into the woody tissue of the tree, helping to build tough but flexible cells.

Trees make excellent windbreaks: A tree placed on the windward side of a house can substantially reduce heating bills.

The morning breeze carries dust from the plowed fields of nearby farmland, which collects on the oak leaves. A single tree may have 10 to 30 acres of leaf surface, all able to draw dust and pollutants from the air. Air passing through the tree is thus purified, and humidified as well. As air passes through the tree, it picks up moisture exhaled from the leaves, a light burden of pollen grains, a fine mist of small molecules produced by the tree, some bacteria, and fungal spores.

Some of those spores have landed below the tree, spawning

several species of fungus that grow symbiotically amid the roots, secreting nutrients and antibiotics that feed and protect the tree. A vole has tunneled into the soft earth beneath the tree in search of some of this fungus. Later this vole will leave manure pellets near other oaks, inoculating them with the beneficial fungus. That is, if the owl who regularly frequents this oak doesn't snatch up the vole first.

This tree's ancestors provided Native Americans with flour made from acorns, though most suburbanites wouldn't consider this use. Blue jays and squirrels frolic in the oak, snatching acorns and hiding them around this and neighboring yards. Some of these acorns, forgotten, will sprout and grow into new trees. Meanwhile, the animals' diggings and droppings will aid the soil. Other birds probe the bark for insects, and yet others depend on the inconspicuous flowers for food,

Later in the day, clouds, half of them created by trees remember, begin to build. Rain droplets readily form around the bacteria, pollen, and other microscopic debris lofted from the oak. These small particles provide the nucleation sites that raindrops need to form, thus, trees act as cloud-seeders to bring rain.

As the rain falls, the droplets smack against the oak leaves and spread out into a fine film, coating the entire tree, all 10 to 30 acres of leaves, plus the branches and trunk, before a single drop strikes the ground. This thin film begins to evaporate even as the rain falls, further delaying any through-fall. Mosses and lichens on this old oak soak up even more of the rain. We've all seen dry patches beneath trees after a rain: A mature tree can absorb over 1/4 inch of rain before any reaches the earth; even more if the air is dry and the rain is light.

The leaves and branches act as a funnel, channeling much of the rain to the trunk and toward the root zone of the tree. Soil close to the trunk can receive 2 to 10 times as much rain as that in open ground, and the tree's shade slows evaporation, preserving this moisture.

As the rain continues, droplets leak off the leaves and splatter on the ground. Since this tree-drip has lost most of the energy it gathered during its fall from the clouds, little soil erodes beneath the tree. Leaf litter and roots also help hold the soil in place. Trees are supreme erosion-control systems.

The water falling from the leaves is very different from what fell from the sky. Its passage through the tree transmutes it into a rich soup, laden with the pollen, dust, bird and insect droppings, bacteria and fungi collected by the leaves, and many chemicals and nutrients secreted by the tree. This nutritious broth both nourishes the soil beneath the tree and inoculates the leaf litter and earth with soil-decomposing organisms. In this way, the tree collects and prepares its own fertilizer solution.

The rain eases toward sundown, and the sky clears. The upper leaves of the tree begin to chill as night falls, and cold air drains down from the canopy, cooling the trunk and soil. But this chill is countered by heat rising from the day-warmed earth, which warms the air under the tree. The leafy canopy holds this warmth, preventing it from escaping to the night sky, so nighttime temperatures are warmer beneath the tree than in the open.

The leaves, however, radiate their heat to the sky and become quite cold, often much colder than the air. All these cold surfaces condense moisture from the air, and the resulting dew drips from the leaves and wets the ground, watering the tree and surrounding plants. Leaves can also gather moisture from fog: On foggy days, the mist collects in such volume that droplets trickle steadily from the leaves. On arid but foggy coasts, tree-harvested precipitation can be triple the average rainfall. By harvesting dew and fog, trees can boost available moisture to far beyond what a rain gauge indicates.

As we gaze at this huge oak, remember that we're barely seeing half of it, at least 50 percent of this tree's mass is below the ground. The roots may extend tens of feet down, and horizontally can range far beyond the span of the tree's branches. These roots loosen and aerate soil, build humus as they grow and die, etch minerals free from rocks with mild acid secretions, and with sugary exudates provide food for hundreds or even thousands of species of soil organisms that live with them."[2]

Forests Multiply the Rain

Forests create rain from winds blowing inland from an ocean or large lake. That is why when forests are destroyed rainfall declines. Bill Mollison explains how forests affect total precipitation in *Permaculture: A Designer's Manual.*

"The water in the air is what evaporated from the surface of the sea or lake. It contains a few salt particles but is clean. A small proportion may fall as rain, 15-20 percent, but most of this water is condensed out of clear night air or fogs by the cool surfaces of leaves, 80-85 percent. Of this condensate, 15 percent evaporates by day and 50 percent is transpired. The rest enters the groundwater. Thus, trees are responsible for more water in streams than the rainfall alone provides.

Of the rain that falls, 25 percent again re-evaporates from crown leaves, and 50 percent is transpired. This moisture is added to clouds, which are at least 50 percent tree water. These clouds travel inland to rain again. Thus trees may double or multiply rainfall itself by this process, which can be repeated many times over extensive forested plains or foothills.

As the air rises inland, the precipitation and condensation increases, and moss forests plus standing clouds may form in mountains, adding considerably to total precipitation and infiltration for the lower slopes and streams.

Whenever winds pass over tree lines or forest edges of 12 m, 40 feet, or more in height, Ekman spirals develop, adding 40 percent or so to rainfall in bands, which roughly parallel the tree lines.

Within the forest, 40 percent of the incident air mass may enter and either lose water or be rehumidified.

And, in every case, rain is more likely to fall as a result of organic particles forming nuclei for condensation, whereas industrial aerosols are too small to cause rain and instead produce dry, cloudy conditions.

Thus if we clear the forest, what is left but dust?"[3]

Great Lakes of Water Storage

Trees also intercept and draw on underground water reserves for growth, and then pump the water into the air again. Imagine the visible above ground forest as water, and all but about 5-10 percent of this mass is water. Then imagine all the water that is contained in the soil, the organic matter, the trees and plants, and root material. The forest is actually a huge great lake of stored and actively recycling water. No other water storage system is as efficient or beneficial to life as that of the forest.[4]

Snowmelt Water Increased

A couple years ago, legislation was proposed to allow more logging in Colorado forests because it was believed that clear cutting would

increase melt water and so increase reservoir levels at lower eleva-
tions. It does not work and here is why.

Although trees intercept some snow, the effect of shrubs and
trees is to entrap snow at the edges of clumps, and hold 75-95 percent of snowfall in the shade. Melting is delayed for many days compared with bare ground, so the release of snowmelt is more gradual.
Of the trapped snow within trees, most is melted, while on open
ground almost all of the snow moisture evaporates directly into the
air. Thus, the beneficial effects of trees on high slopes are not
confined to humid coasts. On the high cold uplands of the American west, the thin streaks of winter snow either blow off the bald
uplands, to disappear in warmer air, or else they sublime directly to
water vapor in the bright sunlight of winter. In neither case does the
snow melt to the groundwater. It is gone without direct productive
effect, and no streams result on the lower slopes.

Even a thin belt of trees traps large quantities of driven snow in
drifts. The result is a long, slow release of meltwater to river sources
in the highlands, and stream-flow at lower altitudes. When the
forests were cleared for mine timber in 1846 at Pyramid Lake,
Nevada, the streams stopped flowing, and the lake levels fell. Add to
this effect river diversion and irrigation, and whole lake regions
which had been rich with fish and waterfowl become like dust-
bowls. The Cuiuidika'a Indians who live there lost their fish, waterfowl and freshwater in less than 100 years. The cowboys of the
West won the day, but ruined the future to do so.[5]

OTHER IRREPLACEABLE FOREST SERVICES

Protect The Soil

We have seen in previous chapters how forests build and protect
the earth's irreplaceable topsoil. When forests are clearcut, soil mineral loss increases about 1000 times.[6] Here is a current example of
what happens when forests are unable to provide this ecological
protection.

Nepal has lost over 30 percent of its forest cover to fuel-wood
gathering and subsistence farming in just the past few decades. For
the thousands of years that tribal people lived there, elaborate hillside
terraces had provided a predictable supply of food for the nation's
population. Today, most of those terraces are crumbling under the

erosive force of rains that race down Nepal's steep slopes, no longer slowed by forests.

Women in Nepal, as in most developing countries, are the ones primarily responsible for gathering firewood as well as growing, gathering and preparing food. Because of the rapid deforestation in Nepal, Nepalese women have recently had to add between one and four hours to their normal ten-hour workday just to walk to and from the increasingly distant sources of wood. Within the near future these sources will also be exhausted. Nepal will probably travel the same road that Haiti has tragically followed.[7]

Prevent Desertification

A rainforest tree will draw three million gallons of water up through its roots and release it into the atmosphere as water vapor during its lifetime. While it may seem that this would deplete the soil of water, actually, the reverse is true: trees draw water into the soil, the first step in a complex cycle that prevents land from becoming desert.

Without forests first pumping millions of tons of water into an area's atmosphere, there's little moisture released into the air to condense into clouds and then fall again as rain. The result is that just downwind of the place that was once forest but is now denuded, the rains no longer fall and a process called desertification begins. This has happened over much of north and eastern Africa, leading to massive famines as the rains stop, crops fail and the top-soil is blown away. What is left is desert. Largely because of the destruction of upwind forests, over 1,500 acres of land are becoming desert worldwide every hour.

Most rainfall on non-forest land is either absorbed into the soil and becomes surface ground water, or it is transported along culverts, ditches, sewers, streams and rivers, eventually reaching the ocean. On our continental landmasses, only trees effectively cycle large quantities of water back to the atmosphere. For comparison, think of the evaporation from a 40 acre lake. Forty acres of surface area may seem like a lot of potential water to be evaporating into the atmosphere, but that 40 acres is equal to the evaporative leaf surface area of a single large tree.[8]

Create Our Atmosphere

We were taught in elementary school that the oceans and the forests were the chief sources of oxygen for the planet. It turns out that this is only partially correct. The oceans account for less than eight percent of the atmosphere's oxygen, and that is dropping rapidly. There are now millions of acres of ocean that are dying from the dumping of toxic wastes and fertilizers, and changes in water temperature and acidity. Some ocean areas have even become net *consumers* of oxygen. Most cities and deforested areas such as Greece, no longer produce the oxygen they consume.

So trees, it turns out, are the major source of recycled oxygen for the atmosphere. They are our planet's lungs. A fully-grown pine or hardwood tree has a leaf surface area from one quarter-acre to over three acres, depending on the species. Rainforest trees have leaf surface areas as high as 40 acres. Throughout this enormous surface area, sunlight is used as an energy source to drive the conversion of carbon dioxide into oxygen and plant matter. Trees breathe in the CO_2 through that enormous leaf area, and they exhale oxygen as their own waste. Without trees, our atmosphere would most likely become toxic to us. Because rainforest trees have such a huge leaf area compared to our temperate zone trees, the rainforests of the world provide most of the oxygen that you are breathing as you read this page.[9]

If North America and the tropical rainforests become deforested like the Mediterranean and Middle East, will there be enough oxygen for mammals like us?

Carbon Sink

It took hundreds of millions of years for trees, ranging from ancient to modern forests and plants, to pull billions of tons of carbon out of the earth's atmosphere and store it in the earth. The resulting decrease in greenhouse carbon dioxide in the air along with other factors produced the climate we enjoy today, one very different from the climates in the past. Modern forests account for the massive share of the current atmosphere's carbon storage systems. Scientists point out that there's a measurable annual fluctuation in atmospheric levels of carbon dioxide that has to do with plants growing during the summer and pulling down carbon from the air and shedding their leaves in the fall and winter and thus releasing carbon back into the atmosphere as the leaves decompose or are burned.

Many people believe that trees are made mostly from the nutrients in the soil from which they grew. That is a common misconception. Trees are mostly made up of carbon dioxide gas from the air and water—hydrogen and oxygen. Trees are solidified air, water and sunlight. When you burn wood, the "sunlight energy" is released in the form of light and heat. Carbon released from the wood reverses the photosynthesis. The small pile of ash remaining is all the minerals the huge tree had taken from the soil. Everything else was gas from the air: carbon, hydrogen, and oxygen.

Stored carbon release is accelerating due to deforestation at an incredible rate. During the decade of the 1980s, scientists estimate that fully 15 percent of the new carbon dioxide in the atmosphere was released as the result of one single human activity: burning the rainforests in the Americas, mostly to make ranch land for cattle.

Dead Trees Are Habitat

Even when a tree is dead it provides valuable ecological services. Snags or dead trees which remain standing, provide rich habitat for countless species. When these burned or rotten trees are removed from the forest, other species are deprived of a place to live, eat and breed. The snag will also rot away and become nutrients for the next tree. Unfortunately, salvage logging after a fire interrupts this essential habitat and nutrient cycle. When we look at the world with whole-systems eyes, we see that nature recycles everything.[10]

So next time you see a dead tree in your yard, you might just want to leave it standing. If you cut it down, the bugs and birds that need it for habitat will go after your live trees instead.

FOREST LOSS TODAY

David Brower said this about the loss of posterity's old growth forests in *Let The Mountains Talk, Let The Rivers Run*:

"We are entering a twenty-year period that can either spell the end of beautiful trees as we know them, or that can save them. What is really at stake right now is the primeval forest Longfellow admired in *Evangeline*. These are, usually, the closed canopy forests, perhaps the cathedral redwoods, where some of the trees tower 100 meters into the sky, or the Sitka spruce groves of British Columbia, or what is still virgin in the Amazon. What are no longer at stake are the clearcut tropical rain forests of Papua New Guinea, Indonesia, and Malaysia. There will never be places like this on earth again. We can save what's left. It is like saving the Grand Canyon. It must be done if enough of the pages of the poem that is the earth are to remain whole.

Since 1600, the United States has lost 95 percent of its ancient forests. For example, only four percent of the original stand of redwoods is left. This does not mean that we don't have tremendous forests. The difference has been made up by secondary growth. In fact, in many states we are putting back in as much as we are taking off. But in volume or in quality it is not the *original good stuff*, and of course it cannot be. Primeval forests represent the treasure troves of biodiversity and time. That is what makes them irreplaceable. You will never see again what we cut now; you will see nothing like it or the nonhuman community it nurtures.[11] The best pages of the poetry of our inheritance are being ripped out of the book of life for us and our children.

Planet wide, only one-fifth of the planet's original forest cover remains in large tracts of undisturbed natural forests. The total amount of rainforest left on the planet is about the size of the continental United States, and every year, an area the size of Florida is cut down and permanently destroyed."[12]

From 1990 to 2000, the Food and Agriculture organization (FAO) of the United Nations reports that more than 370 million acres of the earth's forest cover, an area the size of Mexico—was converted to other uses. At the same time forests are in decline, demand for forest products is growing. If the loss of 49 million acres per year, typical in the 1990s, continues to increase at two percent per year, the unprotected forest will be gone before the end of the century.[13]

Unlike farms here in the temperate North, the land of a rainforest after clearcutting rapidly becomes scrub or desert. When this happens the farmers cut more trees, and the burning away of the skin of the earth goes on. Beyond a certain point the process will become irreversible. When only 20 to 30 percent of a tropical forest ecosystem remains, it can no longer maintain its climate and it collapses. At the present rate of clearance, it will not be long before the forests no longer have the critical mass they need to exist as a self-sustaining ecosystem. When the forests vanish, the billions of poor who live in those regions will be left with little to support them in the newly harsher climate.[14]

The second day of January 1999 saw a milestone in the efforts to protect the Brazilian rainforest. On that date, it was reported that the Brazilian government, bowing to intense pressures from the International Monetary Fund (IMF) to cut spending, slashed their budget for protecting the rainforest.

In Brazil's rainforests, an area half the size of the United States, which contains two-thirds of the planet's non-glaciated fresh water, are hundreds of indigenous tribes. The $250 million rainforest-protection program's first priority was to survey a 25-million-acre area that would be kept intact forever for their use alone. By cutting the $250 million budget down to $6 million, the program is barely kept alive, and now nothing substantive will be done to protect the trees or the people. In the meantime, the forest is being overrun by loggers, ranchers, miners, farmers and evangelists bent on the salvation of the *heathen* tribes. The trees are being cut and burned at a rate of more than 200,000 acres or about six square miles a day.[15]

That does not include the staggering cost of animal life. According to studies associated with United Nations Economic and Social Commission for Asia and Pacific (UN/ESCAP), approximately 10,000 vertebrates that include birds, amphibians, reptiles and manmals, are destroyed with each square mile of rainforest that is destroyed.[16] This translates to 60,000 animals destroyed per day plus all of their potential offspring lost to posterity.

One more thought for perspective—we have the forests we do today because we are heating, cooking and running industry with fossil fuels. As those supplies are depleted, people will return to the forest to cut the trees for heating and cooking.

MONOCULTURE FOREST FARMS

Monoculture Replacing Biodiversity

In the United States, particularly in heavily-logged areas of the Pacific

Northwest and Alaska, there has been a renewed assault on the great stretches of temperate forest. Although the United States, like several other developed nations, actually shows more area of forested land now than it did a hundred years ago, many of the huge tracts that have been *harvested* and replanted have been converted from diverse hardwoods to a monoculture of softwood conifer forests that no longer support the species that once thrived there.

In national forests throughout the country, logging roads are being built to facilitate more logging of public lands including Sequoia National Monument, under contracts that require the sale of the trees at rates far below market prices. This enormous taxpayer subsidy for the deforestation of public land contributes to both the budget deficit and an ecological tragedy.[17]

Logging Industry Propaganda

Short of visiting Big Reed Pond, or perhaps a few other rare places like it, a Maine resident has no way of knowing that the forests which cover most of the state today bear little resemblance to those that existed when the first European settlers marveled there. Industrial forestry has completely transformed the landscape turning much of the state into a huge non-native tree factory. Unfortunately, the average citizen does not have a clear understanding of the distinctions between a tree factory and a natural forest.

Industry propaganda plays on this ignorance by claiming that its timber management practices are good for wildlife. The industry definition of *wildlife* is a narrow one based primarily on large mammals such as deer, moose, beaver, and bear, all of which abound in the timberlands of northern Maine. Large herbivorous mammals thrive on early regrowth, with its easily accessed foliage and profusion of berries. But large mammals make up only a tiny fraction of the full richness of natural ecosystems, which can be summed up in the term *biodiversity*. Industry propaganda does not make boasts about biodiversity, and for good reason. Industrial timber management is highly prejudicial to much of nature's diversity.[18]

Bad Indicator Species

Ecologist John Terborgh described in *Wild Earth* magazine what makes a poor and a good indicator species for forest health and bio-diversity.

"The timber industry generally manages a landscape as a patch-work of stands of varying age, ranging from recent clearcuts to tracts that are ready for harvest. Such a mosaic will often support more bird species than a virgin forest, which tends to be relatively uni-form except for small gaps produced by fallen trees. The more is better argument thus gives the industry a strong hand to play in designing its public relations campaigns.

Although birds have been the subjects of scores, perhaps hun-dreds, of studies on logging's effects on biodiversity, they are perhaps one of the least appropriate groups to use for the purpose. Birds of some sort utilize almost any habitat, even parking lots and ledges on city buildings, and they are instant colonizers of disturbed sites. Birds are so opportunistic that it is hard to find any habitat, however bat-tered and degraded, that doesn't support at least a few.

But in the larger world of Nature, such opportunism and colo-nizing ability are far more the exception than the rule. Most of the myriad plants and animals that make up biodiversity are small, inconspicuous, sensitive to disturbance and poor dispersers; many even lack the ability to cross commonplace barriers such as roads and agricultural fields. A fuller understanding of the impact of tim-ber management on biodiversity should be derived from a study of these sensitive organisms."

Good Indicator Species

Herbaceous plants are one such group of indicator organisms. Con-tributing roughly 80 percent of the flora of eastern deciduous forests, herbaceous plants are far more representative of plant diver-sity than trees. Unlike birds and many trees, which disperse well and colonize quickly after disturbances, many herbaceous plants are weak dispersers that are slow to recolonize disturbed ground.

This lesson was strongly impressed upon John Terborgh during the nine years he occupied a home at the edge of Duke Forest in Chapel Hill, North Carolina. His house is perched atop a bluff over-looking a small river. Lying upslope is land that was farmed until the Great Depression of the 1930s and now supports a maturing pine forest. Downslope, the terrain is so steep and rocky that, so far as he could judge, it was never cleared or plowed. The spring wildflowers of this steep slope are an annual delight to his botanical proclivities. For more than a month each spring, the slope is alive with trout lilies, irises, pennyworts, hepaticas, anemones, trilliums, orchids and many more. Altogether, some 978 species of plants have been recorded in Duke Forest, the vast majority of them are herbaceous species like those named above.

The demarcation line between the recovering and undisturbed portions of the slope is inscribed by the herbaceous plants. The lush community of native wildflowers stops abruptly with the undisturbed soil almost as if it had been held in place by an invisible hand. Upslope, in the pine stand, native herbs are few. Most of the scattered sprigs of green visible in the understory are Japanese honeysuckle or other invasive alien species. An occasional trout lily, bellwort, wild ginger or hepatica has jumped over the demarcation line, but this tentative reclaiming has not advanced more than a few meters in 60-plus years. He never found an iris, showy orchids, anemone or trillium above the line, an observation that explains why these plants are becoming rarer and rarer, even as forest cover has expanded throughout the East during the last century.[19]

In a study using records maintained by the U.S. Forest Service, Duffy and Meier carefully selected a dozen matched pairs of sites in the southern Appalachians. One of each pair of sites was located in an undisturbed primary stand, while the other was a tract that had been logged just once, usually 90 to 100 years earlier. The pairs of sites were carefully matched for latitude, elevation, exposure, slope, soil and underlying geology.

Duffy and Meier sampled the vernal herbaceous flora at each site using standard methodology. Their results were so startling that they provoked a furious reaction from the timber industry (Elliot and Loftis 1993, Steinbeck 1993). The once-logged stands contained less than half the herbaceous diversity of the primary stands. The differences between the matched pairs of sites were so great that the ranges of values did not overlap. In other words, the differences Duffy and Meier documented were not merely statistically significant; they were dramatically distinct. Even a single episode of clearcut logging takes a toll of diversity that persists for at least a century.[20]

Sizable birds nest in large tree cavities and are examples of birds that can be a good indicator species. Birds such as barred owls or pileated woodpeckers need large trees. You will not find barred owls in young birch and aspen stands in factory forests because trees are not allowed to reach a size that would accommodate a nesting cavity. Like the barred owl's cousin of the Northwest, the spotted owl, you will only find them in mature old growth forests.

OUR TAKER STORY CAUSES FOREST LOSS

The loggers, who are destroying the forest, go about their work with the same dedication as a whaler hunting down the last blue whale. It was their livelihood, their lifestyle and their art. But it is our future. When this unsustainable orgy of cut and run is finally over, the logger, like the buffalo hunter, like the whaler, will exist only in history books. [21] The only issue is whether they will shift to new employment before or after the last forest is gone.

Our Taker culture has not learned from its past history of destroying its own environment. The entire Mediterranean region shows the effects of siltation, overgrazing, deforestation, erosion and salinization. In Roman times, one could walk North Africa's coast from end to end without leaving the shade of trees; now it is a blazing desert.

To see what we are really doing to our forests, read the Native Forest Council's newspaper *Forest Voice* and visit www.forestcouncil.org.

In the past, our Taker culture just moved on to the next forest. Today however, with global reach, after the last forest is gone, there will be nowhere else to go.

10. Climate Change

As of 2005, Mount Kilimanjaro's snowcapped glacier has melted for the first time in 11,000 years. I thought I would not see the photograph or write these words for 20 more years. By mid-century there may be no glaciers left in Glacier National Park.

The consequences of global climate change to our food supply and ecosystems are more significant than just receding glaciers. It is the erosion of life's resilience through the decline of biodiversity and the near extinction of native knowledge of plant cultivars that makes global warming so threatening to humanity.

START OF A HEAT AGE

Even if all greenhouse gas emissions were to stop today, we would still see the earth change and we, its first intelligent species, are both the cause and the spectators. The imminent change of our climate will be as great as between the last ice age and today.

To comprehend the magnitude of the change let us look back to the last ice age, just a few tens of thousands of years ago. The glaciers reached as far south as latitude 35° in North America and to the Alps in Europe. The sea was more than 100 meters lower than it is now, and therefore an area of land as large as Africa was above water and able to grow plants. The tropics were like the warm temperate regions are now. Now imagine the new age of a heating: temperatures and sea level climb until eventually the world is nearly free of ice.

There are likely to be surprises, things that even the most detailed science models can not predict. Think of the ozone hole and remember that was a real surprise. The most extensive computer modeling and monitoring of the earth's ozone layer failed predict its magnitude. Surprises are almost certain to occur like climatic extremes, ferocious storms or as unexpected atmospheric events. Nature is nonlinear and unpredictable and never more so than during a period of change.[1]

RATE OF INCREASE

Carbon dioxide makes up just 1 to 2, 800th of the atmosphere. Together with the other trace gases, even that tiny amount insulates the earth's surface on average to about 59° Fahrenheit warmer, so even a relatively small additional amount can raise the temperature of the planet significantly. [2]

Each year, because of our combustion of oil, gas and coal, we are pumping more than six billion tons of heat-trapping carbon dioxide into our thin layer of atmosphere, so much that in just the past 20 years the concentration of CO_2 in the atmosphere has increased from 280 parts per million to over 370.9 parts per million, the highest level in 420,000 years. Within a few more decades, it is projected to exceed 500 parts per million, thus dramatically warming the planet.[3]

Under the UN's Intergovernmental Panel on Climate Change (IPCC) low emissions scenario, global emissions of carbon will rise to 11.7 billion tons per year by 2050, an increase of 70 percent from 2000.[4]

According to the scientists of the IPCC, average global temperature over the next few decades will rise 3° to 4° Celsius (5° to 7° Fahrenheit), and possibly as much as 7° Celsius (10° Fahrenheit).[5]

Scientific consensus now predicts that we can expect climate change will increase from two to 10 times faster in this century than in the last. The north polar region is melting for the first time in 50 million years, and three times faster than computer models predicted.[6]

On our farm in Ashland, Oregon, the growing season has increased by two months. We used to have to transplant frost-tender tomatoes and peppers after June 1 and harvest by October 1. Today we can plant May 1 and the season lasts past the end of October. This is a stunning change to our local climate in just 10 years.

Fossil Fuel Subsidies Continue

Despite all of the environmental problems of fossil fuels and their threat to global climate, their production continues to be subsidized by many nations at a phenomenal rate, amounting to $300 billion globally per year. The United States alone directly subsidizes these energy systems at more than $20 billion annually. Even this figure, however, does not begin to cover the full costs of fossil fuel systems, including environmental damage, trillions for the war in the middle east, additional investments in military programs to protect vulnerable oil and gas supply lines, and the corrupt regimes of our oil-producing nations around the world.[7]

Deforestation Contributes to Global Warming

As we just discussed, forest loss is also contributing to global warming. When large areas of rainforest are burned, the amount of rainfall recycled to adjacent areas is sharply reduced. If the deforested area is large enough, the amount of rainfall removed from adjacent areas will be enough to cause a reinforcing drought cycle, which slowly kills more trees, thus further reducing rainfall recycling and accelerating the death of the neighboring forests in turn. When the overarching canopy of leaves is removed, the sudden warming of the forest floor leads to the release of huge quantities of methane and CO_2. A kind of biochemical burning takes place. The massive increase in the number of dead tree trunks and branches leads to an explosion in the population of termites, which themselves produce enormous quantities of methane. This is not to mention the CO_2 which is released when the trees themselves are burned. [8]

THREATS OF GLOBAL WARMING

Agricultural Production Disrupted

It is now virtually inevitable that global temperatures will rise to a level never before experienced in the last 100,000 years and possibly longer. The production of food will be disrupted. The latest UN estimates suggest a 10 percent fall in global food output and a 70 percent reduction in American grain exports. This will intensify the problem of feeding the world's rapidly growing population. Even more worrying is the rapid *rate* of global warming, which will almost certainly be too

144   CULTUREQUAKE

fast for natural ecosystems to adapt in a orderly manner. Every ecosystem in the world will be affected in unpredictable ways.[9]

Ocean Level Rising

Seventy percent of the world's fresh water is locked up in Antarctica, where it has been held as ice for hundreds of thousands of years. Covered by ice sheets that are often more than three miles high, the continent of Antarctica covers four to five million square miles, larger than the size of China and India combined. If the ice of Antarctica were to melt and slide off that continental landmass and into the sea, oceans would rise significantly around the world.

In April 1999, it was reported by researchers with the British Atlantic Survey in Cambridge and the University of Colorado via data analyzed on the ground and from satellite photos that global warming has lengthened the annual melting season of Antarctica by three weeks, producing drastic changes to that continent's ice shelves. The Wilkins and Larsen B ice shelves, for example, are in full retreat. In just the four months from November 1998 to February 1999, over 420,000 acres of the Larsen B shelf's total of 1.7 million acres caved away. In just the month of March 1999, the Wilkins shelf lost over a quarter million of its three million acres, and the process has dramatically speeded up in the years since.

For the first time in history the Northwest Passage is open. According to the National Snow and Ice Data Center's Arctic Sea Ice News Fall 2007, the passage was nearly ice-free for several weeks.

The reason? Average temperatures in Antarctica—relatively stable since the dawn of humanity—have risen 4.5° Fahrenheit since 1950, pushing the summer temperatures there above the critical freezing point of 32° Fahrenheit.[10]

Global warming is melting the Arctic ice faster than expected, and the world's oceans could rise by about one meter by 2100, swamping homes from Bangladesh to Florida.[11]

Deforestation

Forget the carbon for a moment. Trees will die from global warming. In a few years when I walk outdoors here in the Siskiyou mountains of southern Oregon, instead of seeing slopes of healthy fir I may find trees with brown and yellowing leaves and needles, thinning crowns, dead branches and rotting stumps. Or maybe, after what the World Resources Institute calls a transition period, "a shrubby woodland that is adapted to a wider variety of environmental conditions" will appear.

This vast decline, this forest dieback, is not some distant possibility. A report described to a congressional committee in 2006 found that widespread reproductive failure, forest dieback and beetle kill is estimated to begin between 2000 and 2050. A University of Virginia study predicted what Michael Oppenheimer of the Environmental Defense Fund called biomass crashes in the pine forests of the Southeast U.S. over the next forty years if the warming continues. Birch trees and many evergreens in the Northeast may have a hard time surviving even in the next 10 to 20 years.[12]

Water Shortages in the Southwest U.S.

After studying the temperature and stream flow records of the Colorado river, scientists have concluded that if a 2° Celsius increase in temperature occurs, the flow of the Colorado could fall by nearly a third. If this increase in temperature is accompanied by a 10 percent fall in precipitation as predicted, the water supply in the upper Colorado would fall by 40 percent. Even if precipitation *increased* 10 percent, runoff would still drop nearly 20 percent.

Across the West, the picture is similar—in the Missouri, Arkansas, Texas Gulf and California irrigation regions, water availability could fall by 40 percent or more. In the Missouri, Rio Grande and Colorado basins, even current water needs would not be met after the expected climatic changes. "One model we're looking at," says Texas agriculture commissioner Jim Hightower, "predicts a 25 percent increase in the demand for irrigation water." The water currently comes from the Ogallala aquifer, the great subterranean lake that irrigates the plains and is already badly depleted. "You can't pump more water if the well has already gone dry."[13]

End of Stable Weather

In December of 2007, *High Country News* ran a news report about the severe drought then plaguing the West. Ski slopes were brown, wildfires were burning in California and New Mexico, and weather forecasters were predicting an ultra-dry Western winter. By the time the issue hit the streets, those streets and everything else were buried in snow, and it didn't stop falling until spring. Thirty six people died in avalanches in the U.S. by the end of April.

Perhaps scoffing at models and forecasts is the wisest thing to do, given the wacky weather the region has experienced over the last several months. In mid-April, for example, a winter storm dumped up to three feet of snow in Colorado's San Juan Mountains, closing a major highway. A few days later, huge winds swept across the region, dumping red dust all over that new snow, speeding up the snowmelt, causing flooding, and fueling two wildfires in Colorado, one of which killed three people.

Global warming is adding more energy to the atmosphere, which in turn is causing greater variation in the weather. For example, 2007-2008 Colorado winter precipitation was as high 150 percent of normal, while only 200 miles away, parts of New Mexico received less than 50 percent of normal precipitation. As I write this, parts of the West are experiencing record high and lower temperatures all in the same week.

For a week, at least, avalanche season coincided with wildfire season, and the idea that the weather, or even the climate, can be predicted was thrown out the window.[14]

Methane Release Feedback Loop Accelerates Global Warming

Methane is over 20 times more effective in trapping heat in the atmosphere than carbon dioxide. An enormous amount of methane is locked up in the tundra and in the mud of the continental shelves. These are, in essence, methane ices; the ocean muds alone may hold 10 trillion tons of methane.

If the greenhouse effect is beginning to warm the oceans, if it is starting to thaw the permafrost, then eventually those ices will start to melt. Some estimates of the potential methane release run as high as .6 billion tons a year, an amount that could more than double the present atmospheric concentration of methane. This would be a nasty example of a feedback loop: warm the atmosphere and release methane; release methane and warm the atmosphere.

Samples of ice from Antarctic glaciers show that the concentration of methane in the atmosphere has fluctuated between 0.3 and 0.7 parts per million for the last 160,000 years, reaching its highest levels during earth's warmest periods. In 1987 methane composed 1.7 parts per million of the atmosphere. There is now two and a half times as much methane in the atmosphere as there was at any time through three glacial and interglacial periods. And concentrations are rising one percent a year.[15]

Ozone Loss Feedback Loop

Other feedback loops also pose strategic threats. Consider, for example, the way in which the two best-known crises, global warming and ozone depletion, reinforce each other in a complex positive feedback loop. Global warming increases the amount of water vapor in the atmosphere and traps infrared heat in the lower part of the sky which would otherwise radiate back out to space through the stratosphere. As a result, the stratosphere actually cools as the lower atmosphere warms. A cooler stratosphere with more water vapor means more ice crystals in the ozone layer, especially in the Polar Regions, where chlorofluorocarbons (CFCs) mingle with the ozone in the presence of the ice, thus depleting the ozone at a faster rate. The thinner the ozone layer, the more the ultraviolet radiation strikes the surface of the earth. The ultraviolet radiation strikes vegetation that normally absorbs vast quantities of CO_2 through photosynthesis and seriously disrupts its ability to do so effectively. As the vegetation absorbs less CO_2, more of it accumulates in the atmosphere, causing still more global warming, and still more stratospheric cooling. The cycle is reinforced and magnified. It feeds upon itself.[16]

Migration Impossible for Some Species

We already discussed vanishing animal migration habitats because of human settlement. Now global warming threatens the remaining migrating species.

In past episodes of climate change—such as the warming after the last ice age—species could shift their range as the temperature warmed. But this time, it's going to be different. Today, the extremely rapid rate of temperature rise will likely outstrip the migration capacities of many species. At the end of the last ice age, for example, trees could colonize new areas at a speed of up to a half a mile a year, by spreading their seeds and gradually establishing new saplings. But projected warming rates will far outstrip this rate of adaptation: climatic zones in the twenty-first century will be shifting north seven times faster than most plant species can follow them.[17]

But even if the trees manage to migrate, wildlife will be in trouble. Animals do not know they are in parks, and they are not as adaptable as people. As the temperature warms, the elk will move north out of Yellowstone. So will the bison and the grizzly bears and the dozens of other plants and animals that find safety there. When a bison steps across the park line, he is, of course, fair game for hunters, who already line the boundaries at the proper season.

The hunting laws can be changed, of course, but hunters are not the only danger the animals face. The way north is cut by roads and fences, is crossed by cars and is divided up into small fragmented parcels. Montana isn't exactly crowded, but just a couple hundred miles north of Yellowstone and you're in Great Falls, which is no place for a bison herd. In the Kalahari desert of Botswana, when a drought sent a quarter-million wildebeest north in search of water, incalculable numbers of them died along a hundred mile fence set up to protect cattle. We have confined nature to small parcels; the shifting climate will find thousands of species blocked by farm fences and fields, four-lane highways, housing developments and other man-made barriers as they try to escape to cool safety.[18]

Polar Bear Extinction

One hundred years ago, the white bear once roamed the forests of New England and the Canadian Maritime provinces. Now it is called the polar bear because that is where it now makes its last stand.

Polar bears now face extinction in this century if the Arctic continues to melt at its present rate. The sea ice around the North Pole on which the bears depend for hunting is shrinking so swiftly it could disappear during the summer months by the end of the century, the Arctic Climate Impact Assessment (ACIA) says.

Scientists in the study believe the survival of the estimated 22,000 polar bears in the region is hanging by a slender thread, as they suffer from both chemical pollution and dwindling feeding grounds. Polar bears traditionally hunt on floating sea ice for seals and other prey. But the ice has retreated so much during the recent summers, the carnivores are having to swim farther from one floe to the next in search of food.

As a result of this extra effort, many bears are failing to build up the necessary fat reserves during the important hunting period of spring and early summer to take them through the bitterly cold winter months when females nurse their young. The sea ice in the Hudson Bay area of Canada, for instance, breaks up about two and a half weeks earlier than it did 30 years ago, according to Ian Stirling of the Canadian Wildlife Service.[19]

Ocean Life Threatened

Seabirds from California to Oregon have been devastated by a 20° Fahrenheit average water temperature increase since 1950, which has redirected the flow of cold, nutrient-rich ocean waters away from the coast. That, in turn, has led to a 40 percent decline in the zooplankton, which is the food supply for shrimp and other small marine creatures. Fish and squid live on the shrimp, and the birds live on the fish. In just the years between 1987 and 1994, for example, four million sooty shearwater birds died along that coast, reducing their population by over 90 percent.[20]

The threshold of thermal tolerance is also being crossed for tropical coral reefs, which have been struck by severe mass bleaching episodes in recent years—the direct result of the warming seas. Bleaching reached catastrophic levels in the 1995 El Niño event when a sixth of the entire tropical coral reef ecosystem on the planet was destroyed. Disasters of this scale are likely to become commonplace within the next two decades. Within thirty to fifty years severe bleaching could be a chronic event causing the vast majority of corals to die.[21]

Global Species Loss

In a paper recently published in *Nature*, Chris Thomas and his colleagues concluded that between a fifth and a third of species could be wiped out by global warming as soon as 2050. "These estimates," the authors concluded, "show the importance of rapid implementation of technologies to decrease greenhouse gas emissions."

The Millennium Ecosystem Assessment 2005 also concluded that by the end of the century, climate change and its impacts may be the dominant direct driver of biodiversity loss and changes in ecosystems globally.[22]

ABRUPT ICE AGE

What could be more confusing than global cooling being caused by global warming? But some very respected thinkers back this scenario.

A 2004 U.S. Department of Defense report regarding climate change was commissioned by Andrew Marshall, a legendary DOD figure, nicknamed "Yoda" for his sagacity. As head of the Pentagon's secretive Office of Net Assessment, Marshall has offered national security assessments to every president since Richard Nixon.

This assessment pegs climate change as a far greater danger to national security than even international terrorism. The report is titled, *An Abrupt Climate Change Scenario and Its Implications for United States National Security.* According to the Pentagon study, the question is not if abrupt climate change will happen, but when. It could be, according to the report's authors, as soon as the next three years, with the most devastating fallout potentially occurring between 2010 and 2020.

At that point, we could find ourselves in the midst of a new ice age in which mega-droughts devastate the world's food supply, drinkable water becomes a luxury worth going nuclear over, 400 million people are forced to migrate from uninhabitable areas, and riots and wars for survival become commonplace.[23]

If the Great Conveyor Belt of ocean currents, which includes the Gulf Stream, were to stop flowing, the result would be sudden and dramatic. Most scientists involved in research on this topic agree that the culprit will be global warming melting the glaciers on Greenland and the icepack in the Arctic and thus flushing cold, fresh water down into the Greenland Sea from the north. When a critical threshold is reached, the climate will suddenly switch to an ice age that could last minimally 700 or so years, and maximally over 20,000 years.

BARRIERS TO A SOLUTION
Warming Will Coast on for Decades

Even if all greenhouse gas emissions stopped tomorrow, the climate would continue warming for decades, probably by double the 0.6° Celsius so far experienced over the last century. This would make the planet hotter than at any time since the last ice age. The upper range of the IPCC scenario will take us into uncharted waters, with average temperatures higher than they have been for the last forty million years, well outside the range ever experienced by humanity or the other species with which we share this planet.[24]

Required CO2 Reduction is Great

Technology alone will not solve the problem. This is rooted in the extent of the action needed to combat environmental threats. The IPCC says developed countries need to reduce their emissions of greenhouse gases by 60-80 percent between 1990 and 2050 if global warming is to be seriously affected. Given that the latest predictions of sea level rises are higher than those used by the IPCC, this reduction target is likely to be more on the inadequate side than the safe side. To get anywhere near that kind of reduction, the Western world will need to reduce its car and power use drastically.

For a thorough overview of global warming see Vice President Al Gore's documentary *An Inconvenient Truth*.

OUR BEST SOLUTION - A LOT MORE TREES

To be honest, fast or slow, our Taker culture is going to burn all of the fossil fuels it can economically extract. Population growth will wipe out any carbon footprint reductions. We can't make the ocean's any bigger, but at least we try to can stop their decline and so maintain their crucial role in sequestering greenhouse gases.

That leaves trees. The only place left to put trees where there is water is on farms in place of annual crops. Trees can sequester more greenhouse gas than corn or soybeans because a tree is full-grown in the spring when an annual plant is just a sprout. So start planting more trees! Eat more nuts and orchard crops. It just might be the most effective thing we can do to stop global warming.

The annual increase in atmospheric carbon is about three gigatons. Highest yielding temperate woody plants can fix $1.82 \times 10^{(13)}$ grams of carbon/$10^{(6)}$ hectares/year. Since there are some $1,500 \times 10^{(6)}$ hectares under cultivation in the world, a conservative calculation shows that planting one-quarter of world's annual crop lands to woody plants would result in $5 \times 10^{(15)}$ g of carbon (five gigatons) absorbed above that absorbed by present crops, enough to completely counteract the carbon dioxide overload.[25]

11. Peak Oil and Energy Descent

From the beginning our industrial civilization has been like a bonfire upon the earth, burning the earth's one time fuel supplies—drawing down natural resources, fossil fuels and minerals. When the fuel is gone, this civilization will itself burn out.

Imagine a bonfire with half the wood burned. The bonfire still burns brightly, our cities can be seen shining at night from space, but the fire will soon start to dwindle. Unless more fuel is added, it will slowly burn down. It will smolder for a while and then die out.

About half of the oil is gone. The second half will be harder to get with diminishing returns. We could burn more coal, but it would be an ecological disaster. We are starting to do it anyway. We could use nuclear, but its fuel is also finite and would leave ten thousand generations cursed with its radioactive waste. Our civilization has no energy Plan B.

The second half of the oil age will go a lot faster than the first half. When oil was discovered in 1859 in Titusville, Pennsylvania, there were neither cars nor airplanes. Today we are going full speed, pedal to the metal. World oil demand is increasing as China and India's appetite is skyrocketing.

Just as the global economy demands more wood for the bonfire, production is peaking and will start to decline. We have overshot the earth's energy carrying capacity. Welcome to the new world of peak oil and energy descent.

FOSSIL FUELS

Growing Population Using Stored Sunlight

About 900 years ago, humans in Europe and Asia discovered coal below the surface of the earth. This coal was the surface of the ancient mats of vegetation 300-million-years-old. Actually, it is stored sunlight. By burning it humans were, for the first time, able to use sunlight energy that had been stored in the distant past. Before this, our ancestors had to maintain acreages of forestland because they needed the wood for heat to survive the cold winters in the northern climates. Forests captured the current sunlight energy, and they could liberate that captured sunlight in a fireplace or stove to warm a home, cave, yurt or tipi during the long dark days of winter.

The exploitation of coal reduced their reliance on current sunlight, allowing them to cut more forestland and convert it into cropland. By making more croplands available, they were able to produce more food for more humans, and the population of the world went from 500 million people around the year 1000 to one billion living humans in 1820.

This represents a critical moment in human history, for this is when our ancestors started living off our planet's sunlight savings.

Because our ancestors could consume sunlight that had been stored by plants millions of years ago, they began to consume more resources in food, heat, and other materials than our planet had historically been able to provide. The planet's human population grew beyond the level that the earth could sustain if humans were using only local current sunlight as an energy and food source.

We see this same trend today: the availability of a fuel leads to a population that depends on it and will suffer if it is taken away. Had our ancestors run out of coal, nature would have taken over and limited their population.

Instead, our ancestors discovered another bank account they could tap, another reserve of ancient sunlight: the plant matter that hundreds of millions of years ago sank to the ocean floor and was compressed by heat and pressure into what we now refer to as oil.

Oil was first widely used around 1850 in Romania. The real boom began, however, in 1859, when oil was discovered in Titusville, Pennsylvania, in the United States. At that time, the world's population numbered just over one billion people, and the human race was fed both by the current sunlight falling on crop-lands and by a substantial amount of ancient sunlight stored as coal that was mined in Europe, Asia, and North America.

Discovery of abundant supplies of oil, however, kicked open the door to a truly massive store of ancient sunlight. By using this ancient sunlight locked up within carbon as a heating and energy source, and by replacing farm animals with tractors, our ancestors dramatically increased their ability to produce food. Draft animals such as horses and oxen run on current sunlight, the grass they eat each day. Thus they are limited in the amount of work they can do—whatever they can eat and convert to energy in one day—compared with an oil fueled tractor that can burn in one day as much sunlight as would be consumed by hundreds of horses.

It turned out that people could use oil for far more than just fuel. So as we moved into the Twentieth century, we began "spending" more and more of our saved-up sunlight.

Oil can be converted to synthetic fabrics, nylon, rayon, poly-ester, resins and plastics for construction of almost anything, including the keyboard on which this manuscript is being typed. Because we could make clothes from oil, we needed less sheep-grazing land and cotton-growing land, thus allowing us to convert even more land to food production.

The massive leap in our food supply that began just after the Civil War caused our planet's population to go from just over one billion humans around the time of the discovery of oil to two billion in 1930.

By then, we were beginning to use oil to run farm machinery extensively, and for other purposes that also increased agricultural production, for example converting natural gas into fertilizers and manufacturing pesticides. The cumulative effect was that food pro-duction exploded, and so did the population. While it had taken three million years to produce our first billion people, and 130 years to produce our second billion, the third billion took just 30 years.

In 1960, world human population hit three billion.

It took just 14 years, from 1960 to 1974, for us to grow to four billion humans worldwide.

We added another billion in just 13 years, hitting five billion in

1987, and our next billion took only 12 years, as the world's human population hit six billion in 1999—all thanks to fossil fuels.[1]

Fossil Fuel Energy Slaves

As Americans, more than any other people, we have learned to take our high-energy standard of living for granted.

Here are some examples for a better perspective. One gallon of gas will take a 3-ton SUV 20 miles at 60 miles an hour down the road. How long would it take to push their 3-ton SUV 20 miles down the road?

One barrel of oil, 42 gallons, equals the productivity of 25,000 man-hours.[2] A 100-horsepower automobile cruising down the highway does the work of 2,000 people. If we were to add together the power of all of the fuel-fed machines that we rely on to light and heat our homes, transport us, and otherwise keep us in the style to which we have become accustomed, and then compare that total with the amount of power that can be generated by the human body, we would find that each of us Americans has the equivalent of over 50 energy slaves working for us 24 hours each and every day. In energy terms, each middle-class American is living a lifestyle so lavish as to make nearly any sultan or potentate in history swoon with envy.[3]

It would take four to six people 10 hours to push the SUV 20 miles without stopping for a break.

This gives you some idea of the density of oil. There is nothing out there in the suggested fuel alternatives has have anything like this dense power and portability.

Hubbert Peak

Scientist M. King Hubbert first coined the term peak oil in 1956, when he developed the theory of the Hubbert Peak, defining the moment when oil supplies reach their apex and then begun a downhill slide. In 1956, he projected a Hubbert Peak for the U.S. to occur in 1970. He was four years off. The oil crisis was in 1974. In 1975 he predicted a worldwide Hubbert Peak for 1999 or 2000. World oil production actually peaked in 2008 at 81.73 million barrels per day.[4] Hubbert died in 1989.

CURRENT OIL FORECASTS

18, 11, 3, 3 the Countdown has Started

Several new large oil fields came online in 2005, momentarily adding extra capacity. These are probably the last of the 500 million barrel mega fields, since none has been discovered in the past few years despite an intensive search. Eighteen new mega projects started producing in 2005, and were followed by 11 more in 2006. However, 2007 saw the opening of only three new projects, followed by three more in 2008. This will not keep up with declining production or depletion in older fields, much less the increase in demand. The Oil Depletion Analysis Centre (ODAC) has stated that world production is now seeing a one million barrel per day depletion rate.[5]

Since it takes, on average, six years from the first discovery of a major oil field to start producing oil, any other new projects approved now would be unlikely to add further supplies until after 2016.

Industry consultants IHS Energy recently reported that 85 percent of all the oil ever discovered is now in production, and only half the total produced last year was replaced by new field discoveries. Annual consumption has now exceeded new discoveries every year since the early 1980s. Overall, worldwide oil discoveries have been declining steadily for the past 40 years.[6]

It's worth noting that it is unlikely that we will soon find easily accessible new pools of oil. Most of the world has been digitally X-rayed using satellites, seismic data and computers. In the process of locating 41,000 oil fields 641,000 exploratory wells have been drilled. Almost all fields that show any promise are well known and are factored into the one trillion barrel estimate the oil industry uses for world oil reserves.[7]

Yes, new technology may enable us to increase the amount of oil extracted from any given field—perhaps, in some instances, even doubling the ultimately recoverable amount. But for the most part, government and industry estimates have already accounted for such technology based reserve growth.[8]

USGS Reserve Estimates Exaggerated

Why would a government agency like the U.S. Geological Survey

(USGS) publish a report that gives an extravagantly optimistic view of global oil resources? The Energy Information Agency (EIA) of the Department of Energy (DOE) has released similarly exaggerated projections. What's going on here?

A clue is contained in a sentence buried in the EIA "Annual Energy Outlook 1998 with Projections to 2020". It reads, "These adjustments to the USGS and Materials Management Service (MMS) estimates are based on nontechnical considerations that support domestic supply growth to the levels necessary to meet projected demand levels." In other words, supply projections were altered to fit demand projections. As industry insiders have known for years, USGS and EIA data on current and past production are reliably accurate, but their future projections are essentially political statements designed to convey the message that there is no foreseeable problem with petroleum supply, that the American people should continue buying and consuming with no cares about the future. This is not a new situation: in 1973, Congress demanded an investigation of the USGS for its failure to foresee the 1970 US oil production peak.[9]

Oil Producers Reserves Exaggerated

Although Hubbert died in 1989, his work was carried on by J. Colin Campbell, author of *The Golden Century of Oil: 1950-2050: The Depletion of a Resource*, a book that originated as part of a study of worldwide oil supplies and consumption commissioned by the Norwegian government in 1989. In that book and other sources, Campbell and other scientists point out that oil-producing countries often inflate their estimated oil reserves to qualify for higher OPEC production quotas so they can borrow money from the World Bank using their supposed oil supplies as collateral.[10]

Price Instability

In July 2008, the price of crude oil reached an historical high level of US $147 per barrel. However, as a consequence of falling demand over the following six months, the price declined by well over 60%.

Oil prices have gone up over 800 percent since 1999. This amid strong signs that global oil production may have already peaked, as declines around the world are not being offset by new production.

New fields may come online but the respite will be very short-lived. There may be a few mega projects, about a six-day supply for the planet in each, which may produce momentary price declines but the trend is irreversible. Official bodies like the Paris-based International Energy Administration (IEA) are openly wishing that demand growth might slow in 2005, when actual figures already prove this wish unrealistic. China's oil demand is expected to grow by 33 percent in 2006. Industrialized and developing nations are expanding their economies as fast as possible to generate cash and liquidity as a means of securing more oil.[11]

OPEC Cannot Raise Production Enough to Hold Down Prices

With its output already near a 25-year high, OPEC is stretched to meet rising demand, encouraging the investment community to bet that oil's bull run can go further. IEA figures put the total spare capacity of all 11 countries in OPEC at just 330,000 barrels per day (bpd), down from six million bpd in 2002. Conventional Saudi spare capacity is zero. An IEA report from August 2004 indicates Saudi Arabia needs up to 800,000 bpd of newly discovered oil each year just to offset declining fields and maintain its current production level.[12]

World oil demand has risen to 87 million bpd as of 2008, up from 83.7 million bpd over the first nine months of 2005, projections from the IEA showed.

OPEC is not getting much help from non-cartel oil producers. Norway, the world's third-biggest crude oil exporter, said it had limited capacity to boost output. OPEC has urged big non-OPEC suppliers, including Russia and Mexico, to also raise production.[13]

WORLD OIL PRODUCTION IS PEAKING

Richard Duncan, of the Institute on Energy and Man, has compiled the following data on projected conventional oil production peaks for 44 nations comprising seven regions. Combined they account for more than 98 percent of the world's oil production, as of data through the end of 1999. The following data is extracted from Duncan's World Oil Forecast #5, as reported to the Geological Society of America, Summit 2000, Pardee Keynote Symposia, Reno, November 13, 2000.

I have presented just the regional totals here. For details of the peak by each of the 44 countries and many other topics in this chapter, see *The Party's Over: Oil, War and the Fate of Industrial Societies* by Richard Heinberg.

region	peak year
North America	1983
South and Central America	2006
Europe	2006
Former Soviet Union	1987
Middle East	2009
Africa	2006
Asia-Pacific	2004
world peak	2006 [14]

Past The Discovery Peak

The rate of discovery of new oil in the lower-48 U.S. peaked in the 1930s; discovery worldwide peaked in the 1960s. Today, in a typical year, we are pumping and burning between three and four barrels of oil for each new barrel discovered. Demand for oil continues to increase, on average, at about two percent per year.[15]

Here is similar recent news from major private oil companies.

ConocoPhillips, the Houston-based amalgam of Continental Oil and Phillips Petroleum, announced in January 2005 that new additions to its oil reserves in 2004 amounted to only about 60-65 percent of all the oil it produced that year, entailing a significant depletion of those existing reserves.

ChevronTexaco, the second largest U.S. energy firm after ExxonMobil, also reported a significant imbalance between oil production and replacement. Although not willing to disclose the precise nature of the company's shortfall, chief executive Dave O'Reilly told analysts that he expects "our 2004 reserves-replacement rate to be low."

Royal Dutch/Shell, already reeling from admission in 2005 that it had overstated its oil and natural gas reserves by 20 percent, recently lowered its estimated holdings by another 10 percent, bringing its net loss to the equivalent of 5.3 billion barrels of oil. Even more worrisome, Shell announced in February 2005 that it had replaced only about 45-55 percent of the oil and gas it produced in 2004, an unexpectedly disappointing figure.

These and similar disclosures suggest that the major private oil companies are failing to discover promising new sources of petroleum just as demand for their products soars. According to a recent study released by PFC Energy of Washington, D.C., over the past 20 years the major oil firms have been producing and consuming twice as much oil as they have been finding.

Demand Continues To Increase

The worldwide decline in new discoveries has profound implications for the global supply of energy and, by extension, the world economy. Given the current surge in energy demand from China and other rapidly-developing countries, the U.S. Department of Energy (DOE) predicts that for all future energy needs to be satisfied, total world oil output will have to climb by 50 percent between now and 2025; that is from approximately 87 million to 130 million barrels per day. That staggering increase in global production, an extra 40 million barrels per day, would be the equivalent of total world daily consumption in 1969. Absent major new discoveries, however, the global oil industry will likely prove incapable of providing all of this additional energy. Without massive new oil discoveries, prices will rise, supplies will dwindle and the world economy will plunge into recession, or worse.[16]

We do not Have to Run Out to Have Problems

The few Americans who are even aware that there is a gathering global energy predicament usually misunderstand the core of the argument, that we don't have to run out of oil to start having severe problems with industrial civilization and its dependent systems. We only have to slip over the all-time production peak and begin a slide down the side of steady depletion.

The term global oil-production peak means that a turning point will come when the world produces the most oil it will ever produce in a given year and, after that, yearly production will inexorably decline. It is usually represented graphically as a bell shaped curve. The peak is the top of the curve, the halfway point of the world's all-time total endowment, meaning half the world's oil will still be left. That seems like a lot of oil, and it is, but there's a big catch: It's the half that is much more difficult to extract, far more costly to get, of much poorer quality and located mostly in places where the governments hate us the most. A substantial amount of it will never be extracted.[17]

2050 Supply Forecast

The Geneva, Switzerland-based international petroleum industry consulting firm Petroconsultants' study, *The World Oil Supply 1930-2050*, notes that even with consumption dampened by world-wide reductions in oil usage because of increased prices and the probable worldwide depression that this would cause, declining supplies will cause oil production in 2050 to be at levels similar to the 1960s, when the planet only had three billion people. But most demographers expect that in 2050 the world population will exceed nine billion. Imagine: nine billion people alive, but fuel for only three billion. This would leave six billion people, almost the entire population of the planet today, living on the edge of famine.[18]

LOWER RETURN ON INVESTMENT AND EFFICIENCY

Energy Return on Exploration and Recovery

Technology rarely offers us a free ride; there are new costs incurred by nearly every technological advance. In the technologies involved with energy resource extraction, such costs are often reflected in the ratio of energy return on energy invested (EROEI). How much energy do we have to expend in order to obtain a given energy resource? In the early days of oil exploration, when we used simple technologies to access large, previously untapped reservoirs, the amount of energy that had to be invested was insignificant compared with the amount of oil extracted. As oil fields have aged and technologies have become more advanced and costly, that ratio has become less favorable.

This is reflected in figures for rates of oil recovery per foot of drilling. During the first 60 years of oil drilling until 1920, roughly 240 barrels of oil were recovered, on average, for every foot of exploratory drilling. In the 1930s, as new geophysical exploratory techniques became available and the six billion-barrel East Texas field was found, the discovery rate reached a peak of 300 barrels per foot. But since then, during successive decades of drilling, discoveries per foot of drilling have dropped steadily to fewer than 10 barrels per foot. And this decline has occurred during a period of intensive exploration, using ever more advanced technologies, such as 3D seismic and horizontal drilling. Thus, while new technologies have enabled the discovery of more oil, the EROEI for the activity of oil exploration has plummeted.

The same will no doubt be true of technologies used to increase the amount of recoverable oil from existing reservoirs: we will indeed be able to get more oil out of wells, but we will have to invest more energy to obtain that oil, with an ever-decreasing EROEI.

How important is EROEI? When the EROEI ratio for oil exploration declines to the point that it merely breaks even, that is, when the energy equivalent of a barrel of oil must be invested in order to obtain a barrel of oil the exercise will become pointless.[19]

For example, it may still seem profitable to recover oil as prices rise, but when you are using more energy to get oil out of the ground than you are getting out of the oil, then it is time to stop and simply leave it in the ground.[20]

Return on Use — Efficiency

Despite all of our recent advances in energy efficiency, our total petroleum usage, nationally and globally, continues to increase each year. In terms of depletion rates and production peaks, increased efficiency of use means nothing unless we are actually reducing the total amount of petroleum extracted and burned. That is not happening. We are not reducing our dependency on oil; it is still growing. The recession slowed the growth, but it did not reverse it.

There are limits to the benefits from efficiency, since increasing investments in energy efficiency also reach diminishing returns. Initial improvements tend to be easy and cheap; later ones are more costly. Also, population increases quickly wipe out our efficiency gains. Higher milage plus more cars equals no net gain or even more consumption. Also, the energy costs of retooling or replacing equipment and infrastructure can sometimes wipe out gains. Suppose you are currently driving a five-year-old car that travels 20 miles per gallon (mpg) of gasoline. You see a similar new car advertised that gets 30 mpg. It would appear that by trading cars, you would be conserving energy. However, it's not that simple, since more than half of the energy consumption attributable to each vehicle on the road occurs during the manufacturing before that vehicle has traveled its first mile.[21]

Here is a second example from agriculture. The amount of fuel used directly on a cornfield to grow a kilogram of corn fell 14.6 percent between 1959 and 1970. However, when the calculation includes the fuel used elsewhere in the economy to build the tractors, make the fertilizers and pesticides, and so on, it turns out that the total energy cost of a kilogram of corn actually rose by three percent during that period.

The results of these findings are first, that many efforts toward energy efficiency actually constitute a kind of shell game in which direct fuel uses are replaced by indirect ones, usually in the forms of labor and capital, which use energy elsewhere; and second, the principal factor that enabled industrial countries to increase their energy efficiency in the past few decades, the switch to energy sources of higher yield, is not a strategy that can be used indefinitely in the future.[22]

THE WORLD HAS NO PLAN B:
ALTERNATIVES CANNOT REPLACE FOSSIL FUELS

Hydrogen

Hydrogen is the lightest element, and it combines readily with oxygen. When it does so, it burns hot, and its combustion product is water—no greenhouse gases, no particulate matter or other pollutants. For these and other reasons, hydrogen would seem to be an attractive alternative to fossil fuels.

There are no underground reservoirs of hydrogen. Usable hydrogen has to be manufactured from hydrocarbon sources, such as natural gas or be extracted from water through electrolysis. The problem, however, is that the process of hydrogen production always uses more energy than the resulting hydrogen will yield. Hydrogen is not an energy source, but is an energy storage medium like a battery.[23]

In terms of energy efficiency, we would be better off burning natural gas or using solar or wind electricity directly, rather than going through the extra step of making hydrogen. The Second Law of Thermodynamics insures that hydrogen will be a net-energy loser every time since some usable energy is lost whenever energy is converted from sunlight to photovoltaic electricity, from electricity to hydrogen or from hydrogen back to electricity.

Another problem is the reliance on natural gas for hydrogen production. Hydrogen proponents assume the continued, abundant availability of natural gas. Without some transitional hydrocarbon source, there is simply no way to get to a hydrogen economy: there is not enough net energy available from renewable sources to bootstrap the process of hydrogen production while supporting a viable economy. Prospects for maintaining, much less increasing, the natural gas supply in North America appear uncertain. Within only a few years, decision makers will be confronting the problem of prioritizing dwindling natural gas supplies. Should they fund the transition to a hydrogen economy or heat people's homes during the winter?

Given the already low net energy from renewables as well as the net energy losses from both the conversion of electricity to hydrogen and the subsequent conversion of hydrogen back to electricity, it is difficult to avoid the conclusion that the hydrogen economy touted by well-meaning visionaries will by necessity be a much lower energy economy than we are accustomed to.[24]

Solar

There is another problem with development of alternatives, and it is a big one. Consider, for example, solar power. Solar cells capture current sunlight, so we can use the energy immediately. But we have gotten ourselves into a bind—everything about how we produce solar cells depends on oil.

Solar cells are made of several rare-earth minerals, which requires that hundreds of tons of earth be mined to extract a few pounds of the minerals. This mining is done with huge machines fueled by oil. New flexible solar cell may change this, however.

An alternative might be to use plastic instead of glass to cover solar cells, but plastic is made from oil and requires significant energy to refine and process.

What happens when the oil runs out—when we no longer have stored-up ancient sunlight? Where will the solar cells come from?

We can't use today's solar cells to make more solar cells. Today's cells can barely power a small car; they certainly cannot capture enough current sunlight to create enough electricity to power a bulldozer, to haul freight across the country or heat a blast-furnace or a glass factory to make more solar cells.[25]

Although solar cells are a convenient way to generate electricity at locations remote from the power grid, and they may be able to contribute during a transitional period from energy growth to energy descent, a high-tech society running on solar cells is simply a dream. The basis of this view somewhat depends in part on methods for assessing the net energy yield of solar cells. In other words, do they collect more energy over their useful life than they cost to manufacture and maintain?

Emergy, spelled with an "m," measures the net direct and indirect energy input in solar calories.[26] Two emergy studies of installed solar systems in Austin, Texas and Nashville, Tennessee in the 1990's showed Emergy yield ratios of 0.41 and 0.36 respectively. Anything less than one is a net loss.[27] Read Howard T. Odum's book *A Prosperous Way Down: Principles and Policies* to learn more about the important field of Emergy.

Wind

There are similar problems with wind power: while there may be an inexhaustible supply of wind along the shoreline and in some mountain passes, capturing it efficiently requires high-tech turbines, built of high-quality steel and other materials that can be fabricated only with energy derived from fossil fuels. When those parts wear out, in the absence of oil, we are left with the classic low-tech wooden windmills of Holland, extracting enough current wind energy to pump the seawater out of a two or three acre field.[28]

Ethanol and Other Bio Fuels

Cornell University professor David Pimentel, who has performed a thorough net-energy analysis of ethanol, found that an acre of corn ultimately yields, on average, 328 gallons of ethanol. It takes 1,000 gallons of fossil fuels to plant, grow and harvest one acre of corn. Additional energy must be used in distilling the ethanol. In sum, 131,000 BTU are needed to make 1 gallon of ethanol, which has an energy value of only 77,000 BTU. This gives ethanol an EROEI of roughly .59, meaning a 41 percent net loss of energy.

A recent USDA study came to a more optimistic conclusion: it claims that ethanol offers a 34 percent energy profit. This translates into an EROEI of 1.34. The practical difference between Pimentel's .59 and the USDA's 1.34 is slight. In either case, if the entire US automotive fleet were to run on pure ethanol, nearly all of the continental US would be required in order to grow the feedstock.[29] Never mind that we can barely feed the population we currently have and one-sixth of the world goes to bed hungry every night.

Nuclear

There are two ways to get energy from nuclear power. One is the light water reactor, which is what we use in this country. By the way, every fifth home and every fifth business today would be dark if we did not have nuclear power in use. It produces 20 percent of all of our electricity. But there is not all that much fissionable uranium in the world, so we are not going to get there with light water reactors.

France produces about 80 percent of its electricity from nuclear. They mainly use the other way of producing nuclear power— breader reactors. Breader reactors do what the name implies, they make more fuel than they use, but with big problems of enrichment, shipping the dangerous fuel and disposing of the byproducts which last for 250,000 years. That presents enormous challenges for us and for the next 10,000 generations who will have to deal with the waste.[30]

The most massive wastes are, of course, the reactors themselves once they have become unserviceable. There is a lot of discussion on the trivial economic question of whether they will last for twenty, twenty-five or thirty years. No one discusses the humanly vital point that they cannot be dismantled but have to be left where they are, probably for hundreds of thousands of years, an active menace to all life, silently leaking radioactivity into air, water and soil. No one has considered the number and location of these sites which will relentlessly accumulate. Earthquakes, of course, are not supposed to happen, nor wars, nor civil disturbances, nor riots that could occur anywhere at anytime. Disused nuclear power stations will stand as unsightly monuments to our present values—that the future counts for nothing compared with short-term economic gain now.[31]

The destructive properties of uranium are unleashed the moment it is mined from the ground. The victims are usually indigenous peoples of the earth; uranium contaminates their food, their drinking water and it turns their sacred places into restricted dumpsites. Over 70 percent of the world's uranium resources lie buried in lands inhabited by indigenous peoples. These dumpsites go unprotected.

Native people tell us that uranium should stay in the ground but their voices are lost in the wind. Tribal people possess the knowledge of the past that could help heal and restore the earth but their views are in conflict with the nuclearized, neo-colonial mindset of the multinational energy corporations. We in the West are in possession of the most advanced strain of ignorance the world has ever developed. Native people don't think this way. By resisting the repeated incursions of industrial society into their lands, their cultures and their religions, they have heroically preserved a world-view, which carries the core belief that the earth is sacred. It's time we listened.[32]

From another perspective, air conditioning, pumping water to irrigate lawns and waste water treatment account for almost 20 percent of U.S. electricity use. Flush toilets, air conditioning and lawns may be costing us nuclear power.

Oil Shale

As of 2020, the U.S. shale industry peaked without ever making money. Over the past decade and a half, the shale industry totaled $300 billion in net negative cash flow, wrote down another $450 billion in invested capital, and saw more than 190 bankruptcies since 2010, according to a new report from Deloitte. The U.S. shale industry more than doubled oil production over the past half-decade, a phenomenal increase in output. But "the reality is that the shale boom peaked without making money for the industry in the aggregate," the consulting firm wrote in a searing indictment of the shale industry. The financial problems endemic to shale drilling have been known for quite a while, but the Covid-19 pandemic blew up the industry's growth trajectory. Crashing oil prices and a new reality are now driving a "great compression" for shale.

Walter Youngquist sums up the situation well, "Adding up the water supply problem, the enormous scale of the mining which is needed, the low, at best, net energy return, and the huge waste disposal problem, it is evident that oil shale is unlikely to yield a significant amount of oil, as compared with the huge amounts of conventional oil now being used."[33]

Oil Sands

Oil sands are likewise reputed to be potential substitutes for conventional oil. The Athabasca oil sands in northern Alberta, Canada, contain an estimated 870 billion to 1.3 trillion barrels of oil, an amount equal to or greater than all of the conventional oil extracted to date. Currently, Syncrude, a consortium of companies, and Suncor, a division of Sun Oil Company, operate oil-sands plants in Alberta. Syncrude is currently producing over 200,000 barrels of oil a day. The extraction process involves using hot water flotation to remove a thin coating of oil from grains of sand, then adding naphtha, a petroleum distillate, to the resulting tar-like material in order to upgrade it to a synthetic crude that can be pumped. Currently, two tons of sand must be mined in order to yield one barrel of oil. As with oil shale, the net-energy figures for oil sands are discouraging. It takes the equivalent of two out of each three barrels of oil recovered to pay for all the energy and other costs involved in getting the oil from the oil sands.

Furthermore, the primary method used to process oil sands yields an oily waste water. For each barrel of oil recovered, two-and-a-half barrels of liquid waste are pumped into huge ponds. The Syncrude waste pond measures 22 kilometers in circumference. Six meters of murky water floats on a 40 meter-thick slurry of sand, silt, clay and unrecovered oil. Residents of northern Alberta have initiated lawsuits and engaged in activist campaigns to close down the oil sands plants because of the devastating environmental problems associated with their operation, including the displacement of native peoples, the destruction of boreal forests, death of livestock and an increase in human miscarriages.

Replacing the global usage of conventional crude—87 million barrels a day—would require about 350 additional plants the size of the

PEAK OIL AND ENERGY DESCENT

existing Syncrude plant. Together, they would generate a waste pond 8,750 sq. km, or about half the size of Lake Ontario. But since oil sands yield less than half the net energy of conventional oil, the world would need more than 700 plants to supply its needs, and a pond of over 17,500 sq. km—almost as big as Lake Ontario. Realistically, while oil sands represent a potential energy asset for Canada, it would be foolish to assume that they could make up for the decline in the global production of conventional oil.[34]

COLLAPSE - POWER DOWN

Richard Duncan of the Institute of Energy and Man reached this conclusion when he began to correlate world energy use and population data in terms of overshoot and collapse: "The life of industrial civilization will be a horribly short pulse lasting roughly 100 years from 1930 to 2030, with its high point corresponding to the peak of global per capita energy use which occurred in 1979."[35]

It is probably simplistic to equate the coming peak in oil production with the end of industrialism. There are nine major interconnected events that could be considered harbingers of the end of the current age of cheap energy. Three of them have already happened:

1. The peak in global per capita energy production. During the period from 1945 to 1973 world energy production per capita grew at 3.24 percent per year. From 1973 to 1979, growth slowed to .64 percent per year. Since 1979, energy production per capita has declined at an average rate of .33 percent per year. Thus the global peak in per-capita energy production occurred in 1979. Since then population growth has outpaced the growth of energy production.

2. The peak in global net-energy availability. Throughout the past couple of decades, more total energy has continued to be produced each year, on average, from all sources combined, but the amount of energy spent in obtaining energy has increased at a faster pace. This is especially true for oil, coal, and natural gas, for which net yields are falling precipitously. That is it requires more drilling effort to obtain a given quantity of gas or oil now than it did only a few years ago and more mining effort to obtain the same amount of coal. The peak in the total net energy available annually worldwide has almost certainly already passed, but it is unclear exactly when. A good guess would be that the net-energy peak occurred between

1985 and 1995.

3. The peak in global oil extraction. As discussed earlier in this chapter, this peak probably occurred in 2008 at 81.73 million barrels per day. We will know in certainty only in retrospect.

4. The global peak in gross energy production from all sources. This is likely to coincide closely with the global oil extraction peak.

5. The energy-led collapse of the global economy. Even if an economic collapse occurs first for other reasons, for example as fallout from the bursting of the American banking or stock-market bubble, war in the Middle East or the implosion of more scandal-ridden American corporations, energy constraints will eventually hit the global financial system.

Energy scarcity will cause a recession of a new kind, one from which anything other than a temporary or partial recovery will be impossible. If people are deliberate and forward thinking we will create a different kind of economy in the future, building steady-state, low-energy, sustainable societies characterized by high artistic, spiritual and intellectual achievements. But the industrial-growth global economy we are familiar with will be gone forever.

The timing of this event will depend upon the global oil production peak. Reduced use or powering down could buy us a little more maneuvering room, but eventually demand will continue to rise and supply will slowly start to fall. As this gap widens, it will pull the economy down with it.

6. The collapse of the electricity grids. This will probably occur at different times and at different rates in different regions, partly depending on the robustness of the grids themselves. It will also depend on which resource was used to generate the electricity, such as coal, nuclear power, hydro or wind, and on the continued local availability of those resources.[36]

As the net energy available to industrial societies wanes, resources devoted to the electrical grids will become more expensive. At a certain point, demand for electricity will begin to consistently exceed supply. From then on, the electrical power grids may become threatened. Periodic brownouts and blackouts as we have seen in recent years may become common. In that case, the only way to maintain the grids would be to increase the price of electricity sufficiently to discourage nonessential uses. This would have a significant impact on the economy.

Within years of the first widespread blackouts it may become impossible to maintain the grids at their present scope, and efforts may be made to reduce the size of grids and to cannibalize components that can no longer routinely be replaced. Eventually it might no longer be possible to maintain the electrical grids in any form. If and when they come down for good, it's lights out—literally. The party will truly be over.

7. The collapse of the information infrastructure. The daily operation of the information infrastructure of industrial societies is directly dependent on regional electrical grids. When they become impossible to maintain, unless an alternative renewables-based electrical infrastructure is already in place, the information infrastructure of industrial societies will collapse and virtually all electronically coded data will become permanently irretrievable.[37] Among other things, the internet will go away.

8. The collapse of suburbia. The movie *The End of Suburbia* explores the American way of life and its prospects as the planet approaches a critical era, as global demand for fossil fuels begins to outstrip supply. James Howard Kunstler explains, "We poured our national wealth into the construction of a living arrangement that has no future, and the future is nowhere. The infrastructure of suburbia was the greatest misallocation of resources in the history of the world.

The Europeans have very different ways of life and standards of living. They have cars but are not car-dependent, certainly not to the degree we are. They did not destroy their pedestrian towns and cities. We did. They did not destroy their public transit. We did. They did not destroy local agriculture or the value-added activities associated with it. We did. If the West was put under a new oil embargo, the Europeans would still be able to eat and get around. We would not."[38]

9. More resource wars. As this process unfolds, resource wars such as the one in Iraq will become more prevalent. The war on terrorism is a smoke screen to take the gloves off during the end game for oil and keep markets open for American corporations. Anyone who opposes this is labeled a terrorist. You are either with us or against us. U.S. Vice President Dick Cheney has said, "This war will not end in our lifetime."[39]

WE HAVE FLEXIBILITY NOW

Hubbert was quoted as saying that we are in a "crisis in the evolution of the human society. It's unique to both human and geologic history. It has never happened before and it can't possibly happen again. You can only use oil once. You can only use metals once. Soon all the oil is going to be burned and all the metals mined and scattered."

Statements like this one gave Hubbert the popular image of a doomer. Yet he was not a pessimist; indeed, on occasion he could assume the role of utopian visionary. We have, he believed, the necessary know-how; all we need to do is overhaul our culture and find an alternative to money. If society were to develop solar energy technologies, reduce its population and its demands on resources, and develop a steady-state economy to replace the present economy which is based on unending growth, our species' future could be rosy indeed. "We are not starting from zero," he emphasized. "We have an enormous amount of existing technical knowledge. It's just a matter of putting it all together. We still have great flexibility but our maneuverability will diminish with time."[40]

On the other hand, I would say that as we have applied more technology, we have created new problems from unintended consequences. The most appropriate solution to our reduced energy future may be more local renewable systems like permaculture.

Permaculture is a holistic design system that follows nature as a model. It emphasizes planting perennials instead of annuals—building top soil and bio diversity—creating beneficial connections. It can be scaled from backyards, to farms and communities. Permaculture is bound by the ethics of care for the earth, for people and to share the surplus.

12. Bubble Economy

Today we are witnessing the slow deflation of our economy—fewer and fewer people have money and they are spending less of it. There is a limit to how far a growth economy can go on a finite planet. Mother nature always bats last and now she is coming to bat with *peak everything.* Our whole economy is a Ponzi scheme of converting the earth to money. At this point it is probably wise to start to back down from the house of cards and begin a restorative economy.

FINANCIAL MARKETS

Total U.S. Debt

America has built up a staggering amount of debt. At the time of the 1929 stock market crash, total U.S. debt was 176 percent of GDP. Today, total debt today stands at a whopping 304 percent of GDP and it is growing all them time. Every chart points to higher debt: corporate borrowing, consumer debt, home mortgages, the trade deficit, municipalities and the federal budget. [1]

This debt can only be serviced if the economy continues to grow. If it stops growing or shrinks for any extended amount of time and for any reason, including peak oil, the financial market bubble will burst. The toys for debt game is over.

Public Debt

When obligations of federal, state and local governments are added, taxpayers are on the hook for $61.7 trillion, or $531,472 per household to cover the lifetime benefits of everyone eligible for Medicare, Social Security and other government entitlement programs. We are running deficits in the trillions of dollars, not the hundreds of billions of dollars we're being told.[2] Expect the 2009 deficit to be $1.4 trillion.

The United States is financing these outlays by going into debt to Japan, China, Taiwan, South Korea, Hong Kong and India. This situation has become increasingly unstable as the United States requires capital imports of at least $2 billion per day to pay for its governmental expenditures. Any decision by Asian central banks to move significant parts of their foreign exchange reserves out of the dollar and into the euro or other currencies in order to protect themselves from dollar depreciation would produce a meltdown of the American economy.

On February 21, 2005, the Korean central bank, which has some $200 billion in reserves, quietly announced that it intended to "diversify the currencies in which it invests." The dollar fell sharply, and the U.S. stock market, although subsequently recovering, recorded its largest one-day fall in almost two years. This small incident is evidence of the knife-edge on which we are poised.[3]

Peak Oil

Since the September 11, 2001 terrorist attacks in New York, crude oil prices have risen a dramatic 500 percent. The increase translates into significantly higher costs for heating homes, driving cars and for commodity prices across the globe.[4]

Trade Deficit

Since 1976, the U.S. began running a trade deficit that has since cumulatively ballooned to $4.5 trillion by 2009.[5]

The 2008 current account deficit, which includes investment flows and other transfers as well as trade, topped $673 billion or 4.6 percent of GDP.[6]

Paul Volker, former Federal Reserve Chair, warned in a February 11, 2005 speech at the Stanford University Center for Economic Research conference, "Below the favorable surface [of the economy], there are as dangerous and intractable circumstances as I can remember . . . Nothing in our experience is comparable . . .

But no one is willing to understand this and do anything about it . . . We are consuming . . . about six percent more than we are producing. What holds the world together is a massive flow of capital from abroad . . . it's what feeds our consumption binge . . . the United States economy is growing on the savings of the poor . . . A big adjustment will inevitably become necessary, long before the social security surpluses disappear and the deficit explodes . . . We are skating on increasingly thin ice."[7]

Currency Exchange — The Global Casino

In the eighteenth century, Adam Smith noticed that even acts of selfishness can work to the common good in a limited market. But global capitalism is different. Its most traded commodity is money itself. Money can grow without your having to do anything useful. The gold standard, which held this tendency in check by limiting the amount of money available in cash, was abandoned in the 1930s. Deregulation followed in the 1980s and then, in the 1990s, computerization accelerated international money transactions to real time. Instead of there being just enough money to trade some of the things we make and do, all of the sudden there was three times as much money in the world as the total value of all goods and services combined. What this means is that a full two-thirds of all financial wealth is supported artificially by speculation alone.

Almost all trade is speculation on the fluctuation of currencies as $1.5 trillion careens around the world each and every day. Only two percent of global trade relates to things society makes and does. Our pensions are invested in this house of cards. Sixty years ago John Maynard Keynes feared this might happen, saying, " . . . the position is serious when enterprise becomes the bubble on a whirlpool of speculation." People have come to expect something for nothing in the stock market. Surpluses gained during our brief fossil fuel bubble have artificially created the middle class and suburbia. Once the bubble has burst, so may the middle class.

But surely the global capitalists would explain things more positively? Not if you listen to the top two currency traders. George Soros, who single-handedly bet against the pound in 1992, wrote, in *The Crisis of Global Capitalism*, "The central contention of this book is that market fundamentalism is today a greater threat to open society

than any totalitarian ideology." And, of the 1997 Asian financial crisis, "Instead of acting like a pendulum, financial markets have
recently acted more like a wrecking ball, knocking over one economy
after another."

Bernard Lietaer, who, before Soros dislodged him, was
described as the world's top currency trader, says that the real economy is now a sideshow of the global casino and is therefore alarm-
ingly unstable, with a fifty-fifty chance of meltdown. Corporations
distrust the money system to such an extent that they are avoiding
its use wherever possible. Pepsi-Cola, for example, withdraws its
profits from Russia in the form of vodka, and the Middle East gets
nuclear power stations in exchange for oil. A quarter of all trade in
goods and services is barter.[8]

˙ Speculation

The Wall Street speculative bubble is a cannibalizing scheme. Wall
Street is taking money from workers and the physical economy to
give to the obscenely wealthy insider investors. Each stock, bond or
derivative in the U.S.—most are owned by the financier oligarchy—
represents a claim against the American economy.

With a stock the claim is called a dividend; for a bond it's called
a yield. If we consider all the wealth produced in the U.S. through
such sectors as manufacturing, mining, farming and so forth, then
as of today the wealth extracted through the financial sector in Wall
Street is about 80 percent of the total. Wall Street speculation, as
distinguished from investment, produces nothing real, no factories,
no jobs, nothing—just wealth for the wealthy insider speculators.[9]

Derivatives Powder Keg

I hope I have convinced you that the best place for your retirement
money is not the stock market. In addition to the threat of the financial bubble bursting, there is no new wave of Internet stocks on the
horizon to boost the market except perhaps an alternative energy
bubble. Continued economic growth will be coming to an end.

The $787 billion bailout plan is just the tip of probably a $7 trillion bad housing loan problem. The current global banking bailouts
may make the situation worse by igniting hyperinflation from all of
this liquidity generated out of thin air. Hyperinflation may cause the

$50 trillion derivative markets to explode in a financial supernova. The credit default swaps (CDS) would be the first to blow, driving interest rates to double digits which would light the fuse to the $50 trillion interest rate swaps (IRS) powder keg. See Bob Chapman's website www.theinternationalforecaster.com.

If you have a big mortgage and car payments, what would you do if you were laid off for a year or more? My second piece of advice then is to get out from under your mortgage while you still can. Invest in some good soil and a community of hard working, like-minded people. You are better off in a yurt on good land that you own than you are in a house or apartment that you don't.

CANNOT REFORM THE ECONOMY

Our Taker culture is 10,000 years old. Corporations have been around since the 1600s. If our culture or the free market were going to end poverty and provide for all, they would have by now. The only thing our culture has proven it can do well over the past 10,000 years is produce poverty and hunger, concentrate wealth into the hands of a few and exploit nartural resources.

Albert Einstein said, "We can't solve problems by using the same kind of thinking we used when we created them." We cannot *fix* the economic system we have with a new ethic or new institutions. Capitalism, socialism or communism all have the same end result—concentration and exploitation. The brilliance of the capitalist system is that it all you have to do to perpetuate it is consume. Even going green still involves consuming.

I could write an entire book about what is wrong with corporations, globalization, markets, and private property, but it would not make any difference. You could reform corporate charters to make directors responsible for the harm they cause to communities, individuals and the environment, but you would still have poverty. You could end globalization and free trade, but you would still have inequity and injustice. You could reform markets to reflect all externalized costs, but you would still have resource exploitation and pollution.

As long as our Taker culture continues with the meme that says the world belongs to people for their use, humanity will always have economic systems that exploit nature and concentrate wealth.

13. Totalitarian Agriculture

As you remember, about 10,000 years ago one branch of the family of *Homo sapiens* decided it was exempt from the natural *law of limited competition*. They decided that the gods never meant for them to be bound by it. And so they built a civilization that flouts the law. Within five hundred generations, the blink of an eye in the biological time scale, this branch of *Homo sapiens* brought the rest of the living world to the brink of extinction. There must be something fundamentally wrong with what we Takers are doing.[1]

MAKES US US

One particular style of agriculture has been the basis of our culture from its beginnings 10,000 years ago to present times. It defines our culture and is found in no other. It is ours, it is what makes us who we are. For its ruthlessness toward all other forms of life and for its unyielding determination to convert every square meter on this planet to the production of human food—totalitarian agriculture.

Ethologists, students of animal behavior, and a few philosophers who have considered the matter know that there is a practical form of ethics practiced within the community of life—apart from us, that is. This unspoken code serves to safeguard and promote biological diversity. According to this code of ethics, species may compete but they may not wage war. Practitioners of totalitarian agriculture violate this code at every opportunity. We hunt down our competitors, we destroy their food and by destroying their habitat we deny them access to food. Totalitarian agriculture is based on the premise that all the food in the world belongs to us. There is no limit to whatever we may take for ourselves and deny to all others.

Totalitarian agriculture was not adopted in our culture out of sheer meanness. It was adopted because it is more productive than other styles of agriculture, and there are many other styles. Totalitarian agriculture represents productivity to the max, as Americans like to say. It represents productivity in a form that literally cannot be exceeded—in the short run.

Many styles of agriculture, not all, but many, produce food surpluses. Totalitarian agriculture however, produces larger surpluses than any other style. You simply cannot out produce a system designed to convert all the food in the living world into human food.[2]

We believed, and still believe, that we have the one right way for people to live, but we needed totalitarian agriculture to support our missionary effort. Totalitarian agriculture gave us huge food surpluses, which were the foundation of every military and economic expansion. No one was able to stand against us anywhere in the world, because no one had a food-producing machine as powerful as ours. Our military and economic success confirmed our belief that we have the one right way for people to live. We still believe that today. For the people of our culture, the fact that we are able to defeat and destroy any other society is taken as proof of our moral, intellectual and cultural superiority.

Remember, there are many types of agriculture practiced by native or Leaver people around the world. However, none of them violate the natural law and none of the Leaver people have the meme that there is only one right way to live. Native peoples have lived in what is now called the United States since before the agricultural revolution, yet by the start of the European expansion, there were only 1.8 million people with about 1,000 productive acres per person. As David Brower said, this was the "original good stuff:" huge tracks of old growth forests, herds of millions of bison, and a broad biodiversity from sea to shining sea.

Culture of Fear

Once you begin turning all the land around you into cropland, you begin to generate enormous food surpluses, which have to be protected from the elements and from other creatures including other people. Ultimately the food has to be locked up. Though it surely wasn't recognized as such at the time, locking up the food spelled the end of tribalism and the beginning of the hierarchical life we call civilization.[3]

This is when the *culture of fear* came into existence. After this point, if you did not work within the Taker culture, you did not eat. To grow food you had to have access to private land. To get the money to do that, you had to work within the system. The loophole of being able to gather and grow your own food on the commons was closed later.

PEACE KEEPING LAW

The *peace keeping law* is the natural *law of limited competition* that has ensured that life continues today in its great diversity. It is this diversity that has enabled life to survive on earth for four billion years.

However, there are three things that the Takers do that are never done in other natural communities. These are common practices in our civilization, but they violate the natural law of limited competition.

May Not Exterminate Competitors

First, Takers exterminate their competitors, which is something that never happens in the wild. In the wild, animals will defend their territories and their kills, and they will invade their competitor's territories and preempt their kills. Some species even include competitors among their prey, but they never hunt competitors down just to kill them, the way ranchers and farmers do with wolves, coyotes, foxes, and crows. What animals hunt, they eat.

It should be noted, however, that animals will also kill in self-defense, or even when they merely feel threatened. For example, baboons may attack a leopard that hasn't attacked them. The point is that, although baboons will go looking for food, they will never go looking for leopards.

In the absence of food, baboons will organize themselves to find a meal, but in the absence of leopards they will never organize themselves to find a leopard. In other words, when animals go hunting, even extremely aggressive animals like baboons, it is to obtain food, not to exterminate competitors or even animals that prey on them.

If competitors hunted each other down just to make them dead, then there would be no competitors. There would simply be one species at each level of competition: the strongest.

May Not Destroy Food

By creating monoculture farmland, Takers systematically destroy their competitors' food to make room for their own. Nothing like this occurs in natural communities. The rule is: Take what you need, and leave the rest alone.

May Not Deny Access To Food

Takers deny our competitors access to food. In the wild, the rule is: You may deny your competitors access to what you are eating, but you may not deny them access to food in general. In other words, you can say, "This gazelle is mine," but you can't say, "All the gazelles are mine." The lion defends its kill as its own, but it doesn't defend the herd as its own.

Our Taker policy is: Every square foot of this planet belongs to us, so if we put it all under cultivation, then our competitors are just plain out of luck. If they become extinct, so be it. Our policy is to deny our competitors access to all the food in the world. That is something no other species does.

Bees will deny access to what's inside their hive in the apple tree, but they won't deny you access to the apples.

In summary, the Leaver code of living defines the limits of competition in the community of life. You may compete to the full extent of your capabilities, but you may not hunt down your competitors or destroy their food or deny them access to food. In other words, you may compete but you may not wage war.

Diversity is the Secret to Success of Life on the Planet

What would have happened if this law of limited competition had been repealed ten million years ago? What would the community be like?

There would only be one form of life at each ecological niche. If all the competitors for the grasses had been waging war on each other for ten million years, an overall winner would have emerged by now. The community we have described would have a total of a few hundred species. The community of life as it is today consists of about 30 million species, although many are hanging by a thread.

But, what is wrong with a global community that consists of nothing but grass, gazelles and lions? Or a global community that consists of nothing but corn and humans?

A community like that would be ecologically fragile. It would be vulnerable. Any change in existing conditions and everything would collapse.

Diversity is the survival safety net for the community of life itself. This is called the *law of life*. Diversity is the very secret of success of life on earth.

A community of 30 million species can survive almost anything short of total global catastrophe. Within that 30 million will be thousands that could survive a global temperature drop of 20 degrees, which would be a lot more devastating than it sounds. Within that 30 million there would be thousands that could survive a global temperature rise of 20 degrees. But a community of a hundred species or a thousand species would have almost no chance to survive at all.

Diversity is exactly what is under attack here. Every day dozens of species disappear as a direct result of the way Takers compete outside the law.

What we are doing is not simply a blunder. We are not destroying the world because we are clumsy. We are destroying the world because we are at war with it.[4]

Finishing off Mother Culture

Mother Culture could accept the fact that mankind's home is not the center of the universe. She could accept the fact that people evolved from the common slime. But she will never accept the fact that humanity is not exempt from the peace keeping laws of the community of life. To accept that would go to the core of her world view and would likely finish her off.

Obviously Mother Culture must be finished off if we are going to survive, and that is something the people of our culture can do. She has no existence outside of our minds. Once you stop listening to her, she ceases to exist.

If people do not allow that to happen, then the law of limited competition will do it for them. If Takers refuse to live under the law, then they simply will not live. You might say that this is one of the law's basic operations: those who threaten the stability of the community by defying the law will die.

Accepting nature's law has nothing to do with it—you may as well talk about a man stepping off the edge of a cliff and not accepting the effects of gravity. The Takers are in the process of eliminating themselves. When they have done so, the stability of the community of life will be restored and the damage done will be repaired.

There are many people who understand this and are ready to take a new direction before it is too late.[5]

Ancient Humans Hunting Some Species To Extinction is Different

Recent evidence reveals that ancient human hunter-gatherers hunted some species to extinction. Yes, it means man lived as harmlessly as a hyena or a shark or a rattlesnake. Whenever a new species makes its appearance in the world, adjustments occur throughout the community of life, and some of these adjustments are fatal for some species. For example, when the swift, powerful hunters of the cat family appeared late in the Eocene, the repercussions of this event were experienced throughout the community—sometimes as extinction. Species of easy prey became extinct because they could not reproduce fast enough to replace the individuals the cats were taking. Some of the cat's competitors also became extinct, for the simple reason that they too could not compete; they just were not big enough or fast enough. This appearance and disappearance of species is precisely what evolution is all about.

Human hunters of the Mesolithic period may well have hunted the mammoth to extinction, but they certainly did not do this as a matter of policy, the way farmers of our culture hunt coyotes and wolves simply to get rid of them, or the way ivory hunters slaughter elephants for their tusks. Ivory hunters know full well that every kill brings the species closer to extinction, but Mesolithic hunters couldn't possibly have guessed such a thing about the giant elk or the mastodon.

The point to keep in mind is this: It is the policy of totalitarian agriculture to wipe out unwanted species. If ancient foragers hunted any species to extinction, it certainly wasn't because they wanted to wipe out their own food supply.[6]

SOIL LOSS AND DEGRADATION

Topsoil is like an immense organic solar battery, which efficiently stores the sunlight energy falling on the earth. Industrial agriculture, and even modern organic agriculture, in many cases depletes and exhausts the soil on which it depends. The rich loamy topsoil of the Midwest that was measured to be as much as seven feet deep at the time of European conquest now measures as little as seven inches in depth in some places.

Recently, the first global assessment of soil loss, based on studies of hundreds of experts, found that 38 percent, or nearly 1.4 billion acres, of currently used agricultural land has been degraded.[7]

So, if topsoil is an immense solar battery for the earth, then the battery has been reduced by 38 percent of it's capacity in many regions. That has happened in a tiny fraction of the time it took for our biosphere to store such a tremendous quantity of energy in the first place.

This one-time-only draw down of millions of years' worth of work of our biosphere is rapidly drawing to a close.[8]

Tilling Kills Soil

It is important to understand how industrial agriculture actually depletes the soil. The following two descriptions are from Toby Hemenway's *Gaia's Garden: A Guide To Home-Scale Permaculture*:

"What's really happening during tilling? By churning the soil, we're flushing it with fresh air. All that oxygen invigorates the soil life, which zooms into action, breaking down organic matter and plucking minerals from humus and rock particles. Tilling also breaks up the soil, greatly increasing its surface area by creating many small clumps out of big ones. Soil microbes then colonize these fresh surfaces, extracting more nutrients and undergoing a population explosion.

All this is great for the first season. The huge blast of nutrients fuels tremendous plant growth, and the harvest is bountiful. But tilling of the soil releases far more nutrients than the plants can use. Much of the new fertility leaches away in rains. The next year, when the tilling is resumed, more organic matter burns up, again releasing a surfeit of fertility. The unused portion is again leached. After a few seasons, the soil is depleted, the humus is gone, the mineral ores are played out, and the prematurely exuberant soil life is degraded. Now the farmer must add fertilizer and the gardener must renew the soil with bales of organic matter and plenty of work.

Also, the constant mechanical battering destroys the soil structure, especially when perpetrated upon too-wet soil, and we're all impatient to get those seeds in, so this happens often. Frequent tilling smashes loamy soil crumbs to powder, and compacts clay clods into hardpan. And a tilling session consumes far more calories of energy than are in a year's worth of food. That's not a sustainable arrangement."[9]

We cannot create biological energy any more than we can create fossil fuel energy. But we can preserve the biological energy which already exists. With proper care we *can* build soil. But we cannot build soil with the fossil fuel driven methods of modern industrial agriculture.[10]

Fertilizer Depletes Soil

"Here's what happens to soil life after an overzealous application of chemical fertilizer. Pouring a big bag of inorganic fertilizer on the ground creates an excess of mineral nutrients. Now the food in short supply is carbon. Once again, the soil life roars into a feeding frenzy, spurred by the more-than-ample nitrogen, phosphorus, and potassium in typical NPK fertilizers. Since organisms need about 20 parts carbon for every part of nitrogen, it isn't long before any available carbon is pulled from the soil's organic matter and tied up in living bodies. These organisms exhale carbon dioxide, so a proportion of carbon is lost with each generation. First the easily digestible organic matter is eaten, then, more slowly, the humus. Eventually, nearly all the soil's carbon is gone, and the soil life, starved of this essential food, begins to die. Species of soil organisms that can't survive the shortages go extinct locally. Some of these creatures may play critical roles, perhaps secreting antibiotics to protect plants, or transferring an essential nutrient, or breaking down an otherwise inedible compound. With important links missing, the soil life falls far out of balance. Natural predators begin to die off, so some of their prey organisms, no longer kept in check in this torn food web, surge in numbers and become pests.

Sadly, many of the creatures that remain after this mineral over-dose are those that have learned to survive on the one remaining source of carbon: your plants. Burning carbon out of the soil with chemical fertilizers can actually select for disease organisms. All man-ner of chomping, sucking, mildewing, blackening, spotting horrors descend on the vegetation. With the natural controls gone, and dis-ease ravishing every green thing, humans must step in with sprays. But the now-destructive organisms have what they need to thrive, the food and shelter of plants, and they will breed whenever the now essential human intervention diminishes. The farmer is locked on a chemical treadmill. It's a losing battle, reflected in the fact that we use 20 times the pesticides we did 50 years ago, yet crop losses to insects and disease have actually increased, according to USDA statistics,

The other harm done by injudicious use of chemical fertilizers is to the soil itself. As organic matter is burned up by wildly feeding soil life, the soil loses its ability to hold water and air. The desperate soil life has turned to feed on the humus itself, the food of last resort. With humus and all other organic matter gone, the soil loses its fluffy, friable structure and collapses. Clay-based soil compacts to concrete; silty soil desiccates to dust and blows away.

In contrast, ample soil life boosts both the soil structure and the health of your plants. When the soil food web is chock-full of diver-sity, diseases are held in check. If a bacterial blight begins to bloom, a balanced supply of predators grazes this food surplus back into line. When a fungal disease threatens, microbial and insect denizens of your soil are ready to capitalize on this new supply of their favorite food. Living soil is the foundation of a healthy farm."[11]

Soil Loss

The superficial success of America's farms masks an underlying problem. A third of the original topsoil in the United States is gone, and much of the rest is degraded. Soil productivity in the semi-arid Great Plains fell by 71 percent during the 28 years after sodbusting leading to the dust bowl disaster. Notwithstanding some recent progress in reviving sound soil conservation practices, topsoil is still eroding much faster than it is being formed. Growing a bushel of corn by conventional methods can erode two to five bushels of top-soil. In the 1980s, a dump truck load of topsoil per second was passing New Orleans via the Mississippi River. A decade later, 90 percent of American farmland was still losing topsoil faster, on average 17 times faster, than new topsoil was being formed. In other words, every six years 100 years of topsoil creation is being lost. In many developing countries the rate is greater.[12]

Worldwide, soil abuse is unprecedented. Salinization is affecting ever-larger areas of irrigated land. About 24 billion tons of soil a year are eroding from the world's land surfaces due to forest clearing, farming on steep lands and other inappropriate food production methods.[13] This process is turning 40,000 acres a day into desert.[14]

As more soil is lost, U.S. farm output will be reduced by 20 percent over the next 20 years. Most ancient civilizations collapsed because they destroyed their topsoil, but few of today's policymakers seem mindful of that history.[15]

WATER LIMITATIONS

Agriculture uses about two-thirds of all the water drawn from the world's rivers, lakes and aquifers. Irrigation waters only 16 percent of the earth's cropland, three-fourths of it in developing countries, but produces 40 percent of the world's food. In many areas, groundwater is being over pumped and depleted just like the oil fields. In the United States about one-fourth of the groundwater that is pumped for irrigation is over-drafted. Salting and other side effects of poor irrigation and drainage management have already damaged more than a tenth of the earth's irrigated cropland, some irreversibly.

Since 1945, degradation of soil and water resources has affected nearly three billion acres, roughly the area of China and India combined. Four-fifths of those degraded acres are in developing countries where governments and farmers lack capital to repair the damage. Nearly half the acres have too little water for usual restoration methods to work. Of the one-ninth of the earth's land that was considered arable in 1990, little remains really healthy and losses are accelerating.[16]

Beef Worsens Problem

Two-fifths of America's feedlot cattle are being fed grain grown from water taken from the rapidly depleting Ogallala aquifer. Using current agricultural methods growing enough grain to put on one extra pound of beef costs up to 100 pounds of eroded topsoil.[17] Furthermore, about 13,250 gallons of water are needed to produce one pound of beef, whereas one pound of wheat requires only about 60 gallons.

A lot of land is also used to keep the animals and to grow the grain used to feed them. It takes eight or nine cattle a year to feed one average U.S. meat eater. Each cow needs about one acre of green plants, corn or soybeans a year. So, it takes about nine acres of feed plants a year for the meat one person eats, rather than the half acre needed if the plants were eaten directly. The amount of grain needed to provide meat for one person is enough to feed about 20 people for a year. In the U.S., livestock eat enough grain and soybeans to feed over a billion people. About 16 pounds of grain are needed to make a pound of beef. A reduction of meat consumption by only 10 percent would result in about 12 million more tons of grain for human consumption. This grain could feed all of the 60 million people who starve to death each year.[18]

MORE INDUSTRIAL AGRICULTURE SIDE EFFECTS

Monoculture Ending Agricultural Diversity

The FAO estimates that more than three-quarters of agricultural genetic diversity was lost in this past century. As agribusiness utilizes only high-yield, high-profit varieties we fail to save the seed stock of thousands of other tried-and-true varieties.

The Rural Advancement Foundation International (RAFI) conducted a study of seed stock readily available in 1903 versus the inventory of the U.S. National Seed Storage Laboratory (NSSL) in 1983. RAFI found an astonishing decline in diversity. We have lost nearly 93 percent of lettuce, over 96 percent of sweet corn, about 91 percent of field corn, more than 95 percent of tomato and almost 98 percent of asparagus varieties.

The majority of apple varieties are extinct today; only two varieties alone account for more than 50 percent of the current apple market.

Similarly, in 2000, 73 percent of all the lettuce grown in the United States was iceberg. The relatively bland variety is often the only choice consumers have.

Packaging attempts to hide the fact that we are essentially eating the same set of ingredients over and over, even though they go by different names. Rarely do their ingredients contain anything out of the ordinary. A full 95 percent of the calories we eat come from only 30 varieties of plants, according to the FAO.

A highly consolidated distribution process encourages large supermarket and restaurant chains to feature industrially grown products over more diverse foods produced by small-scale sustainable growers. Just a few huge food distributors dominate the process. They deal almost exclusively with equally massive food producers and pass along their lack of choice to the consumer.[19] Every step is streamlined to cut costs.

Industrial agriculture has become an affront to nature's complexity and integrity. According to agroecologist Miguel Altieri, "Modern agriculture implies the simplification of the structure of the environment over vast areas, replacing nature's diversity with a small number of cultivated plants and domesticated animals." Altieri notes that about 70 plant species are grown on roughly 1.5 billion hectares of cropland worldwide. By comparison, consider the 40,000 species of flora that occur on just two percent of the world's land surface encompassed by Colombia, Ecuador, and Peru.[20]

Biopiracy

Not only is our agricultural biodiversity being wiped out, corporations are stealing what is left through the patenting of seed varieties and the development of genetically modified (GM) terminator seeds that force farmers to buy new seeds every year. Patenting ancient seed varieties by companies like Monsanto is stealing from poor farmers the world over by forcing them to buy seeds that they have saved for generations. Patenting seeds also further impoverishes farmers by forcing them to pay royalties on seeds that they formerly saved, to pay penalties for unauthorized production, and forcing them to purchase more chemical inputs.

Two thirds of Third World people in the South depend on

access to biodiversity for their livelihoods and needs. In India, 70 percent of seeds are saved or shared farmer's seed. When corporations steal and control those genetic resources through patents, the poor are directly deprived.

Instead of preventing organized economic theft, the World Trade Organization (WTO) under Trade-Related Intellectual Property Rights (TRIPs) protects the powerful and punishes the victims. National courts are also enforcing the life form patenting. See Vandana Shiva's *Biopiracy: The Plunder of Nature and Knowledge* to understand the global threat posed by genetically modified organisms and the patenting of life forms.

The Canadian Supreme Court found in 2004 that it did not matter whether canola farmer Percy Schmeiser knew or did not know that his canola field was contaminated with Monsanto's Roundup Ready gene plants. He had to pay for their technology anyway. In Percy Schmeiser's case, he had been saving his own canola seeds for 50 years. Monsanto's patented canola seeds blew off of passing trucks and onto his farm. The court found that regardless of how the seeds got there, including wind or flood, Percy Schmeiser had to pay for Monsanto's genetically modified seeds for his entire crop. Visit www.percyschmeiser.com for more information about his case.

This commoditization of life itself is the apex of what some call the *information age*. Life and information is now monopolized by and for corporations. Corporations have formed an information cartel by controlling the information portals, filing patenting, controlling university research and, of course, controlling our media and our government.

Monoculture Increases Pests

Under primitive agricultural conditions, the farmer had few insect problems. Those arose with the intensification of agriculture—the devotion of immense acreages to a single crop. Such a system set the stage for explosive increases in specific insect populations. Single-crop farming does not take advantage of the helpful principles by which nature abides; it is an agriculture engineered strictly by the human intellect. Nature has great variety in the landscape; people seem to have a passion for simplifying it. Diversity keeps insect species in balance.[21] The key is to be sure there is abundant habitat for these creatures.

Monocultures are rare in nature in part because they create paradises for plant diseases and insects. As science writer Janine Benyus puts it, "They are like equipping a burglar with the keys to every house in the neighborhood—they're an all-you-can-eat restaurant for pests."

The conventional practise of dousing infested plants and soil with pesticides may have seemed like a good idea at first, but it is becoming increasingly clear that using technology to override natural processes has not worked. In 1948, at the start of the era of synthetic pesticides, the United States used 50 million pounds of pesticides a year and lost 7 percent of the pre-harvest crop to insects. Today, with a nearly 20-fold increase in pesticides use, almost a billion pounds a year, the insects get 13 percent, and total U.S. crop losses are 20 percent higher than they were before we got on the pesticide treadmill.[22]

Pesticides Kill Beneficial Insects

Toby Hemenway describes in *Gaia's Garden* how counterproductive pesticide use is. "Timing is everything in a aphid infestation. Unfortunately, just about the time the beneficial lady beetles reach the numbers necessary to control the aphids, the farmer notices the outbreak and sprays insecticide. This kills most of the aphids as well as the lady beetles. The fast-breeding aphids recover within a few weeks, but the lady beetles, who have no food until the aphids are in good supply, remain at critically low numbers. Just when the lady beetles, feeding on the small population of aphids, begin to breed again, the farmer sees that a few aphids are still out there. Fearing another plague, he sprays again, really hammering the struggling lady beetles. A few rounds of this cycle and the lady beetles are all dead, while some aphids are bound to survive. Now the pests are predator-free and can multiply unchecked and the farmer is on an expensive and toxic insecticide treadmill. He or she has eliminated nature's safeguards, and must spray and spray, or take the time, and the short-term crop loss, to restore the natural balance."[23]

Monoculture Reduces Food Security

The tendency to create broad international markets for a single product generates vast monocultures that reduce biodiversity, thus diminishing food security and increasing vulnerability to plant diseases, insect pests and weeds. These problems are especially acute in developing countries, where traditional systems of diverse crops and the methods to grow them are being replaced by monocultures that push countless species to extinction and create new health problems for rural populations.[24]

Landlessness

Landlessness is one of the major problems of industrial agriculture and globalization that deserves mentioning. The migration from farms in rural areas has fueled an explosion in third world cities.

Local food systems, small land owners, indigenous systems and family farming are not compatible with global corporate operations. We face a very aggressive international campaign to undermine small farmers, get them off their traditional lands and make way for industrial agricultural systems with absentee owners that produce monocultures for export. The net outcome is that once-viable, self-reliant communities are being made landless, homeless, cashless, and hungry; there are few jobs available in the industrial agriculture model that emphasizes machine and pesticide-intensive production or biotechnology. Meanwhile, food-growing activities that had been the economic, social and spiritual heart of community life are wiped out taking the heart of the local cultures along with them.[25]

Once self-reliant farmers are becoming dependent on welfare systems for survival or fleeing to already overcrowded cities, searching for the rare factory job in competition with all the other new arrivals. Furthermore, the industrial agriculture companies do not grow food for the local people. They favor high-priced, high-margin luxury items such as flowers, potted plants, beef, shrimp, cotton and coffee, for export to already overfed countries. Local farmers' traditional knowledge and agrarian culture are displaced by a managerial and industrial culture which concentrates on growing crops for cash instead of food.

This has been true as much in the United States as anywhere else in the world. Seventy years ago there were nearly seven million American farmers. Today there are only about two million, even though the U.S. population has doubled. Between 1987 and 1992, America lost an average of 32,500 farms per year, about 80 percent of which were family-run. A mere 50,000 farming operations now account for 75 percent of U.S. food production.[26]

FOSSIL FUEL DEPENDENCE

Production

Modern industrial agriculture has become energy-intensive in every respect. Tractors and other farm machinery burn diesel fuel or gasoline; 40 percent of the world's food supply depends on nitrogen fertilizers produced from natural gas[27]; pesticides and herbicides are synthesized from oil; seeds, chemicals and crops are transported long distances by truck; and foods are often cooked with natural gas and packaged in oil-derived plastics before reaching the consumer.

If food-production efficiency is measured by the ratio between the amount of energy input required to produce a given amount of food and the energy contained in that food, then industrial agriculture is by far the least efficient form of food production ever devised.

Traditional forms of agriculture produced a small solar-energy surplus: each pound of food contained somewhat more stored energy from sunlight than humans, often with the help of animals, had to expend in growing it. That meager margin was what sustained life.

Today, from farm to plate, depending on the degree to which it has been processed, a typical food item may embody input energy, calories, between four and several hundred times its value in food energy. This energy deficit can only be maintained because of the availability of cheap fossil fuels, a temporary gift from the earth's geologic past.[28]

For example, in high input fruit and vegetable cultivation, the energy output/input ratio is between 2 and 0.1, or one calorie of food energy output requires up to ten calories of energy input. For intensive beef production the ratio is between 0.1 and .03, and may reach extreme values of 0.002 for winter greenhouse vegetables. All of these ratios refer to he energy consumed up to the farm gate and exclude processing, packaging and distribution.[29]

Processing

Industrial agriculture, according to Professor Mark D. Shaw, now uses 16.5 percent of all energy used in the United States. This 16.5 percent is used in the following ways:

On-farm production	3.0 percent
Manufacturing	4.9
Wholesale marketing	0.5
Retail marketing	0.8
Food preparation (in home)	4.4
Food preparation (commercial)	2.9

Apologists for industrial agriculture frequently stop with that first number showing that agriculture uses only a small amount of energy. The other numbers, amounting to 13.5 percent of national energy consumption, are more interesting, for they suggest the way the food system has been expanded to make room for industrial enterprise.

Between farm and home, producer and consumer, we have interposed manufacturers, a complex marketing structure and food preparation. I am not sure how this last category differs from manufacturing, and I would like to know what percentage of the energy budget goes for transportation, and whether or not Professor Shaw figured in the miles that people now drive to shop. Nevertheless, the industrial economy grows and thrives by lengthening and complicating the essential connection between producer and consumer.[30]

PEAK AGRICULTURE

Grain Reserves Exhausted

As of 2008, U.S. government grain surpluses have evaporated because, with record high prices, farmers are selling their crops on the open market, not handing them over to the government through traditional price-support programs that make up for deficiencies in market price. Worldwide, food prices have risen 45 percent in the past nine months of 2007–2008, posing a crisis for millions, says the United Nations' Food and Agriculture Organization.[31]

Land Limitations

In the 1980s the total amount of land in the world devoted to agriculture expanded at only 0.1 percent a year and the amount of arable land actually declined because of the effects of past agricultural expansion, soil erosion, desertification and salinisation. After 10,000 years of agriculture about 11 percent of the world's surface is now used for growing crops and there is little new land left suitable for agriculture. What remains is either too steep as in the Andes, too acid, too dry as in most of Africa or is in the tsetse fly areas of Africa where trypanosomiasis, sleeping sickness, is rife.

About a quarter of the world's surface has been taken over for grazing animals and although arable land could extend into this area, the net increase in food production would be small and past experience suggests that these soils, if plowed, are likely to suffer from severe soil erosion. The only other land that could be used for agriculture lies in the tropical forests where the soils are generally poor and can produce crops only for only a limited time.[32]

Peak Oil — The End of Cheap Food

Expanding agricultural production, based on cheap energy resources, enabled the feeding of a global population that grew from 1.7 billion to over 6.7 billion in a single century. Cheap energy will soon be a thing of the past. How many people will post-industrial agriculture be able to support? A safe estimate would be this: as many people as were supported before agriculture was industrialized, that is, the population at the beginning of the twentieth century or somewhat fewer than 1.5 billion people.[34]

I would cut this number by 20 to 30 percent to account for environmental degradation. Without fossil fuels, we will not be starting where we left off. As we know, our overshoot has significantly reduced the earth's original carrying capacity. There has been considerable emergy built up in the form of infrastructure and machinery, but without fossil fuels or spare parts it will be of little use. By the end of this century, there may only be enough food for about one billion people.

PART III

Restoration Revolution

14. Leaver Wealth

As Takers we have been struggling for 10,00o years to invent a lifestyle that works and have failed. We have invented many things that have worked, such as cars, airplanes, televisions, toasters and the internet, but a lifestyle that works for people's benefit and well being has always eluded us.

We are having a hard time building enough prisons to hold all our criminals. The nuclear family is struggling. Incidence of drug addiction, domestic violence, divorce, child abuse, suicide, mental illness, and even terrorism continue.

The fact that we have not been able to invent a lifestyle that works for us and for the earth is not surprising because our culture is based on a flawed premise.

The tribal lifestyle works because it was subject to the same evolutionary processes and ecological restraints that produced workable lifestyles for deer, whales, birds and bees. Tribalism was tested from the time people began and what worked survived and what did not work did not survive. The fact that we are here today after three million years proves that tribes work for people.

LEARNING FROM WHAT WORKS

Evolutionarily Successful

Tribes during the first three million years of human life were ethnic groups, extended families with a common language, common laws and customs, and so on. Their social borders were generally, but not absolutely, closed to members of other tribes to ensure tribal integrity. Captives of war were an exception, but a member of the Ute, for example, couldn't ordinarily just decide to become a Navajo.[1]

The story the Leavers have been enacting here for the past three million years is not a story of conquest and rule. Enacting their story does not give them power beyond their evolutionary position within nature. Enacting it gives them lives that are satisfying and meaningful. They are not seething with discontent and rebellion, not incessantly wrangling over what should be allowed and what forbidden, not forever accusing each other of not living the right way, not living in terror of each other, not going crazy because their lives seem empty and pointless, not having to stupefy themselves with drugs to get through the days, not forever searching for something to do or something to believe in that will make their lives worth living.

This is not because they live close to nature or have no formal government or because they are innately noble. This is simply because they are enacting a story that works well for people, a story that worked well for three million years and that still works well where Takers have not yet managed to stamp it out.[2]

Erratic Retaliator

We talked earlier about the *law of limited competition* which applies to all species. Species also compete within themselves in various ways. The way of competition within tribal peoples is the strategy of erratic retaliator. This strategy developed over hundreds of thousands of years and perhaps even millions. It is as natural to humans as hibernation is to bears, migration is to birds and dam building is to beavers.[3]

The erratic retaliator tribal competition strategy is *give as good as you get*. In practice *give as good as you get* means that if the neighboring tribe is not bothering you, do not bother them, but if the neighbor tribe does bother you, then be sure to return the favor.

Another element is, *do not be too predictable*. This means that even if the neighbor tribe is not bothering you, it will not be a bad thing if you make a hostile move against them from time to time. They will of course retaliate, giving as good as they get, but this is just the price to be paid for letting them know that you are there and have not gotten soft.

Then, once the score is even between the tribes, they can get together for a big reconciliation pow-wow to celebrate undying friendship and do some matchmaking because, of course, it does not do well to breed endlessly within a single tribe.[4] Other tribes also produce goods that can be traded for.

While tribes occasionally compete or come into conflict, they more often cooperate, as seen in the rituals of the potlatch and pow-wow. One tribe may view another with disdain, but there are few historical records of tribal people engaging in genocide. Another tribe may be attacked, but it will never be completely wiped out. After all, the other tribes are useful. Perhaps most important, by being a *them* the other tribes help a local tribe to maintain its identity as an *us*.

Although intertribal conflicts sometimes result in deaths, it is rarely a large number, and in the case of most tribes studied over the years, intertribal conflict usually produces no deaths. The function of the intertribal conflict is to help solidify and maintain the boundaries and unique character of each tribe. As such, it is a good thing for the survival of both tribes.[5]

The last component of this strategy is if you are the resident, attack, if you are the intruder, retreat, but do not be too predictable. Human tribes will protect a territory, a permanent piece of real estate to call their home and will protect everything in it. Animals will never go looking for new territory to call their own. An animal goes looking for food and mates, and when it finds them, it draws a circle around them that says to the same species rivals, "The resources inside this circle are taken and will be defended." It does not care about the acreage itself. If the resources in it disappeared, the animal would walk away from it without a backward glance.[6]

This sort of behavior is not at all unusual. Most species resolve their same species conflicts over resources in just such a fashion. It does not pay to get into a serious battle over every acorn, but it also does not pay to back down over every acorn. It is important to be predictable to a certain extent, but it is also important not to be too predictable. For example, your opponent should know that when you start snapping your teeth at him, you are fairly likely to attack. On the other hand, your opponent should not be able to count on your backing down just because he starts snapping his teeth at you.[7]

The erratic retaliator strategy is part of the law of limited competition. It may seem combative, but it is actually a peace keeping strategy.

Knowledge of What Works Well for Ordinary People

Our Taker culture accumulates knowledge about what works well for *things*. Leavers accumulate knowledge about what works well for *people* and other forms of life.

Each Leaver tribe has a system that works well for them because it evolved among them; it was suited to the terrain in which they lived, suited to the climate in which they lived, suited to the biological community in which they lived, suited to their own peculiar tastes, preferences and vision of the world. Knowledge like this, knowing what truly works for people, is called wisdom.

What Takers teach their children is how to make more and better things. Takers do not teach their children what works best for people because they do not know. Every generation has to come up with its own version of what works well for them. My parents, for example, had their version, which was pretty much useless to me, and we are currently working on our version, which may well seem pretty useless to our own children.[8]

Every time the Takers stamp out a Leaver culture, a wisdom ultimately tested since the birth of humanity disappears from the world beyond recall, just as every time they stamp out a species of life, a life form ultimately tested since the birth of life disappears from the world beyond recall.[9]

The tribal lifestyle does not expect its members to be perfect, noble, enlightened or any better than they are. The tribal life does not turn people into saints; it enables ordinary people to make a living together with a minimum of stress year after year, generation after generation.[10]

Taker Pride Keeps Us from Learning from Leavers

Our Taker culture is not working for the vast majority of people and species on the planet, but we still think we have all the answers and refuse to look anywhere else for solutions. People are fascinated to learn why a pride of lions works, why a pod of whales works or why a flock of geese works, but they often resist learning why a tribe of humans works.

What is not tolerable to people of modern society is that these *savages* know something we do not know. After all, we know about culture and civilization. We created the arts and all this modern living. Tribalism is a much less advanced form of culture.

Tribal humans were successful for millions of years and they are no less successful today wherever they manage to survive untouched, but most people of our culture don't want to hear about it.

LEAVER ANIMIST VISION

Animism

If tomorrow we were to wake up and learn that the night had brought forth a new, vital religion so universally acceptable to humanity that all religious disagreement had utterly vanished from the world, this would be considered a great miracle in the history of our spiritual development.

There once was such a religion on this planet. Everyone is more or less aware of this fact, but no one has ever suggested that this was miraculous or even remarkable. No one has ever suggested that this universal religion might have even the slightest claim to validity. Needless to say, this was not one of our Taker religions. It was, and is the religion of the Leavers, and for this reason it is judged not to count as a religion at all. It is considered merely a pre-religion, a crude evolutionary stage that people had to pass through in order to arrive at the enlightened and advanced religions that evoke such murderous fervor among the Takers.

The religion is animism. The only world religion whose name you need not capitalize. It is not a name coined by any adherent of this religion. Who would bother to ask a savage to supply a name? Derived from the Latin word for soul or spirit, in the 1860s and 1870s it came to be applied to the religious notions of primitive peoples. Sir Edward Tyler supplied an early definition in his book, *Primitive Culture*.

Simply put, as Taker scholars understand it, animism represents spirit worship as opposed to the presumably more advanced worship of gods or God. In other words, these poor, ignorant savages have the silly idea that every tree and bush and rock has a spirit. This is what makes it a pre-religion; true religions are concerned with gods, not spirits. Considering the unbridled anthropocentrism of the Taker mentality, it is not hard to figure out why this should be so: Gods are like us, which makes them preeminently deserving of worship.

A spirit in a tree is a what? It doesn't have a name, you can't talk to it or expect it to talk back to you. It's just there. Gods have personality, just like us. Gods have personal lives, just like us. Gods have gender, sex lives and even babies, just like us. They visit the earth and talk to people, get involved in our lives. They listen to our troubles, take sides in our quarrels, look after us on our journeys and see that our enterprises get a little extra help. I speak here of the Olympian gods, the gods of pagan Greece and Rome.

Of course, having a single god is considered to be even more advanced. The bad part about having just one god, however, is that it can only be one sex or the other, which puts it in the middle of the war of the sexes. If it's a he, it tends to see things from the male point of view, and if it's a she it tends to see things from the female point of view. The current controversy over God's sex doesn't strike anyone as being the least bit primitive.

In his own way, the god of the Abraham tradition is even more anthropocentric than the Olympian gods. He loves us, talks to us, listens to us, gives us gifts, takes them back, frames laws for our conduct, gets angry when we fail to obey them, punishes us, forgives us, keeps track of our every thought throughout our lives and at death rewards us with everlasting bliss or damnation. He isn't as big on damnation as he used to be; in some of the more advanced religions, he has quietly closed down hell and boarded it up like a decrepit amusement park. All these things are clear indicators that one is dealing with an advanced religion, a religion worthy of the name. It is not thought to be the least superstitious to believe that God has an especially keen interest in what people do behind closed doors.

The religion of the Leavers is "pre" because it does not involve the worship of anthropocentric gods like these. There are plenty of gods in Leaver mythologies, of course, but these are only local deities, not objects of universal worship or even of local worship, as we use the term. For example, the Amazulu of Mrica say that Unkulunkulu made all things, but they do not worship this creator the way Jews worship Yahweh or the way Christians worship Jesus. And if the Amazulu were to run across a band of Ashanti, they would not expect them to acknowledge the primacy of Unkulunkulu over their Onyankopon. This is supposed to be a sign of their religious backwardness. If the Amazulu were instead to fall upon the Ashanti and slaughter them for refusing to acknowledge the primacy of Unkulunkulu, this would represent a clear step forward on the path of spiritual development, and we would be forced to acknowledge that the Amazulu now had a true religion.

Animism is the only world religion that has never been named or defined by its own adherents. It's the only world religion that has never generated a sacred foundation text; it's hard to imagine how it could have done, since it was never the religion of a single nation or people. It's probably just as well. When you have a text, you almost inevitably have schisms and heretics, divisions by interpretations and divisions by degrees of orthodoxy. All the same, it makes it difficult to answer people's questions.[11]

Fire of Life

The best way to explain the Fire of Life is to tell a story. This story is from Daniel Quinn's, *The Story of B*. For a deeper reading on The Fire of Life and animism see Quinn's autobiography, *Providence: The Story of a Fifty-Year Vision Quest*.

"We are going to take a field trip. This will be a mental one, so you will not have to put on your Natty Bumppo hat. I want you to travel with me to a place I remember as a child, a plains wilderness. . . . Once when I was a kid I remember watching an old western movie on TV called *The Sea of Grass*. I do not know what it was about. All I remember is one scene where Spencer Tracy looks out over this vast sea of grass stretching from horizon to horizon, and the wind's stirring it up and sending it into waves just like the sea. The place I'm talking about wasn't as huge as that, but it was the same kind of place. Close your eyes and see if you can picture such a place.

The important thing to realize is that this is not grass. This is deer and bison and sheep and cicadas and moles and rabbits. Reach down and grab a handful. Go ahead, at least mentally. Have you got it? That's a mouse. And the mouse, the ox, the gazelle, the goat, and the beetle all burn with the fire of grass. Grass is their mother and father and their young are grass.

One thing: grass and grasshopper. One thing: grasshopper and sparrow. One thing: sparrow and fox. One thing: fox and vulture. One thing, and its name is fire, burning today as a stalk in the field, tomorrow as a rabbit in its burrow, and the next day as an eleven-year-old girl named Shirin.

The vulture is fox; the fox, grasshopper; the grasshopper, rabbit; the rabbit, girl; the girl, grass. All together, we're the life of this place, indistinguishable from one another, intermingling in the flow of fire, and the fire is god—not God with a capital G, but rather one of the gods with a little g. Not the creator of the universe but *the animator of this single place.* To each of us is given its moment in the blaze, its spark to be surrendered to another when it's sent, so that the blaze may go on. None may deny its spark to the general blaze and live forever—certainly not me, for all my giant intellect. Each is sent to another someday. You are sent. You are on your way. I too am sent. To the wolf or the cougar or the vulture or the beetles or the grasses, I am sent. I'm sent and I thank you all, grasses in all your forms—fire in all your forms—sparrows and rabbits and mosquitoes and butterflies and salmon and rattlesnakes, for sharing yourselves with me for this time, and I'm bringing it all back, every last atom, paid in full, and I appreciate the loan.

My death will be the life of another, I swear that to you. And you watch, you come find me, because I'll be standing again in these grasses and you will see me looking through the eyes of the fox and taking to the air with the eagle and running in the track of the deer."[12]

Humanity Belongs to the Earth

The premise of the Taker story is the world belongs to humanity. The premise of the Leaver story is humanity belongs to the earth. It is almost too neat. A culture born from human pride and the quest for pleasure will perish. True lasting culture is born within nature, and is simple, humble and pure.

It means that right from the beginning, everything that ever lived was not separate from,but belonged to the earth, and that is how things came to be this way. Those single celled creatures that swam in the ancient oceans belonged to the world, and because they did, everything that followed came into being. Those club finned fish of shore belonged to the world, and because they did, the amphibians eventually came into being. And because the amphibians belonged to the world, the reptiles eventually came into being. And because the reptiles belonged to the world, the mammals eventually came into being. And because the mammals belonged to the world, the primates eventually came into being. And because the primates belonged to the world, *Australopithecus* eventually came into being. And because

Australopithecus belonged to the world, people eventually came into being. And for three million years people belonged to the world, and because he belonged to the world, we grew and developed and became brighter and more dexterous until one day we were so bright and dexterous that we had to call him *Homo sapiens*—us.

If we accept the Taker premise, that the world belongs to humanity, a disaster is sure to follow.

However, if we accept the Leaver premise, that humanity belongs to the world, then creation can go on forever.[13]

The World is Sacred

The world is a sacred place and a sacred process. Leaver people, whether they are agricultural or hunter-gatherers, live with a deep connection to the earth. For them, the planet on which we live is a living organism. It has its own life, its own destiny, and, in a way that the Takers could never understand, its own consciousness. Things that run counter to the earth's laws of life will not work in the long run—although the damage may be too slow to be notice-able on the Taker culture time scale. All we have to do to tell which is which is look at what is happening on the earth.

The Leavers are so clear in their understanding of our place on earth that they often pray for the soul of an animal as they kill it for food. Daily they are thankful for the life given them, and the life around them, all of which is viewed with reverence.[15]

Ute Berry Harvesting Story

Isabel Kent, in a 1985 interview, told how her mother taught her to pick berries.

"My Mom used to say that the berry tree is given to us by Mother Earth. She's given us berries. She's given us all kinds of ani-mals, big, small, and the little ones. If you've seen a chokecherry tree, it's all filled with berries and the birds and animals will not touch it unless you and I go and pick and say 'Oh, this is good.' The birds then have a right to eat it. The upper part is for the birds. The middle part is ours, the human's, the rest, the bottom part is for the animals that cannot climb. That's why we were taught that we don't pick the whole thing. We leave some, because the earth gave us this wonderful food, not just for the human beings but for all of us. So we have to share with the little birds and little wild animals."14

No One Right Way to Live

When you go among tribal peoples, you will find that they do not look to the heavens to find out how to live. They don't need an angel or a spaceman to enlighten them. Their laws and their customs give them a completely detailed and satisfactory guide. I do not mean that the Akoa Pygmies of Africa think they know how all human beings should live or that the Ninivak Islanders of Alaska think they know how all human beings should live or that the Bindibu of Australia think they know how all human beings should live. All they know is that they have a way that suits them. The idea that there might be some universally right way to live would strike them as ludicrous.16

LEAVER WEALTH
Learn from Leaver Success

The people of our Taker culture are in the process of rendering this planet uninhabitable to millions of other species and possibly to ourselves. If we succeed in doing this, life will certainly continue, but at levels considerably more primitive. When I speak of saving the world, I mean saving a diverse world roughly as we know it now, a world populated by elephants, gorillas, kangaroos, bison, elk, eagles, seals, whales and an array of trees, shrubs, plants and microorganisms.

The only other way to save the world is to find a way to get the things humanity needs without destroying the world.

It is my personal theory that the people of our culture are destroying the world not because they are vicious or stupid, but because they are terribly deprived of things that humans absolutely must have, simply cannot go on living without year after year and generation after generation. I believe, given a choice between destroying the world and having the things they really, deeply want, they will choose the latter. But before they can make that choice, they must see that choice.17

I think that Taker people can get what they desperately need without destroying the world by studying the success of Leaver peoples. They must swallow their pride that there is only one way to live.

Cradle-to-Grave Security

The foremost wealth of tribal peoples is cradle-to-grave security for each and every member. This is precisely the wealth that tribes stick together to have. It is impossible for one person to accumulate more of this wealth than anyone else. There is no way to put it under lock and key.[18]

This isn't the result of an innate saintliness or unselfishness of tribal peoples. Baboons, gorillas and chimpanzees enjoy exactly the same sort of security in their social groups. Groups that provide such security are going to hold onto their members much more readily than groups that do not. Again, it is a matter of natural selection. A group that does not take good care of its members is a group that does not command loyalty and probably will not last long.

The fact that ethnic tribes can provide their members with cradle-to-grave security is a true measure of their wealth. The people of our culture are rich in gadgets, machines and entertainment, but we are all too aware of the dreadful consequences of losing a job.[19]

We need to demand for ourselves the wealth that humans had from the beginning, that they took for granted for hundreds of thousands of years. We need to demand for ourselves the wealth we threw away in order to make ourselves the rulers of the world. But we cannot demand this from our leaders. Our leaders are not withholding it. They do not have it to give to us. This is how we must differ from revolutionaries of the past, who simply wanted different people to be running things. We cannot solve our problem by putting someone new in charge.

We must demand it of ourselves. Tribal wealth is the energy that tribal members give each other in order to keep the tribe going. This energy is inexhaustible, a completely renewable resource.[20]

Cradle-to-grave security is possible in tribal communities because of their economic model. The Tribal model is *give support—get support*. The Taker model is *make products—get products*. The Taker model invariably leads to the concentration of wealth and no security.

John Wesley Powell spent several months studying the Ute language in the 1870s. He noted, "An interesting fact is that there is no word signifying rich or poor as having to do with much or little property. When an Indian says 'I am rich,' he means 'I have many friends.' 'I am poor' means 'I have but few.' "[21]

Care for Elders

One indication of the health of a society is its treatment of the elderly. A sensitive, thoughtful society will raise elderly people to positions of greater honor and respect as they grow older. This is not to argue in favor of a society tyrannized by the aged, but one in which seniors are cared for psychologically as well as physically, where their opinions are sought and valued. It is noble and beautiful to give respect to the elders as their physical powers wane, rather than to cast them aside. Neglect for the aged is not only ugly, it's lacking in gratefulness to the generation that cradled us and on whose shoulders we stand. We set an example in the treatment of our parents and grandparents that our children are likely to follow when we are old.

Elders will most willingly share their knowledge. It is a crime that we do not design a way of living that fosters the use of our elders' minds and abilities.

Everyone wants to feel they are needed and valuable. We benefit doubly by providing pleasant, useful work for older people. They benefit through feeling needed and society benefits from their contentedness and their contribution. Some of our most precious cultural treasures have come from the wisdom of our elders.[22]

Fulfillment and Contentment

For all of our millions of gadgets and distractions, we are still not fulfilled. Many have a hollow sense that there is something missing. Today we cannot seem to be rich enough, or good looking enough, or smart enough or consume enough. Consumerism is our sense of lack institutionalized as a sort of state religion. We think of ourselves as wealthy, but we are truly impoverished.

This is the Achilles heal of our culture. Our Taker culture cannot give us the happiness it promises. Despite all of its consumerism, media and religion, we are never fulfilled. Once enough people realize that our culture is never going to work for them, they will simply walk away just like the Maya and the Olmec.

Learning from Ladakh

Few people seem so healthy emotionally, so secure, as the Ladakhis in Himalayan region of India. The reasons are complex and spring from a rich way of life and world view. The most important factor is the sense that you are a part of something much larger than yourself, that you are inextricably connected to others and to your surroundings.

The Ladakhis belong to their place on earth. They are bonded to that place through intimate daily contact, through knowledge about their immediate environment and its limitations. They are aware of the context in which they find themselves. The movement of the stars, the sun, and moon are familiar rhythms that influence their daily activities.

In traditional Ladakhi society, everyone, including aunts and uncles and Buddhist monks and nuns, belongs to a highly interdependent community. A mother is never left on her own, separated from her children. She always remains a part of their lives and those of their children.

Large extended families and small intimate communities form a more secure foundation for the creation of mature, balanced individuals than our isolated Western families. A healthy society is one that encourages close social ties and mutual interdependence, granting each individual a net of unconditional emotional support. Within this nurturing framework, individuals feel secure enough to become free and independent.

If you ask a Ladakhi, "Do you enjoy going to the regional capital Leh, or do you prefer staying in the village?" You are likely to get the answer "I am happy to go to Leh; and if I don't go, I am also happy." It really does not matter so much one-way or the other.

The Ladakhis enjoy a feast more than everyday food, and they would rather be comfortable than uncomfortable, healthy rather than ill. But, in the end, their contentedness and peace of mind do not depend on such outside circumstances; these qualities come more from within. The Ladakhis' relationships to others and to their surroundings have helped nurture a sense of inner calm and contentedness.

Contentment comes from feeling and understanding your self to be part of the flow of life, relaxing and moving with it. If it starts to pour with rain just as you set out on a long journey, why be miserable? Maybe you would not have preferred it, but the Ladakhis' attitude is "Why be unhappy?"[23]

To learn more about the Ladakhi people see the book and movie by Helena Norberg-Hodge, *Ancient Futures*.

Focus on What You Are Gaining

Many people consciously or unconsciously think of evolution as a process of continual improvement. We imagine that humans began as a miserable lot but under the influence of evolution very gradually got better and better until one day they became us, complete with frost-free refrigerators, microwave ovens, air-conditioning, minivans and satellite television.

Because of this, giving up anything would necessarily represent a step backward in human development. So Mother Culture formulates the problem this way: Saving the world means giving things up means reverting to misery. Therefore forget about giving things up and saving the world.

We should not think of ourselves as wealthy people who must give up some of our riches. We should think of ourselves as people in desperate need.

In its root sense, wealth is not a synonym for money; it is a synonym for wellness. In terms of products, we are of course fabulously wealthy, but in terms of human well being and living in harmony with our surroundings, we are pathetically poor. In terms of human wealth, we are the wretched of the earth. And this is why we should not focus on giving things up. How can you expect the wretched of the earth to give anything up?

On the contrary, we must concentrate on getting things, but not more toasters, radios, television sets, and smart phones. These are tools to unplug ourselves from the people around us. We need to build communities of people who want to make a living together, help each other grow and provide each other security. These communities are the seeds of the future.

Thriving in Modern Communities

How can we apply the social strengths of Leaver village lifestyles to our modern culture in an effective way?

We can gather some insights from my colleague, Tracie Sage, who is devoted to rekindling the social roots of village in our lives today. She has been researching, experimenting, learning, and now teaching core elements and practices that build fulfilling relationships, providing the social foundation to support the collective village paradigm. This relieves individual burdens, while creating greater ease for all.

In her words, "Many of us long for more community in our lives. As I speak of community, I'm speaking of the need for more intimate, cooperative, interdependent relationships among our circles of friends, family, colleagues and neighbors—a collaboration that supports basic survival needs and meets our need for fulfilling connections. These are the social roots of 'village' that we've lost and forgotten; yet still want and need in our lives today.

Village or community can be created in various shapes and sizes. Your community could be your neighborhood, your circle of family and friends or it may be a group of people with whom you share land or a common mission.

Whatever form community takes, challenging issues and conflicts often arise that divide or dissolve the community. Alternatively, conflicts are avoided, yet individuals still struggle with feeling isolated, alone or unsupported even in the midst of community.

What will it take to build enduring supportive community?

We'll need to make a radical shift from what is 'normal', conventional and comfortable; we cannot create thriving, collaborative community within the current paradigm. Essentially, we need to shift our time, energy and focus to more quality connections with ourselves and others instead of attempting to buy our happiness.

Here are seven core elements that, when cultivated, help create enduring relationships and thriving community. We have lost the first, second and last elements; the key shifts we must make to rekindle the social roots of village in our lives.

1) A shared commitment to self-awareness practices. Each community member participates in a regular self-awareness practice, including compassionate self witnessing and connecting deeply with his or her own feelings, desires and inner wisdom. Modern approaches to these

practices can take many forms such as yoga, co-listening, meditation or one that your group designs. These practices support the ability of each person to know and express their own feelings and desires, which allows them to be supported by the larger group. It's important for the group well-being that each person is also willing to commit to and be responsible for their own emotional health and growth. See courses at www.turningpointvillage.us.

2) Social well-being processes shared often and consistently to build and deepen trust within community. Some components of these processes include being fully present, honest, respectful and compassionate with each other, listening with all the senses, expressing, clearing, resolving emotionally charged issues, etc. Practices to explore include: Naka-Ima, Co-creative Solutions Process, Nonviolent Communication, ZEGG Forum, and Process Oriented Psychology.

3) Common ground. Being aligned with a common vision—an important uniting element that needs to be simple, clear, acknowledged, and ideally written. The intentional communities ZEGG and Tamera share a common vision of 'Love without Fear'. Commune di Bagnaia has a common vision of collective wealth—each giving according to their means and receiving according to their needs.

4) Shared commitments and agreements—clear and written. Every thriving community I've visited had written agreements as a foundation for community life.

5) Working, creating and playing together. In my interviews with community members, this element is often mentioned as an important way of bonding, whether in the form of team building projects or the creative expressions of music, dance or art. We depend on this element in our current culture but by itself it's not enough to carry us through real life challenges.

6) Willingness to evolve and grow—both individually and as a community. The one thing we can depend on in life is change. Embracing change allows us to move through life's evolutions gracefully and effectively. It brings greater ease, happiness and longevity into communities.

7) Youth empowerment. Creating space for the next generation of visionaries to take on important roles of leadership. At Tamera, this was supported by their approach to school; the children were very articulate and at ease, displaying a strong sense of security and responsibility in their community and in the world."

15. A New Vision Can Save The World

A culture perpetuates itself through its story, or meme. People make the story come true by living it. New story, new culture. It's not quite that simple, but in a way it is.

Human evolution is discontinuous. It rests in a more or less steady state for long periods of time and then is punctuated by an abrupt shake-up that reorders the culture. These shake-ups are either environmental or information-based. Humanities coming changes will be caused by both.

The good news is that the problem is not humanity itself, but the Taker culture we live in. We do not have to change our genes to save the world; we just have to move to new cultures.

Remember, our culture cannot be *fixed* because of its core meme that the world belongs to humanity; we have to go back and look at the success of Leaver peoples and bring forth a new story.

SELF-GENERATING COMMUNICATION NETWORKS

Cultures use communication in the form of stories as their particular mode of reproduction. Earlier we called these stories memes, such as the world belongs to people or civilization is unsurpassable.

These communications are produced and reproduced by a network. These networks of communication are self-generating. Each communication creates thoughts and meaning, which give rise to further communications, and thus the culture self-perpetuates.

As communications recur and create feedback, they produce a

shared system of beliefs, explanations, values and vocabulary—a common context that is sustained by further information. Through this shared context people gain identities as members of the social network, and in this way the network generates its own boundaries. It is not a physical boundary, but a cultural boundary of expectations and loyalty which is continually maintained and renegotiated by the network itself.[1]

PROGRAMS VS. VISION
The Power of Vision

Vision, or story, is to culture what gravity is to matter. When you see a ball roll off a table and fall to the floor, it is clear that gravity is at work. When we see a culture make its appearance and spread outward in all directions until it takes over the entire world, a vision is at work.

When a small group of people begins behaving in a unique way that subsequently spreads across an entire continent a vision is also at work. For example, if I tell you that the small group I have in mind were followers of a first-century preacher named Paul and that the continent was Europe, you will know the vision was Christianity.

Dozens or perhaps even hundreds of books have investigated the reasons for Christianity's success, but none were written before the nineteenth century. Before the nineteenth century people believed that Christianity needed no more explanation to succeed than gravity does. It was bound to succeed. Its success was simply its destiny.

For the same reason, no one has written a book investigating the reasons for the success of the industrial revolution. It is just obvious that the industrial revolution was bound to succeed. It could no more have failed than a ball rolling off a table would rise to the ceiling.

That's the power of vision.[2]

Current Vision is Creating our Problems

Our problems come not from our technology, our diet, violence in the media or any other single thing we do. They arise out of our culture, our view of the world. The reason most solutions offered to solve the world's crises are impractical is because they arise from the same vision that caused the problem. Recycling will not save the world, birth control will not save the world and saving what little is left of the rainforests will not save the world.

Even if all those good things were implemented, the fundamental problems described in Part II of this book would still remain, and would inevitably continue. Even if fusion energy were to become a reality eliminating the need for oil with free electricity for all, it would not save the world. Nothing but changing our way of seeing and understanding the world can produce real, meaningful and lasting change. That change would naturally lead us to begin to control our populations, save our forests, create community and reduce our wasteful consumption.[3]

Vision is Self-Spreading

Every vision is self-perpetuating, but not every vision spreads itself in the same way. In a sense, the spreading mechanism is contained in the vision itself.

Our culture's spreading mechanism was population expansion: grow, then get more land, increase food production, and grow some more. Christianity's spreading mechanism was conversion: accept Jesus, then get others to accept him. The industrial revolution's spreading mechanism was improvement: improve on something and then put it out there for others to improve on.

All spreading mechanisms have one thing in common—they confer benefits on those who do the spreading. Those who get more land, increase food production and grow are rewarded with riches and power. Those who accept Jesus and get others to accept him are rewarded with heaven. Those who improve on something and put it out there for others to improve on are rewarded with respect, fame and wealth.

The benefit conferred should not, however, be confused with the mechanism itself. People becoming rich and powerful did not spread our culture; people going to heaven did not spread Christianity, and people winning respect, fame and wealth did not spread the industrial revolution.[4]

PROGRAMS FAIL

Programs Run Counter to Vision

Programs invariably run counter to vision, and so have to be thrust on people—have to be sold to people. For example, if you want people to live simply, reduce consumption, reuse and recycle you must create programs that encourage such behaviors. But if you want them to consume a lot and waste a lot, you do not need to create programs of encouragement, because these behaviors are supported by our cultural vision.

Vision is the flowing river. Programs are sticks set in the riverbed to impede the flow. The world will not be saved by people with programs. If the world is saved, it will be saved because the people have a new vision. People with a new vision will not have new programs.

Perhaps our new vision will be community survival through interdependence and restoration. Those who spread it are rewarded with survival and cradle-to-grave love and security.

Programs are Reactionary

It is important is to understand the difference between vision and programs. Programs are inherently reactionary. By their nature they always follow, never lead. They only react to something else. Programs are like first aid. This does not make them bad; it just makes them provisional and temporary. Programs must wait for bad things to happen to be useful. Then they scramble playing catch-up.

By contrast, vision does not wait for something bad to happen. It simply pursues something desirable. Vision does not oppose, it proposes.[5]

Excuses for Failure

Programs make it possible to look busy and purposeful while failing. If programs actually did the things people expect them to do, then human society would be heaven: our governments would work, our schools would work, our law enforcement systems would work, our justice systems would work and so on.

When programs fail it is blamed on things like poor design, lack of funds and staff, bad management and inadequate training. When programs fail, look for them to be replaced by new ones with improved design, increased funding and staff, superior management and better training. When these *new* programs fail, as they invariably do, it is still blamed on poor design, lack of funds and staff, bad management and inadequate training.

This is why we spend more and more on our failures every year. Most people accept this willingly enough, because they know they are getting more every year: bigger budgets, more laws, more police, more prisons—more of everything that did not work last year or the year before that.

Old minds think: If it did not work last year, let's do more of it this year.

New minds think: If it did not work last year, let's do something different this year.[6]

NEW MINDS

As you discuss the ideas found in this book with your friends, you will be able to spot the old minds easily. They are the ones who are playing the devil's advocate, proposing and concentrating on difficulties, always nailing the progress of your dialogue down to problems. Focus instead on what you want to happen and how to make it happen, rather than on all the things that might keep it from happening.[7]

If the world is saved, it will be by new minds wanting to live a new way. It will not be because old minds come up with new programs. Programs never stop the things they are launched to stop. Programs have never stopped poverty, drug abuse or crime and they never will. And no program will ever stop us from devastating the world.[8]

Old minds think: how do we solve these problems? Or, how do we stop these bad things from happening?

New minds think: how do we make happen what we want to happen? Or, how do we make things the way we want them to be?[7]

Vision Does Not Need Programs

Although historians now look for the reasons behind Christianity's success, they are not looking for programs. Christianity thrived in the Roman world because the people of that time were ready for it. Historians would no more expect to find programs at work there promoting Christianity than chemists would expect to find angels at work in their test tubes. It might be argued that Constantine's Edict of Milan allowing Christians freedom of worship was a program of support, but in fact it merely permitted what 2.5 centuries of persecution had been unable to stop, much as the twenty first amendment to the U.S. Constitution merely permitted what 14 years of Prohibition had been unable to stop.

In the same way, the spread of our culture has never had to be kept going by a program. It hasn't flagged for an instant, and the same could be said of the industrial revolution.[9]

To say that the industrial revolution is a terrific example of what people can do without programs is an understatement. From the time Giambattista della Porta dreamed up the first modern steam engine nearly 400 years ago until the present, this vast, world-transforming movement has been carried forward by vision alone: *improve on something, then put it out there for others to improve on.*

The industrial revolution was moved forward by the confident realization in millions of minds that even a small new idea, even a modest innovation or improvement over some previous invention could improve their lives almost beyond imagination. Over a few brief centuries, millions of ordinary citizens, acting almost entirely from motives of self-interest, have transformed the human world by broadcasting ideas and discoveries and furthering these ideas and discoveries by taking them step by step to new ideas and discoveries.[10]

The industrial revolution was a flowing river. It needed no programs to get it going or to keep it going. It was not a river in the second century or the eighth or the thirteenth. But, one after another, tiny springs bubbled up and began to flow together, decade after decade, century after century. In the fifteenth century, it was a trickle. In the sixteenth, it became a brook. In the seventeenth, it became a stream. In the eighteenth, it became a river. In the nineteenth, it became a torrent. In the twentieth century, it became a world-engulfing flood. And through all this time, not a single program was needed to further its progress. It was awakened, sustained and enhanced entirely by vision.[11]

WORLDVIEW AND VALUE SHIFT

When people change their values, a change in worldview will not be far behind. A worldview is everything you believe is real—God, the economy, technology, the planet, how things work, how you should work and play, your relationship with your beloved and everything you value. For some, their worldview shifts first and their priorities shift later. For others, it happens the other way around. Most often, there is a mix of the two, with values and worldview shifting alternately, influencing each other.

Worldview changes do not happen often, or we would be like teenagers heaving this way and that on Disney World's Space Mountain Ride. Most of us change our worldview only once or twice in our lifetime, if we do it at all, because it changes virtually everything in our consciousness. When you make this shift, you change your sense of who you are, what you are willing to see and how you interpret it, your priorities for action and for the way you want to live. If your worldview changes, it changes everything.[12]

The intent of *Culturequake* is to give people the information they need to have a shift towards something new—restoration. This process is an unveiling which gives rise to living a new truth. Revealing the truth about our history, state of the world and how change occurs is not a program. It does need to expand and become a new self-spreading vision or story. This is the challenge for ours and future generations.

INFORMATION IS KEY TO TRANSFORMATION

There are two properties of complex systems that pertain to cultural change. First, information is the key to transformation—pass this book to a friend. That does not necessarily mean more information, better statistics, bigger databases, or presence on the Internet, though all of these may play a part. It means relevant, compelling, select, powerful, timely, accurate information flowing in new ways to new recipients, carrying new content, suggesting new visions and ethics that are themselves information.

When its information flows are changed, any system will behave differently. The policy of glasnost, for example, the simple opening of information channels that had long been closed in the Soviet Union, led to the rapid transformation of Eastern Europe beyond anyone's expectations. The old system had been held in place by tight control of information. Letting go of that control triggered a total restructuring of the system.[13]

READINESS FOR A CHANGE

Talk to People who are Ready

Society today is made up of concentric rings radiating out around a new vision. Those in the center have gone through their unveiling and are enlightened to the point they are living a new truth. There are a lot of people doing a wide variety of good work today. Look for example on the internet at the explosion of non-governmental organizations (NGOs).

The first ring out are those who now know they need to live a new way and are seeking solutions. These are people learning, trying new things, reading and taking classes. The second ring out is a much larger group that knows that something is wrong, but has not put their finger on it. They are beginning their unveiling journey. The third group is by far the largest. These are the masses that still have old minds, are dependent on modern culture and are glued to their televisions.

Talk to people in the first and second rings. Here is where you will exchange ideas and create new models together for others to see. This is not preaching to the converted, or talking to ourselves. Think of it rather as talking to people who see your vision and are ready to join you.[14]

Readiness Determines Ease or Difficulty

The decisive factor for whether a new vision takes hold is not ease or difficulty. The relevant measures are readiness and unreadiness. If the time is not right for a new idea, no power on earth can make it catch on, but if the time is right, it will sweep the world like wildfire. The people of Rome were ready to hear what St. Paul had to say to them. If they had not been, he would have disappeared without a trace and his name would be unknown to us.[15]

People will listen when they are ready to listen and not before. Do not waste time with people with old minds who want to argue.

They will keep us immobilized. Look for people who are already open to something new.[16]

Offer the Complete Vision

We must tell the whole truth about our ideals, ethics and purposes. Some activists insist on the political necessity of tempering their real aims; but unless these are clearly articulated, how can they be agreed upon as collective vision? If we do not agree on where we want to go, we probably will not get there. By diluting a message for public consumption, we may fail to inspire those likeliest to be moved by a daring and positive vision of a new culture.[17]

Be positive in your message, that by living closer to the earth we can save the earth and each other. It is good to be serious, but don't dwell on the negative. Talk to people about your vision, they can read the evidence for the need to take action on their own.

Beliefs Need Continual Reinforcement

Let us join hands with each other as of old, and mourn the loss of species and landscapes, remember our billion-year journey and empathize with the myriad creatures. Whenever we do so, an expanded ecological awareness inevitably emerges in us along with a profound experience of community. Rituals might include:

- The Council of All Beings.
- Deep Time, Evolutionary Remembering, The Cosmic Walk.
- Empowerment, or work with feelings.

However, these experiences are ephemeral. Research has shown that unless one finds a way to regularly practice a deep appreciation of all life, consciousness soon fades. A practice can be as simple as giving thanks everyday to the great spirit for your life and the life around you. Thank mother earth from whom all bounty flows.

We need to find or create a family of kindred spirits. We need to find opportunities to meet on solstices, equinoxes, under the full moon, in permaculture and deep ecology workshops or on-line to build these vital support systems into our lives and to spread a new vision.[18]

16. Become the Change You Want to See

DEEP CHANGE IS NEEDED

Because we live within the Taker culture and listen to Mother Culture every day, profound change seems difficult. It is easy to send $25.00 off to the Wilderness Society, but it is much more difficult to reconsider a world view and values we have had since childhood, and then change your lifestyle. Taker culture also offers almost no alternatives. Modern life resolves around consumption and happy motoring instead of small interdependent communities of extended family.

But such a profound change is what we really need to form new cultures and to save the rich biodiversity of life. Nothing else will do but a complete change in our vision. Unless we *become* the change we wish to see in the world, no change will ever take place. Remember, our vision focuses on what we are gaining, not on what we are giving up. In a Leaver community we gain cradle-to-grave security, and freedom from the Taker prison.

DO NOT HAVE TO WAIT FOR ANYTHING

We do not need to have all seven billion of us living like environmental saints tomorrow—or ever, for that matter. To take such a thing as our objective would assure failure. We do not need to achieve the impossible dreams of global enlightenment and unity that people like Al Gore and Mikhail Gorbachev describe as humanity's only hope. We simply cannot, as Gorbachev suggests, wait for "all members of the world community to resolutely discard old stereotypes." We cannot wait for all members of the world community to do anything, because all members of the world community will never do anything as a body.

We cannot wait for our national leaders to save us. For years all we have ever asked of from them are short-term fixes. Why would they suddenly begin thinking like global visionaries?[1]

Because we do not expect to overthrow governments, abolish capitalism or turn everyone in the world into walking Buddhas, we do not have to wait for anything.[2]

If ten people walk beyond civilization and build a new life for themselves, then those ten people are already living the new restoration vision. They do not need the support of an organization. They do not need to belong to a party or a movement. They do not need new programs or laws to be passed. They do not need a constitution. They do not need tax-exempt status.

For those ten, the new culture will have already succeeded.[3]

WALKING AWAY

Social Ecology

The ecology movement should not be a political movement at all; it should be a social movement. "The tragic reality," wrote permaculture co-founder Bill Mollison, "is that very few sustainable systems are designed or applied by those who hold power, and the reason for this is obvious and simple: to let people arrange their own food, energy and shelter is to lose economic and political control over them. We should cease to look to power structures, hierarchical systems or governments to help us, and devise ways to help ourselves."

I highly recommend reviewing the last chapter of Bill Mollison's *Permaculture: A Designer's Manual*, Chapter 14: The Strategies of an Alternative Global Nation. Much of this new model is dervied from the Mondragón Corporación Cooperativa (MCC) in Spain's Basque region. MCC is a federation of democratically-run enterprises that produce and sell a range of goods and services (including appliances and machinery needed to produce solar panels). Set up in 1956 in the Basque town of Mondragón, it relies on democratic methods in its organizational structure and is concerned with generating assets for the benefit of its members and their communities, rather than for shareholders. Today, MCC is the seventh largest company in Spain.

It has about 100,000 cooperative members in about 250 cooperative enterprises that operate in more than forty countries.

Instead of a political deep ecology, the answer lies in a reinvigorated social ecology. Social ecology does not demand that people hold this or that philosophical or ideological position; it proceeds on an empirical basis, building appropriate local and bioregional alternatives using consensus. For decades we have had both highly visible ecological protesters and persistent Green politicians. Disasters have been well documented and lobbying ceaseless, but all the while the destruction of the earth has accelerated, the solvent effects of capitalism on society have been largely unchecked and modern culture has marched ahead.

The task that faces us is not to mold the existing political and economic system into something more amenable to life on earth; there is no evidence that that is even possible. It is senseless to believe that we can take a system based on exploitation, warfare and greed, and by using the same political and economic practices that drive it, make it sustainable.

No, our task must be to replace the system with an alternative society right within its midst, or as Murray Bookchin suggests, "to hollow out loyalty to the power structures until they collapse." This work, which is also the work of permaculturists, organic growers, community activists and good neighbors, embodies the creation of a better society without the mediation of politicians or economic power brokers. It is positive, direct action in communities and workplaces.

Building a new culture is a big job, but the short cut to transformation offered by politics is an illusion. Only individuals and communities can create the future we so desperately need. It may not be glamorous, but it is honest work and it is a realistic alternative to passive consumption of green products, green parties and even green books. The debate we should be having is how best to make social ecology a reality. To paraphrase a misguided politician: go back to your constituencies and prepare to make the government irrelevant.[4]

Hierarchy Has No Defense Against Abandonment

Because revolution in our culture has always represented an attack on hierarchy, it has always meant upheaval. But upheaval has no role to play in moving beyond civilization. If the plane is in trouble, you do not shoot the pilot! Instead, you grab a parachute and jump. To overthrow the hierarchy is pointless; we just want to leave it behind. In fact, we might need them to fill the potholes for a while.

As everyone knows, especially revolutionaries, hierarchy maintains formidable defenses against attack from the lower echelons. It has no defenses, however, against abandonment. This is in part because it can imagine revolution, but it cannot imagine abandonment. But even if it could imagine abandonment, it could not defend against it, because abandonment isn't an attack, it's just a discontinuance of support.

It is almost impossible to prevent people from doing nothing, which is what discontinuing support amounts to.[5]

End the Taker Prison

The inmates of the Taker prison build the prison anew for themselves every generation. Our parent's did their part and we are doing it still. As we dutifully go to school and prepare to take our place in the world of work we are building the prison for your own generation.

As long as the food remains under lock and key, the prison runs itself. The governing we see is the prisoners governing themselves. We are allowed to do that and to live as we please within the prison walls.

The prison is our culture, which we sustain generation after generation. Our parents learned from their parents and so on, back to the beginning in the Fertile Crescent 10,000 years ago.

How do we stop it? By breaking the pattern and learning something different. By refusing to teach our children to be prisoners. Practice home schooling. Take your children to see things, and do things which demonstrate the new vision. Visit U-pick farms and go hiking in the forest together. Sing and dance. Cook wholesome meals.

When seven billion of us refuse to teach our children to be captive in Taker culture, this nightmare will be over. It could take a single generation. Our culture has no independent existence outside of us. If we cease to perpetuate it, it will vanish like a flame with nothing to feed on.

We cannot just stop teaching our children anything. Rather, we must teach them something new. And if we are going to teach them something new, then we must first learn or relearn some new things ourselves. That is why we are learning about Leaver wealth, the laws of life, permaculture and our true and forgotten history.[6]

Historically Walking Away

History has examples of people just walking away from civilization. The Maya simply walked away from their cities and their culture. The Olmec themselves defaced and abandoned San Lorenzo. La Venta Teotihuacan was torched by its own citizens. One day the ditch-tenders of southern Arizona downed tools and walked away, and on another day the villagers and cliff dwellers of Chaco Canyon and Mesa Verde did the same.

All these peoples did something even more outrageous that is almost never alluded to in accounts of this kind. It was bad enough that they abandoned their civilizations, but what they did next is almost unthinkable—they stopped farming. They stopped growing all their own food. They gave up the very best way of living there is.[7]

WHAT YOU CAN DO TODAY

Here are some ideas one could start with today without making a major change in lifestyle. They will not save the world. You could see them as ideas for making the transition to a different more fulfilling way of life. Just as the industrial revolution unfolded over a couple generations, so too will the new tribal revolution.

Stop mowing the lawn and plant a garden there instead. Learn about Permaculture; you might get some interest from your neighbors about your new forest garden. Find how you can create beneficial relationships between plants in guilds and how sheet mulching minimizes weeding and builds soil. Read Toby Hemenway's *Gaia's Garden: A Guide To Home-Scale Permaculture* and watch the *Introduction to Permaculture Design* DVD by Geoff Lawton from www.permaculture.org.au.

Find the nearest permaculture institute teaching design certificate courses in the *Permaculture Activist* magazine, www.permacmatureactivist.net and *Permaculture Magazine*, www.permaculture.co.uk. For example, see the Restoration Farm permaculture education center at www.restorationfarm.org.

Teach your kids and grand kids how to plant a garden, tend it and enjoy the rewards at harvest time. Teach them about preserving and how handy a root cellar is. See Mike and Nancy Bubel's *Root Cellaring: Natural Cold Storage of Fruits and Vegetables*. Also see Carol Hupping's *Stocking Up* as a guide to preserving foods of all kinds.

Plant perennial vegetables that do not require tilling the soil and learn how handy a thick mulch can be for building soil. See Eric Toensmeier's book *Perennial Vegetables: From Artichokes to Zuiki Taro, A Gardener's Guide to Over 100 Delicious and Easy to Grow Edibles*.

If you are going to plant annuals, try to use organic heirloom seeds. There are a number of organic seed companies online that are easy to find. Also, find out about seed saving and learn why these days it is a revolutionary activity. See Marc Rogers's *Saving Seeds: The Gardener's Guide to Growing and Storing Vegetable and Flower Seeds*. Avoid genetically modified seeds, chemical fertilizers, pesticides, and only use minimal tilling. If you do not have land yourself, look into community gardens in your area. And please, plant trees.

Eat organic, vegetarian or vegan if you can. Join a food coop. You will learn about other locally grown healthy foods and save money by buying in bulk. Barter with your neighbors for food, labor and materials.

Keep your family small but your circle of friends and community large. Accumulate practical necessary skills, not money. Stop watching television. You may be surprised how much more relaxed you are and how much more time you have to be with family and friends and to pursue other interests.

Don't build a stick frame house.

BE INVENTIVE

This is our chance to be inventive in adapting a Leaver lifestyle. The search for ways to create a new cultural vision for the world is one of the most demanding, exciting and challenging quests ever undertaken. We now know how to solve our problems for the long-term. We have always known. Leaver people have been showing us how to live for 10,000 years. Finally we are ready to listen. Working toward this goal is the most exciting game in town and the most worth playing.

People casually say, "There is nothing new under the sun." Don't believe it. Doing something like putting wheels on a birdhouse new is not hard. Doing something that is both new and useful, that is more difficult. But, doing something that is new, useful, and better—that is rare challenge indeed. Have fun with it.

If people everywhere used their imagination in the search for a new Leaver lifestyle, we would have an unprecedented pool of skill and talent to draw upon. We would have many new and better ideas for solutions. And this is exactly what is happening.

One measure of a healthy, mature and creative society is that people will value their own development and follow where it leads. As Thoreau wrote, "Do what you love. Know your own bone. Gnaw it. Bury it. Unearth it and gnaw it still."[8]

SELF RELIANCE

The phrase "change the world by changing yourself" is recognized as a spiritual or inward-focused approach to working for a better world. This principle also applies to externally focused concepts such as community building and permaculture design. Developing an edible landscape using permaculture design skills reduces societies hold on you by locking up the food. It can give you a surplus to trade, create connections and generate revenue by teaching your skills to others.

Through self reliance, a group can achieve enough autonomy from modern culture to start living its own lifestyle and to develop its own identity. If you go to work everyday in modern culture, you have to fit in and observe cultural norms. If you live with a group of people who minimize their outside expenses and make a living together, you can live more by your own tune and closer to your truth.

There is also the benefit of reducing entanglement with modern culture. Old-order Amish, for example, use wood instead of rubber wheels on their wagons to reduce their dependence on modern culture. They can build and maintain their own wood steel wheels.

Although many environmental activists regard this approach as politically naive and unrealistic, or simply too slow, there are sound political, historical and ecological reasons for this emphasis on community self reliance.[9]

FIERCENESS

We need a fire in the belly in order to replace our Taker cultural story with a new one. What's needed now is a determination to change the world in positive ways. Being fierce is not the same as cruelty. Our fierceness is what gives us the energy to change things in a positive direction. It is also what mothers feel when their children are threatened. And that is a healthy thing.

We need to re-embrace that fierceness and indignation. It does not arise from ego but from compassion. We cannot let the world be destroyed, and we need to be fierce—not violent or cruel, but steadfast. That's where human determination comes from. It comes from feeling empowered—feeling that I can do this, and damn the torpedoes.[10]

YOU WILL HAVE AN IMPACT

This condition of unknowing forms a context and also a source of hope for our work. Just as we cannot fully grasp the conditions of our existence, so we cannot assess the long-term impact of our actions. Whatever we do, think, or say may precipitate a chain of events that is far beyond our ability to follow or understand.

The idea of karma is that every thought moment reverberates endlessly throughout time. We are also responsible for our actions, which also lead to lasting consequences. We can never understand the deep implications and ramifications of what we do. We cannot take ourselves too seriously, but should never underestimate the impact we might have.[11]

Margaret Mead said, "Never deny the power of a small group of committed individuals to change the world. Indeed that is the only thing that ever has."

17. New Leaver Communities and Resources

This chapter summarizes much of my vision of how to merge today's reality with the Leaver wealth of the past. This is largest chapter in the book. It could be broken into half a dozen small chapters, but then the vision would be fragmented. This chapter uses whole systems thinking to offer one vision.

Because we live in the Taker culture, we do not give ourselves alternatives. The purpose of this chapter is to provide enough ethics, models and resources to let you use your imagination to find modern versions of Leaver lifestyles.

We need to build hybrid communities that borrow what worked from the past and combine it with the best forward-looking communities of today. Ecovillages and intentional communities are a step forward in social organization, but they do not go far enough. They are more interdependent than today's suburbans, share a common vision among members and have greater self-reliance and self-determination. Some consider how they make a living and even consider how they will educate the children, but few consider how the elders will live and be cared for.

I call these new hybrid lifestyles Leaver communities. Leaver in the sense of regaining Leaver wealth that has proven to work sustainably for millions of years, and community in the sense of drawing from the best of modern green communities. Leaver communities take modern green communities to the next level. They will close the whole loop from birth, growth, death, and generation—the cycle of life—cradle-to-grave security.

Members are fulfilled, live in harmony with the earth and don't have to consume mindlessly to be happy. The diversity of life in the landscape is again allowed to flourish.

If you extend the Leaver or tribal community concept to the diversity of human experience you get a wide variety of interpretations. We will see suburbs coalescing into communities where people walk or bicycle on their daily rounds, and pedestrian urban communities develop into urban villages. The key is to change the lifestyle by creating alternatives to the ways of our Taker culture—the more alternatives the better.

This is a huge leap past programs, movements and reforms that may shake things up a little bit but in the end don't change anything. It is a way for people to start walking their talk and becoming the change they want to see.

A NEW VISION

Ecotopian Culture

Ernest Callenbach offers a compelling vision in *Ecotopia Emerging*:

This process will allow us to learn how our bioregion can best support us. Building small but lovely and often innovative houses with our own hands, we will live on city savings until we establish permaculture-style agriculture or develop a green community business. We begin in a way new to most early twenty first century Westerners. We consider ourselves settled and permanent inhabitants of our region, responsible for it, and for passing it on unimpaired to our children. We live in such a way that we build topsoil and biodiversity so that the land might support our descendants unto the seventh generation.

When we cannot see having our children subjected to the lock-step curriculum prescribed by the state, we will found our own cooperative schools. We will become innovative gardeners, keenly aware of variations in soil, plant and animal life, and the sun. We will rehabilitate or replant abandoned orchards, and relearn traditional methods of drying fruit in the sun. We will create cooperative natural food and handicraft stores. *We will plant trees.*

We will mobilize politically and fight off developers, highwaymen and miners. We will seek out the places of early native American habitation and sit on great rocks next to old acorn-grinding holes. We will find comfort in knowing that humans once lived in these spots in balance with the natural order.

Little by little, year after year, our children will grow up knowing the plants and the insects, the fishes and the angles of the sun; knowing the natural stages of creeks and rivers, feeling at home on the land, occupying it not for profit, but for sustenance and survival.[1]

Transition

Leaver communities will be transition communities between the Taker culture and humanity living again in harmony with the earth. The next generation will take the concept further. Our generation will start the journey; we will immediately reduce our ecological footprint and start restoring Gaia's ecosystems through reduced population, consumption and travel. Leaver communities will start to spread the meme that humanity belongs to the earth. For example see the Transition Town network at www.transitiontowns.org.

Self-Sufficient

These communities will be self-sufficient doorways into the future. Ideally, each community will be as close to local food and energy self-sufficiency as possible. Obtaining some food, fuels and modern conveniences from nearby communities through barter is not unrealistic. This would reduce the pressure to generate cash and would reduce each community's exposure to economic, energy or agricultural instabilities.

Live Within Carrying Capacity

One of the primary community goals is to live within our bioregional carrying capacity and to avoid the population food race. Depending on available land, Leaver communities might be limited to a traditional tribal size of about 50 to 150 members.

Families that reach a commonly accepted size, such as one or two children, depending on the age of the parents, should be encouraged to employ permanent birth control so the community does not grow into overshoot. If a family exceeds this size, whether all members live within the community or not, it may be asked to leave the community. It is important to live by example and self-limit our population.

This will be controversial in today's modern culture. However, we need models of steady state communities that are not growing and are living within the carrying capacity of their bioregion.

Community Identity

Leaver communities would have their own cultural identity. They would also be places of inspiration, ritual and education for those who wish to learn. Like monasteries of old, they would be places of spiritual teaching and light.

As indigenous tribes have in the past, tribal communities within the same local bioregion, or local watershed, would likely share a similar culture. This would help to avoid competitive conflicts for resources. Leaver communities that share the same culture may choose to organize for mutual benefit as tribal nations have in the past.

Nobel Peace Prize winner, Wangari Maathai, said this about the importance of culture to a community,

"Cultural revival might be the only thing that stands between the conservation or destruction of the environment, the only way to perpetuate the knowledge and wisdom inherited from the past, necessary for the survival of future generations. A new attitude toward nature provides space for a new attitude toward culture and the role it plays in sustainable development: an attitude based on a new understanding—that self-identity, self-respect, morality and spirituality play a major role in the life of a community and its capacity to take steps that benefit it and ensure its survival.

Until the arrival of the Europeans, communities had looked to nature for inspiration, food, beauty and spirituality. They pursued a lifestyle that was sustainable and that gave them a good quality of life. It was a life without salt, soap, cooking fat, spices, soft drinks, daily meat and other acquisitions that have accompanied a rise in the diseases of the affluent.

Communities that have not yet undergone industrialization have a close connection with the physical environment, which they often treat with reverence. Because they have not yet commercialized their lifestyle and their relation with natural resources, their habitats are rich with local biological diversity, both plant and animal."

Wangari Maathai also notes that globalization is threatening local community cultural identities:

"However, these are the very habitats that are most at threat from globalization, commercialization, privatization and the piracy of biological materials found in them. This global threat is causing communities to lose their rights to the resources they have preserved throughout the ages as part of their cultural heritage."[2] For a thorough discussion of the anti-globalization movement, see *Alternatives to Economic Globalization* by the International Forum on Globalization, www.ifg.org.

Indigenize the White Man

The time of the pioneer is over in North America. The plundering by the pioneers is complete. It is time for people to end the frontier relationship and start a new dance with the land. Limits of the ecosystem and natural law will eventually shape the human way of life to be in harmony with the other communities of life that still remain. The sooner we wake up to this inevitability, the less painful the transition will be.

One tool in the creation of new cultures will be the teaching of the story of North America. Tim Flannery in *The Eternal Frontier* gives us the deep time story of this continent and its peoples. We have an engaging history in North America replete with geologic and ecological diversity and rich cultural development. Knowing this story and telling it to our children is one step on the journey to becoming truly indigenous.[3]

Existing Leaver peoples are our tribal community elders. Whenever possible, we should learn from those who have experienced the Leaver culture directly. Existing tribal cultures contain the last remaining Leaver treasury of the wisdom of how people can live in harmony with nature.

Some Native American groups are attempting to introduce native spiritual values to American activist communities. Among the leaders of this project is Christopher Peters, a Poliklah Indian who lives on the Hoopa Reservation in northern California, and who is the executive director of the Seventh Generation Fund, www.7genfund.org.

In 1991, Peters designed a symposium for the Elmwood Institute, in Berkeley, California, on Native Thinking and Social Transformation. In the planning memorandum for the event, Peters wrote: "As we approach the end of the twentieth century, we witness a world society that is rapidly approaching a must change society. The earth's ecosystem can no longer tolerate the devastating demands of this society's narcissistic definition of prosperity. Much of contemporary literature suggests that a cultural revolution is needed... but unlike other revolutions that perpetrate doom and destruction, this pending rebellion shall be positive, reinstating optimism and renewed favorable expectations for a better society. It will be a revolution *for* something, rather than against something. Embodied within this pending revolution will be a consciousness raising, new paradigm intellectualism, and perhaps, greater cosmic awareness."[4]

Defend Your Bioregion

Let's not give up on activism all together. The most powerful activism is that of a community defending its home. In my previous home town of Telluride, Colorado, a group of dedicated citizens worked almost 21 years to build a public-private partnership to preserve our valley floor as open space. Because development of the valley floor represented a threat to the entire town's identity, we succeeded in a lengthy condemnation court battle and raised $50 million to buy the property. I learned a lot about the value of conservation to a community's identity by serving on the board of The Sheep Mountain Alliance—the organization that led the fight.

Developing a deep sense of place raises the awareness of the importance of protecting the bioregion that supports everyone in the community, tribal or not.

Educating others is one of the strongest methods of protecting local habitat for future generations. It is good to focus on things that restore habitat and biodiversity, protect practical skills for living, build topsoil, community, and local resiliency. This will lead to a new vision of people living in harmony the earth.

Allow Gaia to do what it has to do

Human settlement must allow mother earth to do what she needs to do to restore the biosphere that we all depend on for our survival. We must adapt, spread and amplify the meme that humanity belongs to the earth. Maps must be redrawn away from anthropocentric lines such as roads and cities to bioregions and watersheds. We need to look at the world through new lenses.

Growth is not bad in and of itself. It is a question of what do we want to grow? Do we want to grow cities, pollution and hunger, or do we want to grow biodiversity, topsoil and wetlands?

Again, we must not only self-limit our population to encourage growing in the right way, but we must *reduce* our population. Maybe, as long as communities remain within their carrying capacity, they will naturally have smaller families in future generations. Maybe a family will join the community with four children but each child decides to have only one child after that in order to live within local resources.

Sustainable communities know that the duties and responsibilities of people to each other are equally as important as those of people to nature; that natural laws relate equally to all life forms and elements of landscape. To conduct oneself only in terms of response to other people leaves a potential to evade responsibility for damage to the ecosystem. Beneficial behavior involves managing natural systems for their own sake, not for our immediate and exploitative personal gain.

The Iroquois nation frames this as a seventh generation concept: that our decisions now are carried out in terms of their benefit or disadvantage to our descendants in seven generations time, about 100 years ahead. This helps explain why we always found tribally managed lands to be rich in natural life resources, and why by ignoring this cultural wisdom, we have managed to ruin much of the resources we inherited.[5]

LESSONS FROM OTHER COMMUNITIES

Earthaven

Earthaven Ecovillage is located in the Blue Ridge Mountains of North Carolina. Here are some lessons learned about village building from Peter Bane from the *Permaculture Activist*.

"1. Village reflects an important scale in human settlement, and size matters. We need more people living here to achieve our goals. We have 55 full members and expect to grow to approximately 150. While there are limits, both physical and social, to the rate at which we can grow, many of the aspects of community we hope to realize here depend on our reaching a size we haven't yet attained.

2. Social capital is a scarce resource and we need to hold onto it and build it up carefully and deliberately. The bonds we built in our early years were more valuable than we realized, and we need to continue feeding that pool of invisible wealth in order to afford to expand the community.

3. Real transformations in culture and daily life depended on being able to walk to our neighbor's homes and to village meetings and events. When we couldn't easily visit our friends on foot, we lost cohesion. In our up-and-down mountain landscape that adds a special pressure on development planning that flat landers might not have to deal with, we had to accept higher densities in order to have the contact we wanted.

4. Higher density living is actually more fun and rewarding, provided the density is of people and not of cars and concrete. Living in a rural area on a large property bounded by even larger undeveloped areas, we enjoy a rich bounty of natural beauty and access to wildlife, but as humans we thrive on connection with other humans. This gets much easier when there are more choices, and that means more people within easy reach.

5. The power of cultural patterning is difficult to overestimate. We thought we understood and had made the case to ourselves for most of the above. But we underestimated the force of unconscious centrifugal energies in the culture. These are reinforced daily by the auto-based transport system upon which we still depend, a system that distorts our perceptions of distance, time, and human limitations.

The most important, overarching lesson in village design that we may have learned from our development detour is one that applies across many fields of challenging endeavor: Keep the main thing, the main thing. A village is about people and the connections they can make with each other."[6]

Interdependent — Making a Living Together

The key to a successful, long-term community is that the group is interdependent for their livelihood and survival. Living in close proximity or being like-minded is not enough. The community needs to make a living together. In modern suburbs or cities most people are dependent on the Taker culture system; they are not interdependent on each other. The key to interdependence is finding a group of people who want to make a living together.

It is also important to have a shared ethic. The first three ethics of permaculture are care for the earth, care for people and share the surplus. We have a more ethic at Restoration Farm that our economy must build topsoil, biodiversity and community.

Shared Vision

Since the beginning of humankind, and certainly in times of difficulty or tribulation, people have banded together to ensure their and their families' survival.

The history of intentional communities in the United States demonstrates this. There were peaks of community building activity during the depression that followed the Civil War, during the Great Depression and during the 1960s when many young people thought their government had gone mad as it sent hundreds of thousands of troops to Vietnam.

It seems that another wave of community building is arising today as the economy struggles and banding together is a better way than to go it alone.

Communities formed for this reason, popping up during bad times, usually die out quickly. Once the crisis is over their shared mission is lost, they drift, and eventually disintegrate. If they do survive, they often become small towns and eventually lose their sense of community.

Tom Hartman describes visiting one such community in *The Last Hours of Ancient Sunlight.* "Louise and I visited one of the more famous of the communes, which sprang up in the 1960s, and found that the land and businesses had recently been privatized— shared ownership had been one of their hallmark community values, the communal commitment to vegetarian diet was being ignored by some, and many people spent most of their time in their homes watching television, which was previously forbidden. Louise and I showed up at the outdoor amphitheater famous for its Sunday morning services, and discovered we were the only people there that day: almost all the activities of the community except those having to do with governance and the annual community party had disappeared. In this respect, this once-thriving community has essentially turned itself into a subdivision for aging hippies. Once the shared vision began to crumble, as a result of a crisis in leadership, individual concerns outweighed any sense of mission or purpose and the community turned into a small town. You could say that they are successful in that they are now a shared-survival community. Our observation of it, though, was that it is now very fragile because it's lost its leadership and its sense of mission.

This is the danger of simply jumping into a community without going through the basic exercise of determining your own personal life goals, mission, and purpose. It's the danger faced by the founders of a community if they fail to go through a similar group exercise. When the biggest mission of the members of a community is to provide a roof over their heads, they might as well be living in suburbia. On the other hand, a community can be world transforming when a shared vision is strong, a group mission is acted out daily as part of the life and work of the community, and people come together with shared values and purpose."[7]

David Brower also had some relevant advice on how to build a strong community by sharing common beliefs among early members.

"In the beginning get only the people who think the way you do, who believe. Put your act together with them, and make the idea and the organization as strong as you can, before you launch it to the public. This is the way to build an organization with real power.

Make it very clear what the organization stands for. Let that be known, and let that be the welcome mat for anyone who wants to come under your tent.

If you start worrying from the outset about pleasing too much or offending certain people or certain groups, then you're already lost. You've got to let people know you are not going to sell out, that you are not going to waffle on the basic principles. You can say, 'I haven't reached all my conclusions yet; I may not be all that practical. But this is the way I think it ought to be, and we stand for that.' Then see who joins and what happens."[8]

Put Vision Into Action

While a mission or lifework may seem to be the same as having a strong shared vision, it really goes a step beyond that. The most successful communities are those with a shared vision that is put into action.

This ranges from the lifetime mission of enlightenment as seen in meditation communities to Christian lifestyle or permaculture education. It also includes communities organized around a specific mission, such as caring for abused children, as was the Salem Children's Village's work. For a community, work is important. The work of the community serves as a galvanizing point, a shared effort that is, in the simple act of doing it, a living out of the vision. It is a daily reminder of the community's vision.

There are parallels to this in the life of an individual. When a person does not feel a sense of purpose in their work, their life often meanders rudderless toward an uncertain destiny. They escape into television, alcohol or other compulsive behavior. They are essentially lost, and at the end of their lives, often look back with regret.

People who have a sense of mission about their work, on the other hand, are happier, more motivated, more productive and likely to remain healthy physically, emotionally and spiritually. This link between work and a sense of mission or purpose has been documented in dozens, perhaps hundreds, of psychological studies and industrial analyses in the workplace over the past 50 years. It shows one of the cardinal points about how to create and maintain successful communities.[9]

Diana Leafe Christian's *Creating a Life Together: Practical Tools to Grow Ecovillages and Intentional Communities* is a good guide to start with. For a detailed description of different types of ecovillages, see *Ecovillage Living: Restoring the Earth and Her People* by Hildur Jackson and Karen Svensson.

If you are inclined to live in an ecovillage or an intentional community look at the *Intentional Community Directory* at www.directory.ic.org. Also see *Communities* magazine at www.ic.org for more resources on ecovillages and intentional communities.

LAND

Finidng Land — Start Where You Are

If you do not own property start by finding a community of like minded people. This can be just a small group of friends or as big as an existing community that has land. With a small group of people, find a home with a good sized yard and water for a garden to rent together to possibly own. By sharing a home, you reduce the rent and make owning possible. In the current economy, there are many people having trouble selling their homes and may offer you a *contract for deed*. This enables you to avoid getting a mortgage and works as long as your group can make your payments to the previous owner. It is a win-win.

If you already live with a group of like-minded people, build community right where you are. Start neighborhood potluck dinners to build interest in working together on food, transportation, child care and just making a living.

The End of Private Land

A long-term element in Leaver communities is the goal of eventually eliminating private property. We can no more own the earth than we can own the sky. Our own lifetimes are as ephemeral as snowflakes. For a little while we have the gift of the earth.

Private property is a tool to hoard resources and control people by forcing them to work within the system. Even if you are fortuniate enough to inheret land for free, you still have to generate income to pay taxes and maintenance to keep the land. Those who work the hardest, get the best pieces of land. Land has to be freed from Taker culture not only for its own sake, but also for people's.

Trusteeship of Land

The law clearly distinguishes between ownership or entitlement to a resource, and the rights to its use. Laws of ownership are relatively modern and are foreign to tribal or clan law. Laws of trusteeship are ancient, philosophical and realistic. Ownership, in effect, gives the titleholder a right to exploit in the short-term. Trusteeship governs the resource for the very long-term, with no right to exploit the resource beyond essential needs or replacement time.

The way land passed from tribal management to personal ownership is well documented. Most of us live on lands that were once tribal and are now owned. Very few of us have any rights to the resources of land which is state, church, or corporation-controlled.

However many people are working to reverse this historical trend;

tribes are still forwarding their claims to common ground after 200-400 years of occupation. Thousands of others are forming trusteeship organizations to remove land from the control of private ownership, church, and state control, and to returning it to people who live on and near the land. In fact, many people of good will, as well as traditional people, have seen that private and state ownership has ruined common resources and are returning to the concept of taking local stewardship.

Gifts or deeds of land can be vested in a tax-deductible trust for use by a specific group or the public under certain reasonable conditions. Many community gardens run this way. People with large incomes can actually benefit from tax-deductible land gifts. They can purchase and improve land and gift it at the improved value at a paper profit.

Essential land for local food, fuel, forestry, recreation, and conservation can be thoughtfully planned and secured under a set of public trusts. Acquisition can be by public investment, gift, bequest, tax deductible donation, transfer, condemnation or outright purchase. Thus, the community secures its initial land resource.

Each and every parcel of land needs 3-4 involved, active, and interested trustees. Its plans and purposes should be set for the long-term for 50–100 years ahead. Some areas will be under lease to organize gardens and farms, and some reserved for educational and public bodies for public services. Community forestry on steep and rocky lands will provide fuels, food and building materials for the future. Each household could plant and tend an area, and profit from or manage it; it is also an improving asset that can be sold or transferred. This sort of management preserves and improves the forests, public forestry sold to corporate interests generally does not.[10]

Take Control of the Bioregional Commons

When the above actions are in full swing, then it will be possible to place in the hands of your emerging local institutions the responsibility for your own air, water, land and energy as well as your own communication, trading arrangements and exchange systems. In a word, the land and local culture will again be your own destiny. I am assuming that this means establishing some sort of polity that represents the trees, the animals, the soil and water, as well as human beings, in the councils of decision-making. By the word control I do not mean what the multinational corporation means by control—the right to make a profit no matter what the cost to the resource itself. I mean the empowerment of local neighborhoods, cooperatives and bioregional communities or tribes with the ability to resist being controlled by the corporations and thus to have the freedom to make decisions for the well being of the entire local bioregion.[11]

Rewilding

Rewilding, as envisioned by Dave Foreman, founder of Earth First!, is comprised of core wildernesses surrounded by buffer areas and connected by wildlife corridors. Four continental MegaLinkages are envisioned as the foundation of rewilding the continent. Large carnivores such as wolves, mountain lions and lynx would play a vital role in maintaining or restoring ecological health. For more about this idea see Dave Foreman's book *Rewilding North America: A Vision for Conservation in the 21st Century* or visit the Wildlands Project at www.twp.org or the Rewilding Institute at www.rewilding.org. For more information about reintroducing large carnivores to the American West, visit www.wildearthguardians.org.

Another related book is Ivette Perfecto and other's *Nature's Matrix: Linking Agriculture, Conservation and Food Sovereignty.* The book promotes the idea of conservation though a network of biodiversity-friendly small farms and habitat islands that form clusters. This arrangement allows wildlife to migrate between clusters. We want to avoid isolating fragments of natural vegetation in a landscape of chemical drenched agriculture. The best way to encourage high quality matrices is to work with rural social movements.

Restore the Land

Our goal is to restore the earth for its own sake and for ours. If you acquire land for a community, choose land that needs to be restored rather than pristine land that should be conserved.

We are not inheriting the earth from our parents; we are

borrowing it from our children and sharing with other species. The vision is to start with depleted farmland, degraded pasture, clearcut forest, suburban or urban lot and leave after your lifetime a forest garden and natural habitat. That is your legacy to posterity. Use permaculture or any other technique that builds topsoil and biodiversity.

If you are starting from a blank Midwestern farm field, look into prairie restoration. There are guides and businesses to help restore the prairie with native seeds. One such company is Prairie Restorations. See www.prairieresto.com.

Part of healing the land is closing the nutrient cycles with composting toilets. You can spread the well composted humanure around your fruit trees. Put a sign above your compost toilet that says, "make compost." David Del Porto and Carol Steinfeld have produced a comprehensive guide called *The Composting Toilet System Book: A Practical Guide to Choosing, Planning and Maintaining Composting Toilet Systems, an Alternative to Sewer And Septic Systems.* One of my favorite designs is the Sunny John by John Cruickshank, see www.sunnyjohn.com. Also see the classic *The Humanure Handbook: A Guide to Composting Human Manure* by Joseph Jenkins.

Remove as many roads as possible; literally use excavation equipment to erase them. Roads fragment wild habitat into unstable islands and invite motorized traffic. Imagine the web of life as a great Persian carpet. Roads and development cut the carpet into small unraveling fragments in which genetic diversity is reduced and safe migration is cut off. Roads perform the exact opposite function of the linkages required for rewilding. The study of patterns of distribution of species on islands and island-like formations is called island biogeography.

Water and Wetlands

Farmers and builders have drained most wetlands since the agricultural revolution. Our job is to restore them. Let's leave wetlands in our steps too. Wetlands create habitat for other species. Their edges, like beaver ponds, contain an extremely high concentration of biodiversity and of course, they provide fresh water.

At Restoration Farm we have started to heal our creek that is down cutting and we catch rainwater to water our greenhouses in the winter. For a well illustrated guide on this topic, see Brad Lancasters's two volumes, *Rainwater Harvesting for Drylands and Beyond.*

Process your greywater to create more wetlands. Any wastewater used in the home, except water from toilets, is called greywater. Dish, shower and laundry water comprise 50 to 80 percent of a home's wastewater. Toilet-flush water is called blackwater and must be treated differently. Art Ludwig's *Create an Oasis with Greywater: Choosing, Building and Using Greywater Systems,* is an excellent how to guide to everything greywater.

Since many aquifers are being pumped dry, having natural water is very important. If you live in a dry area, look into P.A. Yeomans *Water for Every Farm: Yeomans Keyline Plan,* as a guide for creating water-conserving keylines, see www.keyline.com.au.

If you are fortunate enough to have a stream flow, you can use a pear-shaped cast iron ram pump to raise water, without using motors or fossil fuels. The water can be used for the household, to create wetlands or for irrigation. See Folk Water Powered Ram Pumps at www.journeytoforever.org and other related sites.

FOOD

Foraging — North American Indians

When Europeans first began streaming into North America four centuries ago, they came from a continent that experienced persistent food shortages. A prevailing symbol of pre-modern Europe is the vision of the four horsemen of the apocalypse: war, famine, disease, and death. These images are not simply bogeymen. War was fairly common and often led to famine, which weakened the populations, leading to diseases and, of course, death. Waves of epidemic disease swept through Europe and the "known world," Asia, Asia Minor and Africa. The climate of Western Europe was often unpredictable, too cold for crops some years, warm enough other years. Often there was not enough food to eat, and it was not unusual that people in one place, say Bavaria, might be starving while people in another, say Tuscany, had a surplus. Not everyone was starving all the time, but almost every area experienced hunger some of the time.

But when they arrived in the Americas, Europeans found plenty to eat. Although they gained scant praise or acknowledgment at the time, we know now that the native Americans were responsible for this. The English arrived in New England at a time when the region had been experiencing epidemic diseases and population declines, which may have been ongoing for generations due to infections brought by the Spanish far to the south. But the legacy of support by the native people of New England was a bounty to the English.

Native Americans managed their world to take advantage of nature's capacity for food production. Where berries would grow, the native people encouraged them. Wherever they went, they planted food crops, especially nut trees. There is evidence that the walnut groves the English immigrants encountered when they arrived were planted by the native people as a food source.

And nature helped—food sources existed in North America in some abundance, especially the chestnut tree, which once comprised one-sixth of the North American forest. In addition, the native Americans knew which wild plants to use as food.

Some argue that the depopulation of the native tribes prior to the arrival of Europeans accounted for some of the abundance of game, including the pigeons. But the forests had long been managed in a way that encouraged game populations. For the most part, the native people did not plant foods that were already available in abundance. Instead of creating a garden of blueberries, they encouraged the productivity of blueberry plantations established by nature. They did not bring the blueberries to the village, the village was established near the blueberries. During the nut and berry seasons, they were busy gathering, drying and preparing foods for storage that were provided by nature under the encouragement of humans. It was edible landscaping on a grand scale. The English, upon arrival, cleared much of the natural forest garden and turned their livestock loose on the shrubbery. The blueberries and other wild food plants of the natural forest garden were destroyed. The English thought they were making *improvements* to the land.[12]

Permaculture

If you cannot find a good location for wild foraging, you may want to create your own edible landscape. Permaculture is the best system I have found that combines native Leaver ethics with a design system that meets the goals of building topsoil, biodiversity and community, and provides a low maintenance food supply.

Permaculture is first based on a set of ethics:

1. care for the earth: Provision for all life systems to continue and multiply.

2. care for people: Provision for all people to have access to

resources necessary to their existence.

3. setting limits to population and consumption: By governing our own needs, we can set resources aside to further the above principles. This ethic is a very simple statement of guidance. It can inform our everyday endeavors: to be neither employers nor employees, landlords nor tenants, to be self-reliant as possible and to cooperate as groups. This ethic has more recently been restated as share the surplus or reinvest the surplus.

For the sake of the earth itself, permaculture co-founder Bill Mollison evolved a philosophy close to Taoism from his experiences with natural systems. As stated in *Permaculture Two*, it is a philosophy of working with rather than against nature; of protracted and thoughtful observation rather than protracted and thoughtless action; of looking at systems and people in all their functions, rather than asking only one yield of them; and of allowing systems to demonstrate their own evolutions. A basic question, that can be asked in two ways, is:

"What can I get from this land, or person?" or "What does this person, or land, have to give if I cooperate with them?"

Of these two approaches, the former leads to war and waste, the latter to peace and plenty.

Most conflicts lay in how questions are posed, and not in their answers. Or, to put it another way, we are looking for the right questions rather than for answers. If the question is correct, the answer will be found within it.

Unity in people comes from a common adherence to a set of ethical principles. Each of us will go our own way, at our own pace, and within the limits of our resources, yet we are all heading for common goals of creating a living and sustainable earth. Those who agree on such ethics, philosophies, and goals form a new global culture.[13]

Permaculture also contains a practical set of ecological design principles and methods for human settlements, which can be applied anywhere. Permaculture allows us to establish highly productive environments that provide food, energy, shelter, and other material and non-material needs. However, permaculture is not about these elements themselves, but rather about the relationships we can create between them by the way we place them in the landscape. These principals are rooted in careful observations of natural patterns. They can be applied to all climates and on any scale from an apartment balcony to a small urban yard, a rural farmstead or a vast forest garden. Using permaculture we can *restore* the earth.

Recognizing the creative role that humans play in the cycles that support life, Bill Mollison and David Holmgren pioneered permaculture in the 1970s. Today, tens of thousands of people all over the planet practice permaculture.

The global permaculture community actively evolves through workshops, journals, books, web sites, design certificate courses and most importantly through personal experimentation. People are inspired by this vision of bounty and ecological balance in their gardens, homes, workplaces, and communities.[14]

If projections of future oil shortages are correct, forest gardening will be essential to post-industrial agriculture. As oil becomes more costly, forest gardens will evolve to supplement and replace annual crop systems that require greater amounts of fossil fuel for their production. Chestnut flour for example, may substitute for wheat and other grain flours. Nut meals may substitute for meat.

Nut and other tree crops produce many benefits to people directly through food production, and indirectly through environmental conservation, carbon sequestration and fossil fuel economies. They also offer aesthetic diversity, beauty and wildlife habitat. If you're going to plant a tree, why not plant a nut or fruit tree?[15]

As a first step, I recommend attending a two-week permaculture design certificate course. We offer these at Restoration Farm education center www.restorationfarm.org. This will give you hands on experience with everything from ethics, sheet mulching, greenhouse design and gardening, grafting, water systems, site design, and whole systems thinking. There are many design certificate courses held every year around the country and around the world. See the *Permaculture Activist* magazine for a calendar of design courses or contact your local permaculture network.

Horticulture

Horticulture is a form of human activity between foraging and agriculture. Permaculture is a form of horticulture. Horticulture in this sense is difficult to define precisely, because most foragers tend plants to some degree and also gather wild food. At some point between the digging stick and the plow people must be called agriculturists. Horticulture usually involves a fallow period, while agriculture overcomes this need through crop rotation, external fertilizers and other techniques. Simply put, horticulturists are gardeners rather than farmers.

Horticulturists rarely organize above the tribe or small village level. Although they are sometimes influenced by the monotheism and messianic messages of their agricultural neighbors, horticulturists usually retain a belief in earth spirits and regard the Earth as a living being. Most horticultural societies are more egalitarian than agriculturists, lacking despots, armies and centralized hierarchies.

Horticulture is the most efficient method known for obtaining food, measured by return on energy invested. Agriculture can be thought of as an intensification of horticulture, using more labor, land, capital and technology. Agriculture, consuming more calories of work and resources than can be produced by food itself, is on the wrong side of the point of diminishing returns. That is a good definition of unsustainable. Horticulture is on the positive side of the curve.

Horticulturists use polycultures, tree crops, perennials and limited tillage, and have an intimate relationship with diverse species of plants and animals. Permaculture, in its promotion of horticultural practices and ideals over those of agriculture, offers a road back to sustainability. Horticulture has structural constraints against large populations, hoarding surpluses and centralized control structures. Agriculture inevitably leads to all of these.[16]

Natural Farming

Many in the Permaculture movement were inspired by Masanobu Fukuoka's book, *The One Straw Revolution,* and his *do nothing* method of natural farming. He asked, "How about *not* doing this? How about *not* doing that?" Ultimately he developed a natural method of farming with comparable yields to industrial agriculture without plowing, applying fertilizer, making compost or using agricultural chemicals. From forty years of experience, he learned that few agricultural practices are really necessary.[17]

Fukuoka developed a philosophy for life based on the realization that humanity knows nothing at all. There is no intrinsic value in intellectual or discriminating knowledge. Non-discriminating knowledge is realized through instinct and comes from an unnamable source. To know nature is to realize that one does not really know anything at all, that one is inherently *incapable* of knowing anything because our understanding is based on the limits of the human intellect. One can believe they know a butterfly, but they cannot create one.[18]

Organic Gardening

Permaculture is mostly based on forest gardening, edible landscapes and using perennials. At the other end of the spectrum are annuals. Elliot Coleman's *The Winter Harvest Handbook* and *The New Organic Grower* are very useful books on the subject of growing annuals organically year-round. He has perfected a system of mobile plastic tunnel greenhouses that are moved throughout the season to increase the number of rotations with the addition of compost and soil amendments.

Solar and Wood Cooking

Once you have your food, you can eat raw foods, which give you the most energy, or you might want to cook some of it. When you have the sun, and more patience than using a microwave requires, look to solar cooking. Visit www.solarcooking.org and www.solarcookers.org. If you want to cook with wood, visit www.ovencrafters.net and www.kachelofen-usa.com for expertise on building efficient wood-burning ovens. Also see David Lyle's *The Book of Masonry Stoves: Rediscovering an Old Way of Warming.*

RENEWABLE ENERGY

There is a lot of information available today for off-the-grid home energy systems. You can find vendors and resources in Home Power magazine, www.homepower.com and in Home Energy magazine, www.homeenergy.org.

I now live in my second solar eletric house. The first was off-the-grid at 11,300' in Telluride, Colorado and my current home is grid-tied in Ashland, Oregon. From experience, I can tell you it takes a lot of panels to just run a home office and modern refrigerator. We have 24 panels, three arrays at the farm. On cloudy days and at night, you are drawing down your batteries or living off grid power.

I also suggest reducing your energy use instead of investing in a larger energy system. Look into energy efficient refrigerators such as Sun Frost, see www.sunfrost.com. I also suggest diversifying your energy input systems. It can be very windy during a stormy or cloudy day.

If you live in mountains or hill country, look into micro hydro. Also, you do not have to live in Greenland to look into geothermal for heating; geo-exchange heating uses the natural temperature of the earth anywhere. You can also heat your water with solar hot water panels.

HOUSING

Natural Building

Please do not build a stick frame house. Most of these dwellings are so inefficiently designed that they are only made livable by burning large amounts of fossil fuel.

You don't have to live in a tipi, although, I believe living in a round space is more peaceful and natural than living in a square space. Look into the Colorado Yurt Company, www.coloradoyurt.com and Pacific Yurts, www.yurts.com. A yurt is an ideal way to get to know your land before building a more permanent home. Later the yurt can be used for guests, social gatherings, yoga or ritual practice.

Build from materials available locally. Try not to clearcut an acre of forest to build your home. There are also cob, adobe, earth bag and rammed earth construction. These techniques combine various amounts of mud, clay, and straw. You can even build a home with agricultural waste material using a Strawjet. Visit www.strawjet.com to learn more about this innovative method.

Two books I have reviewed are Paulina Wojciechowska's, *Building with earth: A Guide to Flexible-Form earthbag Construction* and Ianto Evans and others', *The Hand-Sculpted House: A Practical and Philosophical Guide to Building a Cob Cottage.* You will find a lot of resources on the Internet, but here are a few to start with: www.calearth.org, www.rammedearthworks.com, www.cob-cottage.com and www.adobebuilder.com.

Another earth related building technique is an earthship. Earthships are either built into a hill or the back is buried in earth and the front is glazed. Michael Teynolds's, *Earthship Volume III* will give you a good introduction.

If stone is abundant where you live, think about using it as a building material. Helen and Scott Nearing built exclusively with stone during their 60 years of self-sufficient living. In addition to their book, *The Good Life*, look to Tomm Stanley's *Stone House: A Guide to Self-Building with Slipforms*. Frank Lloyd Wright used a variation of slipform construction in building Taliesin West.

Straw bale construction is ideal for colder climates where insulated exterior walls are needed. There are two ways of using straw in construction: using the straw bales themselves and using muddy straw, which is a mud-clay straw mix pressed into slipforms. Paul Lacinski and Michael Bergeron's *Serious Straw Bale: A Home Construction Guide for All Climates* is one of many good straw building books. Robert Laporte has developed a system of combining an heirloom timber frame with muddy straw called and EcoNest. See his book *EcoNest: Creating Sustainable Sanctuaries of Clay, Straw, and Timber* and www.econest.com

Thermal Mass Floor

One of the key elements in capturing passive solar efficiently to heat your home is a floor with thermal mass. Rammed earth or stone is ideal. If you combine that with solar water heating panels and in floor heat, you will be cozy. One idea I would like to experiment with someday is sinking a masonry stove or Kachelofen a few feet below the main living level and having the flue run under the floor and out the other side. It would have to easily draft, be gas tight and easily cleaned out.

Cautions

When it comes to natural building, I suggest you work with an experienced architect and builder. Get references and go look at their projects. There are a lot of ways to build naturally, but very few people understand them all and which techniques are best for your climate and other conditions. The National Sustainable Building Advisor Program trains green building consultants, www.nasbap.org. Who knows, you may be the ones to research and gain enough experience in natural building in your area and then offer your experience as a tribal business.

If you are going to do it yourself, here are some tips. Build an experiment first, a kid's playhouse, a garden shed, or sauna to see how it works. Learn from your mistakes before taking on the main project. Check with your county about local building codes. You may have to discuss your plans with the county Planning Director and the Planning and Zoning Commission because your ideas may be new to them. Contact the U.S. Green Building Council at www.usgbc.org or www.buildinggreen.com for a more practical guide on this.

Also, couples should have a common vision from the start. A high percentage of couple-built homes result in a strained relationship or divorce. If one person has a dream and the other does not share it, it may lead to trouble.

Community Buildings

As one of your first priorities, develop places to build community. Important community building purposes include: social gathering, cooking, dining, greenhouse, guest quarters, bath house, library, workshop and a place for spirituality. Make your structures as multiple-use as possible. Have the focus of the community buildings reflect the mission of your community. If you become an educational center, you may also need space for a classroom, camping, outdoor kitchen and parking. Plan ahead and be flexible.

EXPERIMENT NOW

Now is the time to experiment. Use this transition time. You can still go to the grocery store if your crops fail. Use the Internet to learn practical techniques, locate local resources and to find new community members. You can still move if the site does not work out. This is another good reason not to commit all of your resources in buildings up front. The yurt is looking better for the first year all the time.

If you are starting with developed farmland, you may be able to live in the farmhouse for the first year as things develop. You do not have to start right into natural building.

In addition to taking courses, you could spend time as an intern to see how you like farming, permaculture or natural building. Many organizations are looking for volunteer help in exchange for work experience, food and lodging. Visit www.roguefarmcorps.org, www.wwoof.org and www.growfood.org for more information about work-trade opportunities.

Do not put all of your eggs in one basket when you are getting started. Diversify and experiment. Don't commit to a single building method, food system or energy source. Have your needs met in multiple ways. Experimenting, learning from mistakes, testing and evolving never end.

LEAVER BUSINESSES

Every tribe has an economy. Frederick Hoxie and Alvin Josephy Jr. give us a glimpse into tribal life in *America In 1492: The World of the Indian Peoples Before the Arrival of Columbus*. The economy was living off the land and limited trading with other tribes.

Today we need to try to mimic the same earth-friendly Leaver economy. The goal is to find some friends to make a living with that does not involve participating in the destruction of the earth. This may be a community owned business to build your interdependence and self-reliance. The business should fulfill the shared vision and ethics of the community. Profits for leaver businesses should go to the community or be gifted to your nonprofit trust and not go to one individual.

If you actually do it and succeed as a tribal community, you will have a lot of knowledge that others could use. You can consider becoming a permaculture institute, natural building educational center or spiritual community to spread and amplify what you learned with others. If you become successful at growing much of your food, it means that you have learned what works well in your bioregion. Trade heirloom seeds and perennial vegetables.

SOCIAL ORGANIZATION

To achieve cradle-to-grave security and create the give support, get support community model we need local decision-making and egalitarian governance. Taker culture is hierarchical; that is one of the characteristics that defines it. We want to avoid such structures in our communities. I suggest that our communities should be allowed to be self-determined, be given local control of resources, and be allowed to unplug from federal, state, and county jurisdictions if they wish to. This, plus no land ownership, would end much of the Taker concentration of wealth and control model.

Leadership

Leadership in a tribe is an advisory role, not an authoritarian one. Early European invaders of the Americas did not understand this; in fact, they considered it a sign of backwardness. So they sought out the chief or *leader* of a tribe, thinking that they could negotiate with that person and everyone else would comply. In fact, tribal leadership is usually held by a committee, and even that committee is more advisory than authoritarian. Power is shared among the members of the tribe, as are resources.

When leadership was needed, it was usually just for a particular task like hunting, medicine or migrating to the next seasonal location. People with these roles were still considered equal with everybody else. They viewed their role as a temporary obligation of service, not an opportunity for domination.[19]

The Great Binding Law of the Iroquois Confederacy

The Iroquois allowed Ben Franklin to attend their tribal meetings, where he learned about their thousand-year-old Great Binding Law of the Iroquois Confederacy. This code existed before Columbus arrived and governs the Iroquois Nation to this day. Franklin studied this governmental system with internal checks and balances, separation of the judicial and legislative functions and elected representatives, and shared it with James Madison and Thomas Jefferson.

The three then integrated many of these ideas into the Constitution of the United States. Franklin, Jefferson and Madison all wrote of this extensively in their papers. Franklin even invited 42 members of the Iroquois Confederacy to attend the Albany Plan of Union in 1754, when the idea of representative democracy was discussed for the first time. Franklin later said in a speech to the Albany Congress: "It would be a strange thing. . . if six nations of ignorant savages should be capable of forming such a union and be able to execute it in such a manner that it has subsisted for ages and appears indissoluble, and yet that a like union should be impractical for ten or a dozen English colonies."

The early colonists decided, however, that they knew better than the Iroquois. While they emulated the bicameral legislature, Supreme Court and clearly defined limits on the power of the central government that the Iroquois had had in place for thousands of years, the colonists had a lingering affection for the monarchy. George Washington, who argued unsuccessfully that as president he should be addressed as "his highness," was among those pushing to add a chief executive, or surrogate king, to our system of government.

In the Iroquois system most of the council representatives were male, but they were elected by the tribe's women. And only the women had the power to remove them from office. The colonists altered this so that only men could elect representatives. And only men could remove them.

They also decided to ignore the Iroquois rule that the elected representatives must submit all decisions of importance, such as waging war, changing national boundaries and altering alliances with other tribes to the local electorate. Instead, the colonists created the system we now have where important decisions are routinely made without consulting the electorate.[20]

An in depth book on the Iroquois nation is *Parker on the Iroquois*, by William Fenton.

Consensus

We know that humanity, tribalism and consensus are well suited to one another having proved successful for 99.7 percent of humanity's existence. During that time humanity lived for the most part in harmony with nature—and without devastating warfare.

Consensus decision making empowers community members and builds wisdom through its diversity. Consensus does not imply unity; it implies mutual acceptance of the context and its variety since it is not possible to act on a majority vote where 49 percent can be overruled by 51 percent.

The heart of the consensus process is that the group keeps on discussing the issue until a mutual understanding is reached. The persons or groups that do not agree will accept the decision anyway, as long as it is not severely detrimental to their own activities or interests. In those extreme instances when a single person or group repeatedly tries to block decisions, the consensus less one principle kicks in.

When everyone else finds that a proper solution has been reached and only one person cannot see it, he is deemed a bungler who has lost his right to be taken seriously. That person is kept at a distance and will not be asked to participate in further negotiations.[21] For more about the consensus decision-making process, see *A Manual for Group Facilitators* from The Center for Conflict Resolution.

Old Goddess Culture—Nonviolence, Partnership

Riane Eisler, in *The Chalice & The Blade*, describes the Leaver culture in old Europe that was overrun by the Takers about five or six thousand years ago. She describes the culture as a partnership between men and women and a religion of goddess worship.

This old European culture has no archeological evidence of war. Old Europeans never tried to live in inconvenient places such as high, steep hills, as did the later Indo-Europeans who built hill forts in inaccessible places and frequently surrounded their hill sites with huge stone walls. Old European locations were usually chosen for their beautiful setting, good water and soil, and availability of animal pastures. The settlements of Vinca, Butmir, Petresti and Cucuteni are remarkable for their excellent views and productive lands, not for their defensive value. The absence of heavy fortifications and of thrusting weapons for war speaks of the peaceful character of these art-loving peoples. Only gradually do fortress-style defenses begin to appear, and that was mainly as protection from the warlike nomadic bands coming from the fringe areas of the globe.[22]

One of the most striking things about Neolithic art is what it does not depict. One theme missing from early Neolithic art is imagery idealizing armed conflict, cruelty and violence-based power. There are no images of noble warriors or scenes of battles. Nor are there any signs of heroic conquerors dragging captives around in chains or other evidences of slavery.

Also, in sharp contrast to the remains of even their earliest and most primitive male dominant invaders, another theme notable for its absence in these Neolithic Goddess-worshiping societies is that of lavish chieftain burials. In marked contrast to later male-dominant civilizations such as Egypt, there is no sign of mighty rulers who take less powerful humans sacrificed at their death with them into the afterlife.[23]

As anthropologist Ruby Rohrlich has noted, most

anthropologists have concluded that women were the inventors of agriculture. Because women were the primary food gatherers and food preparers in Paleolithic societies, they are the most likely ones to have noticed the relation between dropped seeds and the green plants that come up. Because women had responsibility for the care of human babies, they may also have been the ones to feed and care for the abandoned young of wild animals and thus the first to domesticate animals. Women's role in the creation of weaving is suggested by the fact that spinning and weaving are part of woman's traditional roles in nearly all agricultural societies. Women are also the potters in many traditional cultures. Women probably invented pottery because the earliest pots were made to aid women's work of food storage and preparation. If women were the initiators of these new inventions of the Neolithic age, it is not hard to imagine that their status would have been high.

Anthropological research and contemporary experience show the important role of women in small-scale agriculture, horticulture and stock breeding. Men come to play dominant roles in agricultural production when the animal-drawn plow and geographical conditions permit the cultivation of larger fields and in stock breeding when large herds are taken far from the home.[24]

EXTENDED FAMILY

Our Taker culture separates generations into nuclear families. The extended family is all but forgotten. In a tribal community the extended family is one of the keys to cradle-to-grave security. Multiple generations and close friends are present to give support and get support.

Grandparents can, but do not have to, live in the same dwelling. In tight Leaver communities they are close by. If the extended family does live together, it greatly reduces the cost of housing per family and reduces the housing burden on the community.

Elders can more easily assist with practical education and passing down tribal lore. Storytelling is a skill we will have to relearn. Elders do not have to retire and become idle. They can grow into new, less strenuous jobs and remain active in the community, its economy and leadership, for many years. I believe this would be more fulfilling for the entire family and the community.

Some of today's elders may not follow the younger generation with its new vision of tribal communities. However, the middle generation today is the elder generation of tomorrow. The future is where some families may grow into their extended family.

EDUCATION

Our Taker educational system fills young minds with facts of little practical value. It teaches histories and skills to reinforce a failing culture. It teaches students to sit still, listen and not ask difficult questions. It teaches us to do what we are told in order to succeed. It does not teach critical or whole system thinking.

The tribal system works for people the way they are, not the way you wish they were. It is a thoroughly practical system that has worked for ordinary people for hundreds of thousands of years.

During the early years of our childhood, our system is indistinguishable from the tribal system. We simply interact with our children in a way that is mutually enjoyable, and we give them the freedom of the house. We will not let them swing on the chandeliers or stick forks into electric light sockets, but otherwise they are free to explore what they want to explore. At age four or five, kids want to go further afield, and for the most part they are allowed to do so within the immediate vicinity of the home. They are allowed to visit other kids down the hall or next door. In school, these would be social-studies lessons. At this stage, kids begin to learn that not all families are identical. They differ in membership, culture, manners and perhaps they even speak a different language. After this point in our system, children are sent to school, where their movements are controlled for most of the waking day. That does not happen in the tribal system.[25]

Children are universally fascinated by the work their parents do outside the home. In our new Leaver system, parents understand that including their children in their working lives is their alternative to spending tens of billions of dollars annually on schools that are failing. We are not talking about turning children into apprentices. We are just giving them access to what they want to know, and all children want to know what their parents are up to when they leave the house.

Once they are loose in an office, children do the same things they did at home—they dig up all the secrets, investigate every closet, and of course learn how to work everything, from the date-stamp machine to the copier, from the shredder to the computer, from the hoe to the hose. And if they do not know how to read yet, they will certainly learn to read now, because there is very little they can do in an office or on the farm without reading. This is not to say that children would be prohibited from helping. There is nothing children like better at this age than feeling like they are helping mommy and daddy. This isn't something they have learned, it is genetic.

In tribal societies, it is taken for granted that children will want to work alongside their elders. The work circle is also the social circle. How else are they to learn to do things if they are not allowed to do them?[26]

Children no more need schooling at age five or six or seven or eight than they need it at age two or three, when they effortlessly perform amazing feats of learning. In recent years parents have seen the futility of sending their children to regular schools, and the schools have replied by saying, "Well, all right, we will permit you to keep your children at home, but of course you understand that your children still must be schooled. We cannot just trust you to teach them what they should be learning. We'll check up on you to make sure you are not just letting them learn what they need to learn, but are also teaching them what our state legislators and curriculum writers think they should be learning." At age five or six home schooling might be a lesser evil than regular schooling, but after that it is hardly even a lesser evil. Children do not need schooling. They need access to what they want to learn—and that means they need access to the world outside the home.[27]

This is where we pull it all together. What I have described is a whole system and these are the eyes we need to teach our children to look through—not just a single major in college. How does the whole system work, what are the consequences of our actions and why do we have the ethics we do? If we can teach our children to think holistically, they will naturally have a better culture.

18. Inspiring Stories

Whatever you do, wherever you go, you can inspire people with a better vision than the old story that the world belongs to people alone. What good is ruling the world if we destroy it along the way? We can tell others the truth about what is happening, and then give them a better vision, a better story to live by, than simply consuming our way to happiness.

Are we really raising our children when we send them off to school or is the school raising them?

Do we really have a fulfilling relationship with our community when we wave to our neighbor as we mow the lawn, or walk by hundreds of people on the street that we do not know?

How fulfilling is it for our parents to reach the end of their lives at a care facility instead of at home as part of a loving extended family?

There are more inspiring stories to live by than our Taker culture offers us today. Here are some examples of the power of vision.

SAVE THE WORLD WITH A BETTER MEME

Replace Our Meme

The first thing we have to invent is a meme-killer. We need to destroy the meme proclaiming that the world was made for people and that civilization is unsurpassable. It is, after all, just a meme, just a notion peculiar to our culture. It is not a law of physics, it is just something we have been taught, that our parents were taught, as were their parents and their parents all the way back to Giza and Ur and Mohenjo-Daro and Knossos and beyond.

There is no better meme-killer than another meme. How about this: Save the world for our children and all other species by living in harmony with the earth.

Remember, new minds with *no* programs will save the world— new minds with a *new vision*.

Exodus

One of the great examples of the power of vision comes from Exodus, one of the central narratives in the Old Testament. This story is especially useful to us today because it describes how a people made the transition from one cultural story to another. Twelve fractious tribes literally walked out of one old story and created a new one. Exodus is the tale of a cultural shift, a story of how people enslaved for generations broke free of a suffocating story line.[2]

Soviet Union

In modern times we have another promising source of inspiration. Look at what happened in the Soviet Union and Eastern Europe. Twenty years ago, anyone predicting that Marxism would be dismantled so quickly would have been labeled a hopeless visionary or a fool. But once the people of these countries were inspired by the possibility of a new way of life, the disintegration took place almost overnight.

Cultural Creatives

Paul Ray, PH.D., has identified a new constituency he calls Cultural Creatives—now 45 percent of likely U.S. voters. They are bridging an old way of life with a new one. They seem to be unraveling the threads of old garments and weaving new fabric, cutting original designs and sewing together a new one. Cultural Creatives main characteristics are: they tend to oppose corporate globalization and big business and favor ecological sustainability, women's issues, national health care and education, and they have a keen concern for the planet and the welfare of future generations.[3] See his book, *The Cultural Creatives: How 50 Million People Are Changing the World*.

MORE INSPIRING STORIES

Witness To Creation—The Reverence of Life

Perhaps this is the special responsibility of humanity to serve as planetary witness to biospheric creation as it occurs at this moment.

The evolutionary paths and ecological trails that lead to our local place are so complex. A *five kingdoms of life* perspective contributes to an appreciation for biodiversity. It enables us to trace the history of life on earth that leads to this moment.

To become more familiar with the other species in our habitat, it is helpful to interpret those species from a biospheric perspective. That allows us to glimpse their legacy, the remarkable story of how they have come to share this place with us and the role they play in maintaining its ecological integrity. In almost every case, we humans are the newcomer. The stories of these species, whether it's through tracing their ancestry, or understanding their role in biospheric functioning, provide a full picture of what it means to live in a place.[4]

To Be the First Without Being the Last

One of the most inspiring visions for humanity that I have read is by Daniel Quinn in *Ishmael:*

"The meaning of the world—I think the third chapter of Genesis had it right. It's a garden, the gods' garden. I say this even though I myself very much doubt that gods have anything to do with it. I just find this a wholesome and encouraging way to think of it.

And there are two trees in the garden, one for the gods and one for us. The one for them is the Tree of the Knowledge of Good and Evil, and the one for us is the Tree of Life. But we can only find the Tree of Life if we stay in the garden—and we can only stay in the garden if we keep our hands off the gods' tree.

There is a sort of tendency or divine intention in evolution. If you start with those ultra simple critters in the ancient seas and move up step by step to everything we see here now and beyond, then you have to observe a tendency toward complexity, and toward self-awareness and intelligence.

All sorts of creatures on this planet appear to be on the verge of attaining that self-awareness and intelligence. So it's definitely not just humans that the gods are after. We were never meant to be the only players on this stage. Apparently the gods intend this planet to be a garden filled with creatures that are self-aware and intelligent.

Man's destiny would seem to be plain. Amazingly enough it is plain because man is the first of all these. He is the trail blazer, the path finder. His destiny is to be the first to learn that creatures like man have a choice: They can try to thwart the gods and perish in the attempt or they can stand aside and make some room for all the rest. But it's more than that. His destiny is to be the father of them all, I do not mean by direct descent. By giving all the rest their chance, the whales and the dolphins and the chimps and the raccoons, he becomes in some sense their progenitor. Oddly enough, it's even grander than the destiny the Takers dreamed up for us.

Just think. In a billion years, whatever is around then, whoever is around then, says, "Man? Oh yes, man! What a wonderful creature he was! It was within his grasp to destroy the entire world and to trample all our futures into the dust, but he saw the light before it was too late and pulled back. He pulled back and gave the rest of us our chance. He showed us all how it had to be done if the world was to go on being a garden forever. Man was the role model for us all! Not a shabby destiny.

This gives a little shape to the story. The world is a very, very fine place. It was not a mess. It did not need to be conquered and ruled by man. In other words, the world does not need to belong to man, but it does need man to belong to it. Some creature had to be the first to go through this, had to see that there were two trees in the garden, one that was good for gods and one that was good for creatures. Some creature had to find the way, and if that happened, then there was just no limit to what could happen here. In other words, man does have a place in the world, but it's not his place to rule. The gods have that in hand. Man's place is to be the first. Man's place is to be the first without being the last. Man's place is to figure out how it's possible to do that, and then to make some room for all the rest who are capable of becoming what he's become. And maybe, when the time comes, it's man's place to be the teacher of all the rest who are capable of becoming what he's become. Not the only teacher, not the ultimate teacher. Maybe only the first teacher, the kindergarten teacher, but even that would not be too shabby."[5]

SOURCES OF MORE INSPIRATION

Publications

For more positive stories and resources to create a better vision, see *Yes!* magazine at www.yesmagazine.org and *EarthLight* magazine at www.earthlight.org. *Yes!* magazine's mission is support it's readers in building a just and sustainable world. *EarthLight's* mission is to live, communicate and celebrate a story that vitalizes our sacred relationship with the living earth.

Another source for inspiration for me is *Resurgence* magazine from the United Kingdom at www.resurgence.org. Edited by Satish Kumar, *Resurgence* provides a mix of articles on deep ecology, holistic science, globalization, creative living, spiritual wellbeing, sustainable agriculture, arts and crafts and book reviews.

Novels

Two novels stand out in my mind because of their visions of the future. They do not necessarily depict Leaver communities, but they do describe extremely creative possibilities. Both contrast a positive cultural vision with a negative one of America gone awry.

Starhawk's *The Fifth Sacred Thing* presents a world without poverty, hunger or hatred, where a rich culture honors its diverse mix of races, religions and heritages. This sustainable culture develops in San Francisco as society collapses around the world from ecological overshoot. The best and worst of our possible futures are poised to clash, and the outcome rests on the wisdom and courage of one clan caught in the conflict. Starhawk's writing is exceedingly powerful and vivid.

Ernest Callenbach's two book series, *Ecotopia,* describes a new country founded when northern California, Oregon and Washington secede from the Union to create a stable-state ecosystem. Ecotopia is born out of political will instead of collapse. *Ecotopia Emerging* describes the buildup to the breakaway of Ecotopia. *Ecotopia* describes the isolated, mysterious Ecotopia twenty years later when the first officially sanctioned American visitor, a reporter, tours the new eco-country.

Also, if you have not yet read Edward Abbey's Desert Solitaire or The Monkey Wrench Gang, you must. They are also classics.

CONCLUSION

We Are Gaining Something Better

I know this change will take generations—in fact change never stops. But I can start the journey with my children and lead the way for others today. I can teach my children and others a new story. I also want to make the coming energy descent a positive transition to new cultures living closer to the earth. I want to act boldly now to soften the landing for our children.

I see new types of tribal communities tucked away, maybe just in seed form, slowly finding their way, budding into new cultures. When we begin the shift from human *doers* back to human *beings*, we will be able to start restoring the earth.

Just as bees live in hives, whales live in pods, wolves live in packs, and deer live in herds—humanity lives in tribes. We know that belonging to the community of life works because after 150,000 generations we are here today.

I am beginning to find the closer I get to the earth and community, the more in harmony I feel. The opposite also appears to be true. It is difficult for us Takers to re-learn a new way but something inside tells us this is better for us and our home. Let the journey begin.

POEM

This is an inspiring poem that Robert Arthur Lewis handed out at
the 1999 meeting of the World Trade Organization to describe
why he had come to the protests in Seattle.

Why We Are Here

For the World Trade Organization Ministerial Summit,
Seattle 1999

*Because the world we had imagined, the one
we had always counted on is disappearing.
Because the sun has become cancerous
and the planet is getting hotter.
Because children are starving in the shadows
of yachts and economic summits.
Because there are already too many planes in the sky.*

*This is the manufactured world
you have come here to codify and expedite.
We have come to tell you
there is something else we want to buy.*

*What we want, money no longer recognizes
like the vitality of nature, the integrity of work.
We don't want cheaper wood, we want living trees.
We don't want engineered fruit, we want to see
and smell the food growing
in our own neighborhoods.*

We are here because a voice inside us,
a memory in our blood, tells us
you are not just a trade body, you are the blind tip
of a dark wave which has forgotten its source.
We are here to defend and honor
what is real, natural, human and basic
against this rising tide of greed.

We are here by the insistence of spirit
and by the authority of nature.
If you doubt for one minute the power of truth
or the primacy of nature
try not breathing for that length of time.

Now you know the pressure of our desire.
We are not here to tinker with your laws.
We are here to change you from the inside out.
This is not a political protest.
It is an uprising of the soul.

— ROBERT ARTHUR LEWIS

ABOUT THE AUTHOR

Chuck Burr is a philosopher, permaculture teacher, seed farmer, and founder of Restoration Seeds in Ashland, Oregon. He has served on nonprofit boards, been a community radio disk jockey in Telluride, Colorado at KOTO, interned for President Reagan, has been a software entrepreneur, and has an MBA. He has been a traveler, adventurer, mountaineer, and avid rock and ice climber. Chuck is the proud father of Charlie and Bridget.

www.culturequake.com
www.restorationseeds.com

NOTES

1. The Human We Were Taught

1   Clive Ponting, *A Green History of the World: The Environment and the Collapse of Great Civilizations* (Penguin Books USA, 1991) p. 393.

2   William R. Catton, Jr., *Overshoot: The Ecological Basis of Revolutionary Change* (University of Illinois Press, 1982) p. 17.

3   Daniel Quinn, *The Story of B* (Bantam Books, 1996) p. 168.

4   Catton, 1982, p. 17.

5   Donella Meadows, *Limits To Growth: The 30-Year Update* (Chelsea Green Publishing Company, 2004) p. 266.

6   Daniel Quinn, *Ishmael* (Bantam Books, 1992) p. 68.

7   Catton, 1982, p. 24.

8   Meadows, 2004, p. 267.

9   Paul Ehrlich, *The Population Bomb* (Buccanceer Books, Inc., 1971) p. 87.

10 Joanna Macy, *Yes!* (Positive Futures Network, 2006) p. 45.

2. Our Real History

1   Daniel Quinn, *Ishmael* (Bantam Books, 1992) p. 38.

2   Daniel Quinn, *The Story of B* (Bantam Books, 1996) p. 239.

3   Daniel Quinn, *My Ishmael* (Bantam Books, 1997) p. 48.

4   Quinn, 1992, p. 170.

5   New International Version of The Holy Bible (Zondervan Bible Publishers, 1988) p. 5. Genesis 4:3-6, 4:8-10.

6   The Holy Bible, 1988, p. 5. Genesis 4:15-16.

7   The Holy Bible, 1988, p. 5. Genesis 3:20. footnote: "Eve probably means *living*."

8   The Holy Bible, 1988, p. 5. Genesis 3:20.

9   Tom Dale and Vernon Gill Carter, *Topsoil and civilization* (University of Oklahoma Press, 1955) p. 20.

10 Dale and Carter, 1955, p. 7.

11 Quinn, 1996, p. 85.

12 Quinn, 1997, p. 113.

13 Quinn, 1996, p. 242.

14 Quinn, 1996, p. 249.

15 Quinn, 1997, p. 253.

16 Quinn, 1997, p. 38.

17 Quinn, 1992, p. 36.

18 Daniel Quinn, *Beyond Civilization* (Bantam Books, 1999) p. 21.

19 Quinn, 1992, p. 166.

20 Quinn, 1996, p. 96.

21 Quinn, 1999, p. 24.

22 Daniel Quinn, *New Renaissance* (www.ishmael.org/education/writings/The New Renaissances/html)

23 Quinn, 1996, p. 156.

24 Quinn, 1992, p. 80.

25 Thom Hartman, *The Last Hours of Ancient Sunlight* (Random House, Inc., 2004) p. 153.

26 Quinn, 1992, p. 204.

27 Quinn, 1992, p. 84.

28 Quinn, 1999, p. 97.

29 Murray Bookchin, *The Ecology of Freedom: The Emergence and Dissolution of Hierarchy* (, 2005) p. 23.

30 Quinn, 1999, p. 44.

31 Quinn, 1999, p. 35

32 Quinn, 1996, p. 77.

33 Jerry Mander, *In The Absence Of The Sacred* (Sierra Club Books, 1992) p. 7.

34 Quinn, 1996, p. 281.

35 Quinn, 1996, p. 282.

36 Quinn, 1996, p. 276.

3. Population's Exponential Growth

1 Catton, 1982, p. 3.

2 Donella Meadows, *The Reporter* (Population Connection, 2005) p. 32.

3 *Living Planet Report 2004* (World Wildlife Fund For Nature, 2004) p. 18.

4 Eugene Linden, *The Future in Plain Sight* (Penguin Books USA, 2002) p. 55.

5 Paul H. Ray, PH.D., *The Cultural Creatives* (Cultural Creatives, 2000) p. 152.

6 Quinn, 1992, p. 138.

7 Quinn, 1999, p. 113.

8 Quinn, 1996, p. 155.

9 Quinn, 1992, p. 136.

10 Paul Ehrlich, *The Population Bomb* (Buccaneer Books, Inc., 1971) p. 78.

11 Richard Heinberg, *Powerdown: Options and Actions For a Post-Carbon World* (New Society Publishers, 2004) p. 172.

12 David Nicholson-Lord, *Resurgence* (Resurgence, July/Aug, 2006) p. 21.

13 Hartman, 2004, p. 206.

14 Quinn, 1992, p. 141.

15 Quinn, 1999, p. 114.

16 David Johns, *Wild Earth* (The Wildlands Project, 2002) p. 13.

17 Ehrlich, 1971, p. 44.

18 Ehrlich, 1971, p. 156.

19 Jim Merkel, *Radical Simplicity: Small Footprints on a Finite Earth* (New Society Publishers, 2003) p. 162.

4. Overshooting Carrying Capacity

1 Richard Heinberg, *The Party's Over: Oil, War and the Fate of Industrial Societies* (New Society Publishers, 2003) p. 29.

2 Heinberg, 2004, p. 32.

3 Paul H. Ray, PH.D., *The Cultural Creatives* (Cultural Creatives, 2000) p. 288.

4   WWF, 2004, p. 1.

5   Paul Ehrlich, *The Population Bomb*
    (Buccanneer Books, Inc., 1971) p. 8

6   Thom Hartman, *The Last Hours
    of Ancient Sunlight* (Random House,
    Inc., 2004) p. 210.

7   WWF, 2004, p. 18.

8   WWF, 2004, p. 19.

9   Meadows, 2005, p. 33.

10 Clive Ponting, *A Green History
    of the World: The Environment and
    the Collapse of Great Civilizations*
    (Penguin Books USA, 1991) p. 403.

11 Meadows, 2004, p. 222.

12 John Bellamy Foster, *Ecology
    Against Capitalism* (Monthly

Review Press, 2002) p. 81.

13 Catton, 1982, p. 5.

14 Catton, 1982, p. 121.

15 Meadows, 2004, p. 48.

16 Catton, 1982, p. 213.

17 *Human Development Report 2004*
    (United Nations, 2004) p. 155.

18 Merkel, 2003. p. 70.

19 Paul Ehrlich, *The Population Bomb*
    (Buccanceer Books, Inc., 1971) p.
    156.

20 Meadows, 2005, p. 38.

21 Dave Foreman, *Wild Earth* (The
    Wildlands Project, 2002) p. 3.

22 Eileen Crist, *Wild Earth* (The
    Wildlands Project, 2003) p. 63.

5. Culture's Hunger, War, Inequity, and Distress

1   *The Reporter* (Population Connection,
    2005) p. 4.

2   Dave Foreman, *Wild Earth* (The
    Wildlands Project, 2001) p. 2.

3   Foreman, 2001, p.2.

4   James MacKinnon and Jeremy
    Nelson, Adbusters (Adbusters Media
    Foundation, 2002) p. .

5   www.organicconsumers.org/toxic/
    obesity-ca.cfm

6   Meadows, 2005, p. 30.

7   *The Reporter* (Population Connection,

2005) p. 30.

8   Meadows, 2005, p. 32.

9   *The Reporter* (Population Connection,
    2005) p. 4.

10 Hartman, 2004, p. 39.

11 Merkel, 2003, p. 63.

12 Merkel, 2003, p. 60.

13 Dave Foreman, *Wild Earth* (The
    Wildlands Project, 2001) p. 2.

14 www.millenniumassessment.org,
    2005.

15 Merkel, 2003, p. 9.

6. Civilization Destroys Ecosystems

1   Dale and Carter, 1955, p. 5.

2   Dale and Carter, 1955, p. 6.

3   Dale and Carter, 1955, p. 14.

4   Hartman, 2004, p. 106.

5   Hartman, 2004, p. 108.

6   Ponting, 1991, p. 77.

7   Jared Diamond, *Harper's Magazine*
    (Harper's Magazine Foundation,
    2003) p. 47.

8   Al Gore, *Earth in the Balance*
    (Penguin Books USA, 2003) p. 78.

9   Dale and Carter, 1955, p. 11.

10 Dale and Carter, 1955, p. 16.

11 Clive Ponting, *A Green History of the
    World: The Environment and the
    Collapse of Great Civilizations*
    (Penguin Books USA, 1991) p. 406.

7. Ecosystems Collapse

1   David R. Brower, *Let The Mountains Talk, Let The Rivers Run* (New Society Publishers, 2000) p. 14.

2   *Millennium Ecosystem Assessment 20-Minute Presentation* (United Nations, 2005) p. 18.

3   Jeffrey Lockwood, *Wild Earth* (The Wildlands Project, 2002) p. 26.

4   Fritjof Capra, *Resurgence* (Resurgence, 2004) p. 8.

5   Fritjof Capra, *The Hidden Connections* (Random House, Inc., 2002) p. 211.

6   Paul Hawken, *Wild Earth* (The Wildlands Project, 2002) p. 5.

7   Brandt Mannchen, *Wild Earth* (The Wildlands Project, 2001) p. 6.

8   James Lovelock, *The Ages of Gaia: A Biography of Our Living Earth* (W. W. Norton & Company, Inc., 1988) p. 228.

9   Lovelock, 1988, p. 31.

10 Bill Mollison, *Permaculture: A Designer's Manual* (Tagari Publications, 2002) p. 95.

11 Mander, 1992, p. 318.

12 Thom Hartman, *The Prophet's Way* (Park Street Press, 2004) p. 11.

13 Leonardo Boff, *Resurgence* (Resurgence, 2002) p. 22.

14 Brower, 2000, p. 1.

15 Brower, 2000, p. 122.

16 Brower, 2000, p. 166.

17 Catton, 1982, p. 3.

18 Wendell Berry, *The Gift of Good Land: Further Essays Cultural and Agricultural* by Wendell Berry (North Point Press, 1982) p. 127.

19 Hawken, 2002, p. 9.

20 *Millennium Ecosystem Assessment 20-Minute Presentation* (United Nations, 2005) p. 20.

21 Hartman, 2004, p. 92.

22 Hartman, 2004, p. 95.

23 Hartman, 2004, p. 96.

24 Hartman, 2004, p. 1.

25 Roderick Frazer Nash, *Wild Earth* (The Wildlands Project, 2004) p. 25.

26 Brower, 2000, p. 16.

27 *New York Times*, May 15, 2003, p. 16A.

28 Meadows, 2005, p. 30.

29 Hawken, 2000, p. 149

30 Gore, 1993, p. 143

31 Hawken, 2000, p. 149

32 Brower, 2000, p. 14.

33 Hartman, 2004, p. 42.

34 Hawken, 2000, p. 52.

35 Pham, 2005.

36 Hawken, 2002, p. 9.

37 Gore, 1993, p. 146.

38 Capra, 2002, p. 252.

39 Ray, 2000, p. 327.

40 Hartman, 2004, p. 134.

8. Biodiversity Crash

1   Thomas Berry, *The Great Work* (Bell Tower, 1999) p. 164.

2   Mitchell Thomashow, *Bringing the Biosphere Home* (The MIT Press, 2002) p. 51.

3   *Millennium Ecosystem Assessment 20-Minute Presentation* (United Nations, 2005) p. 10.

4   Claud Martin, *Living Planet Report 2004* (World Wildlife Fund For Nature, 2004) p. 1.

5   Gore, 1993, p. 79.

6   Thomashow, 2002, p. 52.

7   The New Renaissance (The Ishmael Community, 2002) p. 5.

8   Thomashow, 2002, p. 54.

9   Dave Foreman, *Wild Earth* (The Wildlands Project, 2002) p. 3.
10 Joel Berger, *Wild Earth* (The Wildlands Project, 2005) p. 27.
11 Foreman, 2002, p. 3.
12 Connie Barlow, *Wild Earth* (The Wildlands Project, 2002) p. 20.
13 Robert Dunn, *Wild Earth* (The Wildlands Project, 2002) p. 28.
14 Thomashow, 2002, p. 53.

15 Gary Paul Nabham, *Cultures of Habitat: Poems of Creatures, Seeds, and Their Places: With New Translations of Native American Songs* (Tangram, 1998) p. 37.
16 Thomashow, 2002, p. 187.
17 Mary E. Gomes, *EarthLight* (EarthLight, 2005) p. 17.
18 Michael Lerner, *Yes!* (Positve Futures Network, 2003) p. 16.

9. Forest Loss and Ecological Services

1   Mollison, 2002, p. 138.
2   Hemenway, 2000, p. 100.
3   Mollison, 2002, p. 150.
4   Mollison, 2002, p. 150.
5   Mollison, 2002, p.146.
6   Mollison, 2002, p. 192.
7   Hartman, 2004, p. 39.
8   Hartman, 2004, p. 44.
9   Hartman, 2004, p. 42.
10 Brower, 2000, p. 149.
11 Brower, 2000, p. 73.
12 Hartman, 2004, p. 44.

13 Meadows, 2005, p. 33.
14 Lovelock, 1988, p. 226.
15 Hartman, 2004, p. 75.
16 Daniel H. Henning, PH. D., *Buddhism and Deep Ecology* (1stBooks, 2002) p. 176.
17 Gore, 1993, p. 120.
18 John Terborgh, *Wild Earth* (The Wildlands Project, 2002) p. 30.
19 Terborgh, 2002, p. 31.
20 Terborgh, 2002, p. 32.
21 Brower, 2000, p. 13.

10. Global Warming

1   Lovelock, 1988, p. 266.
2   Hawken, 2000, p. 235.
3   Hartman, 2004, p. 67.
4   *Living Planet Report 2004* (World Wildlife Fund For Nature, 2004) p. 18.
5   Hartman, 2004, p. 68.
6   Kenny Ausubel, *Whole Earth* (Whole Earth, 2002) p. 32.
7   *Alternatives to Economic Globalization* (The International Forum on Globalization, 2002) p. 153.
8   Gore, 1993, p. 51.
9   Ponting, 1991, p. 405
10 Hartman, 2004, p. 75
11 www.commondreams.org, November 11, 2004.

12 Bill McKibben, *The End Of Nature* (Random House, Inc., 1999) p. 34.
13 McKibben, 1999, p. 119.
14 Jonathan Thompson, *High Country News* (High Country News, May 12, 2008) p. 8.
15 McKibben, 1999. P. 17.
16 Gore, 1993, p. 53.
17 Mark Lynas, *Resurgence* (Resurgence, 2004) p. 7.
18 MicKibben, 1999, p. 137.
19 *Independent/UK*, November 11, 2004.
20 Hartman, 2004, p. 72.
21 Lynas, 2004, p. 7.
22 *Millennium Ecosystem Assessment 20-Minute Presentation* (United

Nations, 2005) p. 30.

23 www.alternet.org/story/17953/, February 25, 2004.

24 Lynas, 2004, p. 7.

25 Chris Bowers, *Resurgence* (Resur-

gence, 2003) p. 45.

26 Philip A Rutter, *Permaculture Activist* (Permaculture Activist, December, 1988) p. 34.

11. Peak Oil and Energy Descent

1   Hartman, 2004, p. 12.

2   Roscoe Bartlett, *Congressional Record* (U.S. Congress, March 15, 2005)

3   Heinberg, 2003, p. 29.

4   The Oil Drum, http://www.theoildrum.com/node/5177, March 17, 2009.

5   Dale Allen Pfeiffer, www.fromthewilderness.com, December 29, 2004.

6   Chris Skrebowski, www.fromthewilderness.com, November 17, 2004.

7   Hartman, 2004, p. 18.

8   Heinberg, 2003, p. 109.

9   Heinberg, 2003, p. 115.

10 Hartman, 2004, p. 18.

11 Michael C. Ruppert, www.fromthewilderness.com, March 11, 2005.

12 Michael C. Ruppert, www.fromthewilderness.com, March 11, 2005.

13 Michael C. Ruppert, www.eddition.cnn.com, March 17, 2005.

14 Heinberg, 2003, p. 103.

15 Heinberg, 2003, p. 108.

16 Michael T. Klare, www.commondreams.org, March 22, 2005.

17 James Howard Kunstler, www.fromthewilderness.com, March 24, 2005.

18 Hartman, 2004, p. 17.

19 Heinberg, 2003, p. 109.

20 Bartlett, 2005.

21 Heinberg, 2003, p. 161.

22 Hainberg, 2003, p. 162.

23 Heinberg, 2003, p. 146.

24 Heinberg, 2003, p. 148.

25 Hartman, 2004, p. 111.

26 Howard Odum, *A Prosperous Way Down: Principles and Policies* (University of Colorado Press, 2001) p. 67.

27 David Holmgren, *Permaculture: Principles and Pathways Beyond Sustainability* (Holmgren Design Services, 2002) p. 96.

28 Ibid.

29 Heinberg, 2003, p. 156.

30 Bartlett, 2005.

31 E. F. Schumacher, *Small Is Beautiful: Economics As If People Mattered* (HarperCollins Publishers, Inc., 1999) p. 112.

32 Jerry Mander, *In The Absence Of The Sacred* (Sierra Club Books, 1992) p. 386.

33 Heinberg, 2003, p. 111.

34 Ibid.

35 Heinberg, 2003, p. 200.

36 Heinberg, 2003, p. 202.

37 Heinberg, 2003, p. 185

38 Paul Routly, www.alternet.org/envirohealth/21737/, April 13, 2005.

39 Geoffrey Lean, www.alternet.org/waroniraq/86515/, May 27, 2008.

40 Heinberg, 2003. P. 91.

12. Bubble Economy

1   Michael C. Ruppert, www.fromthe wilderness.com, March 11, 2005.

2   Dennis Cauchon, *USA Today*, http://www.usatoday.com/news/wasing-ton/2008-05-18-Redink_N.htm, May 19, 2008.

3   Chalmers Johnson, www.inthese times.com/site/main/article/2042/.

4   http://en.wikinews.org/wiki/Oil_prices_up_400 percent25_since_9/11.

5   William Finnegan, *Harper's Magazine* (Harper's Magazine Foundation, 2003) p. 53.

6   Christopher S. Rugaber, *Huffington Post*, March 18, 2009.

7   Ruppert, March 11, 2005.

8   James Bruges, *Resurgence* (Resurgence, 2003) p. 66.

9   Norman D. Livergood, *America, Awake!* (Hermes-Press, 2003) p. 173.

13. Totalitarian Agriculture

1   Quinn, 1992, p. 118.

2   Quinn, 1996, p. 258.

3   Quinn, 1999, p. 70.

4   Quinn, 1992, p. 129.

5   Quinn, 1992, p. 144.

6   Quinn, 1996, p. 256.

7   Meadows, 2005, p. 30.

8   Contra La Guerra, *Permaculture Activist* (Permaculture Activist, 2003) p. 53.

9   Hemenway, 2000, p. 67.

10 Wendell Berry, *The Unsettling of America: Culture and Agriculture* (Sierra Club, 1977) p. 85.

11 Hemenway, 2000, p. 66.

12 Hawken, 2000, p. 192.

13 Herbert Girardet, *Resurgence* (Resurgence, 2003) p. 6.

14 Hawken, 2000, p. 149.

15 Hawken, 2000, p. 193.

16 Hawken, 2000, p. 193.

17 Hawken, 2000, p. 215.

18 Jane Goodall, *The Ten Trusts: What We Must Do to Care for the Animals We Love* (HarperCollins Publishers, Inc., 2002) p. 133.

19 Frans Lantung/Minden, *Fatal Harvest Review* (The Center for Food

Safety, 2002) p. 6.

20 MacKay, 2001, p. 53.

21 Rachel Carson, *Silent Spring* (Houghton Mifflin Company, 1962) p. 10.

22 Hawken, 2000, p. 195.

23 Hemenway, 2000, p. 122.

24 Capra, 2002, p. 195.

25 *Alternatives to Economic Globalization* (The International Forum on Globalization, 2002) p. 173.

26 Lantung, 2002, p. 4.

27 Jamie McSweeney, *Permaculture Activist* (Permaculture Activist, 2005) p. 47.

28 Heinberg, 2003, p. 175.

29 Andy Jones, *Resurgence* (Resurgence, 2003) p. 39.

30 Berry, 1982, p. 128.

31 Sue Kirchhoff, *USA Today*, http://www.usatoday.com/money/ind ustries/food/2008-05-01-usda-food-supply_N.htm, May 1, 2008.

32 Ponting, 1991, p. 403.

33 Ponting, 1991, p. 405.

34 Heinberg, 2003, p. 177.

14. Leaver Wealth

1   Quinn, 1999, p. 103.
2   Quinn, 1992, p. 147.
3   Quinn, 1997, p. 94.
4   Quinn, 1997, p. 88.
5   Hartman, 2004, p. 196
6   Quinn, 1997, p. 81.
7   Quinn, 1997, p. 79.
8   Quinn, 1992, p. 203
9   Quinn, 1992, p. 206
10 Quinn, 1999, p. 61.
11 Quinn, 1994, p. 153.
12 Quinn, 1996, p. 187.
13 Quinn, 1992, p. 239.
14 Jan Pettit, *Utes: The Mountain People* (Johnson Printing Company, 1990) p. 28.
15 Hartman, 2004, p. 198.
16 Quinn, 1997, p. 94.
17 Quinn, 1997, p. 193.
18 Quinn, 1997, p. 182.
19 Quinn, 1999, p. 150.
20 Quinn, 1977, p. 191.
21 Pettit, 1990, p. 1.
22 William Coperthwaite, *A Handmade Life* (Chelsea Green Publishing Company, 2004) p. 109.
23 Helena Norberg-Hodge, *Ancient Futures: Learning From Ladakh* (Sierra Club, 1992) p. 85.

15. A New Vision Can Save the World

1   Fritjof Capra, *The Hidden Connections* (Random House, Inc., 2002) p. 83.
2   John Seed, *EarthLight* (EarthLight, 2005) p. 12.
3   Quinn, 1999, p. 14.
4   Hartman, 2004, p. 2.
5   Quinn, 1999, p. 16.
6   Quinn, 1999, p. 19.
7   Quinn, 1999, p. 9.
8   Quinn, 1999, p. 187.
9   Quinn, 1996, p. 49.
10 Quinn, 1999, p. 15.
11 Quinn, 1996, p. 51.
12 Quinn, 1999, p. 7.
13 Quinn, 1999, p. 189.
14 Ray, 2000, p. 17.
15 Jay Kardan, *Wild Earth* (The Wildlands Project, 2002) p. 16.
16 Quinn, 1996, p. 50.
17 Kardan, 2002, p. 17.
18 Meadows, 2004, p. 269.

16. Become the Change You Want to See

1   Quinn, 1999, p. 98.
2   Quinn, 1999, p. 99.
3   Quinn, 1999, p. 102.
4   Paul Jennings, Ecologist (2005) p. 26.
5   Quinn, 1999, p. 95.
6   Quinn, 1997, p. 128.
7   Quinn, 1999, p. 40.
8   Coperthwaite, 2004, p. 116.
9   Holmgren, 2002, p. 82.
10 Michael Soulé, *EarthLight* (EarthLight, 2005) p. 111.
11 Thomashow, 2002, p. 68.

17. New Leaver Communities

1   Ernest Callenbach, Ecotopia Emerg-
    ing (Banyan Tree Books, 1981) p.
    81.
2   www.alternet.org, November 12,
    2004.
3   Connie Barlow, *Wild Earth* (The
    Wildlands Project, 2002) p. 22.
4   Mander, 1992, p. 386.
5   Mollison, 2002, p. 507.
6   Peter Bane, *Permaculture Activist*
    (Permaculture Activist, 2005) p. 45.
7   Hartman, 2994, p. 317
8   Brower, 2000, p. 179.
9   Hartman, 2004, p. 316.
10 Mollison, 2002, p. 533.
11 Gene Marshall, *Green Synthesis*
    (1992)
12 John Mohawk, *Yes!* (Positive Futures
    Network, 2006) p. 22.
13 Mollison, 2002, p. 2.
14 www.permacultureinstitute.com.
15 Karl Davies, Jr., *Permaculture*
    Activist (Permaculture Activist,

2005) p. 7.
16 Toby Hemenway, *Permaculture
    Activist* (Permaculture Activist, 2006)
    p. 7.
17 Masanobu Fukuoka, The One Straw
    Revolution (Rodale Press, 1978) p.
    15.
18 Fukuoka, 1978, p. 125.
19 Hartman, 2004, p. 194.
20 Hartman, 2004, p. 225.
21 Tony Andersen, *Permaculture
    Activist* (Permaculture Activist, 2001)
    p. 69.
22 Riane Eisler, *The Chalice & The
    Blade* (HarperCollins Publishers,
    Inc., 1995) p. 13.
23 Eisler, 1995, p. 17.
24 Eisler, 1995, p. 67.
25 Carol P. Christ, *Rebirth of the God-
    dess: Finding Meaning in Feminist
    Spirituality* (Routledge, 1997) p. 53.
26 Quinn, 1997, p. 163.
27 Quinn, 1997, p. 165.

18. Inspiring Stories

1   Quinn, 1999, p. 54.
2   Ray, 2000, p. 254.
3   K. Lauren de Boer, *EarthLight*
    (EarthLight, Fall/Winter, 2002) p.
    14.
4   Thomashow, 2002, p. 134.
5   Quinn, 1992, p. 241.

index

bibliography

Adbusters magazine. Adbusters Media Foundation. www.adbusters.org/the_magazine/.

Alternatives to Economic Globalization. San Francisco: International Forum on Globalization, 2004.

Berry, Thomas. The Great Work. New York: Bell Tower, 1999.

Berry, Wendell. The Gift of Good Land: Further Essays Cultural and Agricultural. New York: North Point Press, 1982.

Berry, Wendell. The Unsettling of America: Culture and Agriculture. San Francisco, Sierra Club Books, 1977.

Bookchin, Murray. The Ecology of Freedom: The Emergence and Dissolution of Hierarchy. Oakland, CA: AK Press, 2005.

Brower, David R. Let the Mountains Talk, Let the Rivers Run. Gabriola Island, BC, Canada: New Society Publishers, 2000.

Callenbach, Ernest. Ecotopia Emerging. Ft. Myers, FL: Banyan Tree Books, 1981.

Capra, Fritjof. The Hidden Connections. New York: Random House, 2002.

Carson, Rachel. Silent Spring. Boston: Houghton Mifflin Company, 1962.

Catton, William R., Jr. Overshoot: The Ecological Basis of Revolutionary Change. Champaign: University of Illinois Press, 1982.

Coleman, Eliot, *The Winter Harvest Hadnmbook: Year-Round Vegetable Production Using Deep-Organic Techniques and Unheated Greenhouses.* White River Junction, VT: Chelsea Green Publishing Company, 2009.

Cooperthwaite, William. A Handmade Life. White River Junction, VT: Chelsea Green Publishing Company, 2004.

Christ, Carol P., *Rebirth of the Goddess: Finding Meaning in Feminist Spirituality*: Routledge, 1997.

Dale, Tom, and Vernon Gill Carter. Topsoil and Civilization. Norman: University of Oklahoma Press, 1955.

EarthLight. www.earthlight.org/.

The Ecologist. www.theecologist.org/.

Ehrlich, Paul, The Population Bomb. Cutchogue, NY: Buccaneer Books, 1971.

Eisler, Riane. The Chalice & the Blade.

New York: HarperCollins Publishers, 1995.

Forest Voice newspaper. www.forestcouncil.org/.

Fukuoka, Masanobu. The One-Straw Revolution. Emmaus, PA: Rodale Press, 1978.

Gore, Al. Earth in the Balance. New York: Penguin Books USA, 2003.

Hartman, Thom. The Last Hours of Ancient Sunlight. New York: Random House, 2004.

Hartman, Thom. The Prophet's Way. South Paris, ME: Park Street Press, 2004.

Heinberg, Richard. Powerdown: Options and Actions for a Post-Carbon World. Gabriola Island, BC, Canada: New Society Publishers, 2004.

Heinberg, Richard. The Party's Over: Oil, War and the Fate of Industrial Societies. Gabriola Island, BC, Canada: New Society Publishers, 2003.

Hemenway, Toby. Gaia's Garden: A Guide To Home-Scale Permaculture. White River Jct., VT: Chelsea Green Publishing Company, 2009.

Henning, Daniel H. Buddhism and Deep Ecology. Bloomington, IN: 1stBooks, 2002.

Holmgren, David. Permaculture: Principles and Pathways Beyond Sustainability. Hepburn, Victoria, Australia: Holmgren Design Services, 2002.

Jacke, Dave; Toensmeier, Eric. *Edible Forest Gardens: Ecological Vision and Theory for Temperate Climate Permaculture*. White River Junction, Vermont: Chelsea Green Publishing, 2005.

Johnson, Chalmers. Wake Up!: Washington's Alarming Foreign Policy. www.inthesetimes.com/site/main/article/2042/wake_up/, March 31, 2005.

Kimbrell, Andrew, ed. Fatal Harvest: The Tragedy of Industrial Agriculture. Washington, DC: Island Press, 2002.

Klare, Machael T. The Energy Crunch to Come: Soaring Oil Profits, Declining Discoveries, and Danger Signs. www.comondreams.org, March 22, 2005.

Korten, David C. The Great Turning: From Empire to Earth Community. San Francisco: Berrett-Koehler Publishers, 2003.

Kunstler, James Howard. The Long Emergency: What's Going to Happen as we Start Running Out of Cheap Gas to Guzzle? wwwfromthewilderness.com, March 24, 2005.

Lancaster, Brad. *Rainwater Harvesting for Drylands and Beyond*. Tuscon, Arizona: Rainsource Press, 2006

Linden, Eugene. The Future in Plain Sight. New York: Penguin Books USA, 2002.

Livergood, Norman D. America, Awake! Hermes Press, 2003. www.hermespress.com/covers.htm.

Living Planet Report. www.panda.org/news_facts/publications/living_planet_report/index.cfm.

Lovelock, James. The Ages of Gaia: A Biography of Our Living Earth. New York: W. W. Norton & Company, 1988.

Maathai, Wangari. Nature, Nurture and Culture. www.alternet.org, November 12, 2004.

Mander, Jerry. In the Absence of the Sacred. San Francisco: Sierra Cub Books, 1992.

McKibben, Bill. The End of Naure. New York: Random House, 1999.

Meadows, Donella. Limits to Growth: The 30-Year Update. White River Junction, VT: Chelsea Green

Publishing Company, 2004.

Merkel, Jim. Radical Simplicity: Small Footprints on a Finite Earth. Gabriola Island, BC, Canada: New Society Publishers, 2003.

Millennium Ecosystem Assessment 20-Minute Presentation. New York: United Nations, 2005. www.millenniumassessment.org.

Mollison, Bill. Permaculture: A Designer's Manual. Sisters Creek, Tasmania, Australia: Tagari Publications, 2002.

New International Version of The Holy Bible. Grand Rapids: Zondervan Bible Publishers, 1988.

Norberg-Hodge, Helena. Ancient Futures: Learning from Ladakh. San Francisco: Sierra Club Books, 1992.

Odum, Howard. A Prosperous Way Down: Principles and Politics. Boulder: University Press of Colorado, 2008.

Perfecto, Ivette. *Nature's Matrix: Linking Agriculture, Conservation and Food Sovereignty.* London: Earthscan, 2009.

Permaculture Activist. www.permacultureactivist.net/.

Pettit, Jan. Utes: The Mountain People. Boulder: Johnson Books, 1990

Pfeiffer, Dale Allen. www.fromthewilderness.com, November 17, 2004.

Ponting, Clive. A Green History of the World: The Environment and the Collapse of Great Civilizations. New York: Penguin Books USA, 1991.

Quinn, Daniel. Beyond Civilization. New York: Bantam Books, 1999.

Quinn, Daniel. Ishmael. New York: Bantam Books, 1996.

Quinn, Daniel. My Ishmael. New York: Bantam Books, 1997.

Quinn, Daniel. New Renaissance. www.ishmael.org/Education/Writings/The_New_Renaissance/shtml.

Quinn, Daniel. The Story of B. New York: Bantam Books, 1996.

Ray, Paul H. and Sherry Ruth Anderson. The Cultural Creatives. New York: Harmony Books, 2000.

Rogers, Marc. *Saving Seeds: The Gardener's Guide to Growing and Storing Vegtable and Flower Seeds.* North Adams, MA: Storey Publishing, 1990.

The Reporter magazine. Washington, DC: Population Connection.

Resurgence magazine. www.resurgence.org.

Schumacher, E. F. Small is Beautiful: Economics As If People Mattered. New York: HarperCollins Publishers, Inc., 1999.

Skrebowski, Chris. www.fromthewilderness.com, November 17, 2004.

Starhawk. The Fifth Sacred Thing. New York: Bantam Books, 1994.

Thomashow, Mitchell. Bringing the Biosphere Home. Cambridge, MA: MIT Press, 2002.

Toensmeier, Eric. From Artichokes to Zuiki Taro, A Gardener's Guide to Over 100 Delicious and Easy to Grow Edibles. White River Junction: Chelsea Green Publishing, 2007.

Whole Earth magazine. www.wholeearthmag.com/.

Wild Earth magazine. Richmond, VT: The Wildlands Project.

www.alternet.org.

www.commondreams.org.

www.organicconsumers.ort/toxic/obesity-ca.cfm.

www.permaculture.org.au.

www.permacultureinstitute.com.

Yes!: A Journal of Positive Futures. www.yesmagazine.org/.

Manufactured by Amazon.ca
Bolton, ON

28808481R00171